Pamela

ERICA WILSON'S
Embroidery Book

ALSO BY ERICA WILSON

Crewel Embroidery

Fun with Crewel Embroidery

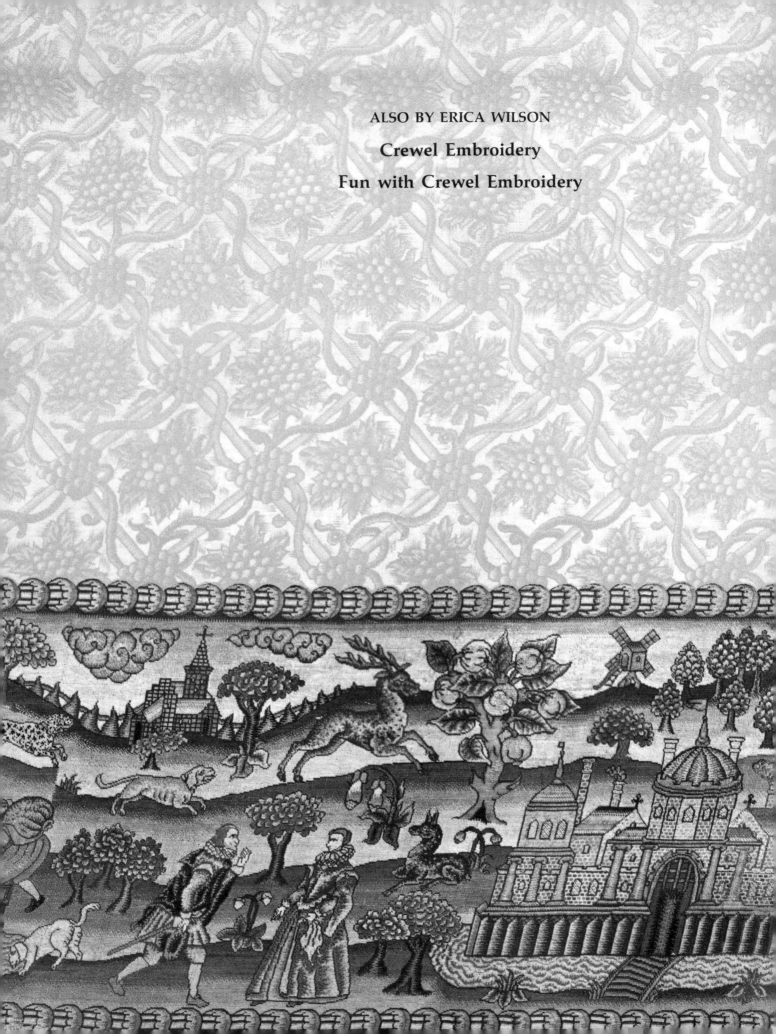

ERICA WILSON'S
Embroidery
Book

CHARLES SCRIBNER'S SONS / NEW YORK

The poem on page v is reprinted with permission of The
Macmillan Company from COLLECTED POEMS by William Butler
Yeats. Copyright 1906 by The Macmillan Company, renewal
copyright 1934 by William Butler Yeats.

The embroideries shown on pages 151, 165, 330, 331 and color
plate 23 are adapted from illustrations by Beatrix Potter in
The Tale of Two Bad Mice, Appley Dapply's Nursery Rhymes
and *The Tale of Johnny Town-Mouse,*
and are reproduced by kind permission of Frederick
Warne and Company, Ltd., London.
Illustrations from *The Tale of Johnny Town-Mouse* on Plate 23
and page 331 copyright © Frederick Warne and Co., Inc., New York,
1918, 1946.

Plates 25, 26, 27 are adapted from an illustration by Ivan Bilibin
in *The Golden Cockerel* by Alexander Pushkin, St. Petersburg, 1907.
Plates 7 and 32, pages 29 and 90
courtesy of Columbia Minerva Corporation.

3 5 7 9 11 13 15 17 19   Q/C   20 18 16 14 12 10 8 6 4

PRINTED IN THE UNITED STATES OF AMERICA
Library of Congress Catalog Card Number 78-123841
SBN 684-10655-8

Had I the heavens' embroidered cloths,
Enwrought with golden and silver light,
The blue and the dim and the dark cloths
Of night and light and the half-light,
I would spread the cloths under your feet, ...
But I, being poor, have only my dreams;
I have spread my dreams under your feet;
Tread softly, because you tread on my dreams.

—WILLIAM BUTLER YEATS

ACKNOWLEDGMENTS

Grateful thanks are extended to the following:

First, my teacher who knew more about needlework than anyone I've ever known—the late Marguerite Randall, principal of the Royal School of Needlework in London. Then Margaret Parshall, who invited me to come to the United States in 1954, and all my pupils whose enthusiasm contributed to the success of the first classes, Mrs. Herman Place, Mrs. Edwin Jameson, Mrs. Thomas Watson, Mrs. Rodney Proctor, Mrs. Peter H. B. Frelinghuysen, Mrs. Barent Lefferts, Mrs. Ernest Vietor, Mrs. Harry Peters, Mrs. Montgomery Hare, Mrs. Huntington Babcock, Mrs. Theodore Roosevelt, Jr., Mrs. Farrar Bateson, Mrs. Ludlow Bull, Mrs. Higginson Cabot, Mrs. William Lamb, Miss Alice Beer, Miss Alice Winchester, Miss Elizabeth Riley, Mrs. Alastair Martin, Mrs. Donald Bush, Mrs. Robert Levy, Mrs. John Marsh, Mrs. B. P. Bouverie, Mrs. Grover O'Neill, Mrs. Erastus Corning, and many more.

I would also like to thank my staff, teachers and friends who over the years have helped me to make this book a reality, Mrs. Hampton Lynch, Lindsay Green, Christina Johnson, May Thierard, Charlotte Matteson, Joan Helpern and Wilayna Bristow who worked so many beautiful designs. Particular thanks go to my patient photographer Frank Guida and especially patient book designer Margareta F. Lyons; and, leaving the most important to the last, my husband, Vladimir Kagan, without whose line drawings, photography, and helpful criticism I could not have produced the book at all, and, finally, my editor, Elinor Parker, who has a way of quietly leading one to believe one is doing it all oneself!

CONTENTS

Coptic medallion with twining incorporated with the weaving stitches. *Victoria and Albert Museum*

INTRODUCTION

TO many people the word "embroidery" summons up visions of tiny silken stitches on fine cloth, usually worked on a doily or a rather redundant table runner. They are wrong. Embroidery is *everything* you can do with a needle on any material including canvas. In fact, it is rather like the word "dog." Just as there are poodles, German shepherds and dachshunds, so there are many "breeds" of embroidery, all beautiful in their traditional sense, and excitingly different when worked with contemporary freedom in new combinations of color and stitch. The bald dictionary definition of embroidery "the decoration of cloth . . . with needlework" gives no idea of the wonderful world of color and texture, or the exuberance of decorative fantasy that has become, through the ages, a part of every country's heritage. Ruskin had a better description when he wrote about "the accomplished phase of embroidery" as . . . "the art of all nations, savage and civilised—from Lapland boot, letting in no snow water, to Turkey cushion bossed with pearl, to Valance of Venice gold in needlework, to the counterpanes and samplers of our own lovely ancestresses."

It has been said that one of the greatest early inventions was that of piercing an eye in a needle. Once this was done, whether in bone, wood, ivory, or even a fishbone with an eye, it was used for decorative as well as useful purposes. Unfortunately so few ancient embroideries have survived that we can only imagine what the great hanging Nero commissioned for the Colosseum must have looked like with Apollo driving his steeds across the starry sky; or how rich Moses' veil in front of the tabernacle must have been, of fine twined linen, in "blue and purple and crimson, and wrought with cherubims thereon." Fascinatingly enough, the few ancient pieces that do remain today show that most of the basic stitches have stayed the same through the ages, all over the world. One of the earliest of these is a twining stitch, incorporated with the weaving of the fabric, very similar to our present day stem stitch. It has been found in embroideries in Egyptian tombs, on ancient Maori costumes from New Zealand, and was depicted on early Greek vases. A woven garment would have the warp threads left bare, so that the stitching could be twisted in, perhaps with the fingers. Medallions made in this way on Coptic clothing often outlasted the original garment, and were then cut out and applied to another. The stitch probably originated in the mists before history when primitive man made "pots to put things in" out of the twists and braids of rushes and grasses.

Apart from stem there are a few other basic stitches which have their roots in history, such as chain, satin, and cross, and from these countless variations have evolved. Their story in its historical setting is like a tapestry itself, making wonderful inspiration for new dimensions in every form of needlework. Just as in Queen Anne's reign in England in the early 1700's, silk and wool were combined in one piece of embroidery to give great effect, or in earlier times needlepoint was applied to velvet with gold thread, contemporary creations can give contrast and variety of texture by the use of wool, cotton, silk, and metal threads. One can experiment with the abundance of new materials, become fascinated with new approaches to color and stitch, and drawing from the techniques of many past centuries, ultimately produce something which is completely of today.

It seems to me that our age, with its appreciation of color, awareness of detail, yet love of simplicity, its excitement and readiness to accept new ideas, provides a climate for creative experiment in any field. Yet all through the ages the knowledge of how to do the stitches has been handed down from family to family and seldom written out. The Royal School of Needlework in London offered a course which I think was unique and which is unfortunately no longer given. Over a period of three years one could study the techniques of many periods and countries, and because one could absorb so many different traditions one developed an awareness of all embroidery. I, therefore, wanted to incorporate the essense of this course in my book as, I hope, an inspiration for those to whom a few of the techniques may be new, and for those who would like to experiment with combinations of both the familiar and the unknown in needlework.

---

* Many stitches can be worked either in the hand or in a frame. Some such as laid work, for instance, depend for their neatness on having the fabric stretched taut in the frame. Padded satin stitch and long and short stitch are others which are much easier when worked on a firm background. Therefore, those stitches for which a frame is essential are marked with an asterisk. *

CREWEL EMBROIDERY

CHAPTER 1

*Here followeth certaine patterns of cut-workes, also sundry sorts of spots, as
Flowers, Birds, and Fishes, etc. and will fitly serve to be wrought, some with
gould, some with silke, and some with crewell, or otherwise at your pleasure.*

From "A Schole house for the Needle"— RICHARD SCHORLEYKER, 1624

Detail of a palampore. *Victoria and Albert Museum*

OPPOSITE. Damietta panel. *Victoria and Albert Museum*

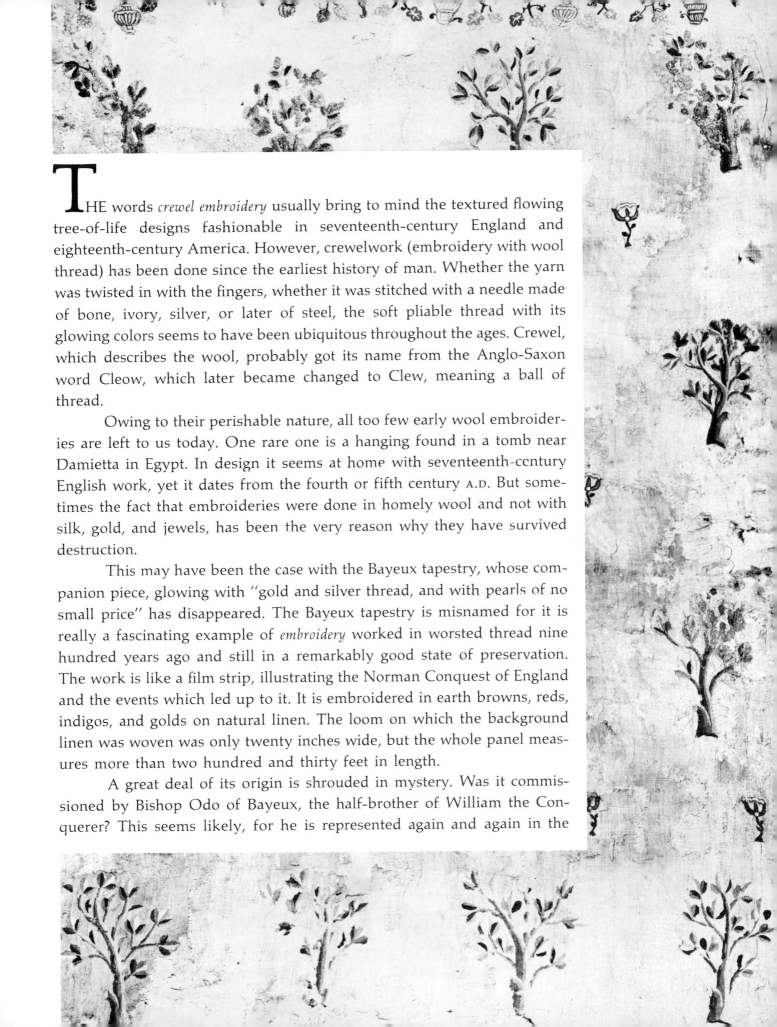

THE words *crewel embroidery* usually bring to mind the textured flowing tree-of-life designs fashionable in seventeenth-century England and eighteenth-century America. However, crewelwork (embroidery with wool thread) has been done since the earliest history of man. Whether the yarn was twisted in with the fingers, whether it was stitched with a needle made of bone, ivory, silver, or later of steel, the soft pliable thread with its glowing colors seems to have been ubiquitous throughout the ages. Crewel, which describes the wool, probably got its name from the Anglo-Saxon word Cleow, which later became changed to Clew, meaning a ball of thread.

Owing to their perishable nature, all too few early wool embroideries are left to us today. One rare one is a hanging found in a tomb near Damietta in Egypt. In design it seems at home with seventeenth-century English work, yet it dates from the fourth or fifth century A.D. But sometimes the fact that embroideries were done in homely wool and not with silk, gold, and jewels, has been the very reason why they have survived destruction.

This may have been the case with the Bayeux tapestry, whose companion piece, glowing with "gold and silver thread, and with pearls of no small price" has disappeared. The Bayeux tapestry is misnamed for it is really a fascinating example of *embroidery* worked in worsted thread nine hundred years ago and still in a remarkably good state of preservation. The work is like a film strip, illustrating the Norman Conquest of England and the events which led up to it. It is embroidered in earth browns, reds, indigos, and golds on natural linen. The loom on which the background linen was woven was only twenty inches wide, but the whole panel measures more than two hundred and thirty feet in length.

A great deal of its origin is shrouded in mystery. Was it commissioned by Bishop Odo of Bayeux, the half-brother of William the Conquerer? This seems likely, for he is represented again and again in the embroidery, and the story is told rather from the Norman point of view. Was it worked by William's wife, Queen Matilda, and her ladies? If so, she most certainly could have had help from any of the schools in England at this time (from 1070 onward) in Canterbury, in St. Albans, or in Winchester, where incidentally there were equally as many men as women embroiderers.

In the tapestry, King Harold is represented with great fairness and respect, and not at all as the villain of the drama, which may indicate that the work was done by English hands. At any rate, the end result is a dispassionate and careful account of a fascinating bit of history. Such details as the comet that appears to Harold as an evil omen (once he has broken his oath to William) and the ghost ships crossing the Channel which may have appeared to him in a troubled dream; William's elaborate preparations for the invasion of England, the building of boats and the loading of them with specially trained chargers and their knights; the way the soldiers pull off their long, horizontally striped woolen hose before wading into the water—all reward the observer with more and more sidelights as the drama unfolds. Below and above the main scenes are narrow borders, which, together with the main panel, intriguingly illustrate everyday life at the time. For instance, the farmer who at any moment may have to take up arms, is plowing his fields and tending the vineyards, and being interrupted as soldiers, camping in the fields, use their shields as tables for an alfresco

Two scenes with detail from the Bayeux Tapestry. *The Phaidon Press, Ltd.*

D·DUX: REVERSVS: EST

meal. While the battle is raging, the main scenes overlap into the border, and the battlefield is shown strewn with naked dead bodies. One of the soldiers, having been taken for dead and stripped of his expensive armor, is actually very much alive and trying to cover himself with a leafy tree branch! So great was the impression made by the fierceness of the invaders that a special clause was inserted into the litany of the day, asking for deliverance from their fury.

The end of the Bayeux tapestry looks unfinished and we can only conjecture what the final scenes might have been. However, the whole style of drawing, with its simplicity, paints such a vivid picture of the Battle of Hastings that we can almost hear the bloodcurdling yells of the soldiers, the Normans with an appeal to the heavens, *"Dex Aie,"* and the Saxons shouting, *"Ut"* ("Get out"), the clanging of axes on shields and chain mail, and the trampling of horses' hooves.

To get a true picture of the background of crewel embroidery in England, however, which finally blossomed into the beautiful bed furnishings and hangings of the sixteenth and seventeenth centuries, we should imagine the life of a noblewoman in a medieval household. On their country estates, well-to-do families led a busy, active life. The lord would hunt, or meet his tenants and stewards, and the lady of the manor, when she had finished giving orders to her servants, supervising the dairy, the bakery, and the gardens, might repair to the solar room or sunroom, where the family passed the time of day. There, on bright days, seated in the window seat, she might embroider on the cloth she had woven with the thread she had spun with her distaff. Or, as one lady said, "I do no other work but read my psalter, work in gold, silk or cruells, play a tune on my harp, checkmate someone at chess, or feed the hawk on my wrist."

Below the solar room the smells of cooking might rise from the rush-strewn great hall, with its high table laden with meats, game pies, cheeses, even wild flower petals preserved in honey. Sometimes these smells would not be savory, for meat kept long without refrigeration needed spices to make it palatable. Though it may seem remote, it was from this need that oriental influences in Western embroidery design began. The Portuguese were first, then the Dutch, and finally the English— setting off on lengthy voyages to bring back lucrative cargoes of cinnamon, cloves, ginger, and pepper. Soon from China and eventually India came "musk, rhubarb, pearls, tin, porcelain, and silk and wrought stuff of all kinds."

The fortune-seeking London merchants who formed the East India Company in 1600 soon found that the "wrought stuff"—flowered chintzes and such romantic-sounding names as paduasoy and lutestring silks—were an important part of their trade. Hand-painted calicoes were in such demand that they almost ruined the domestic market, and eventually had to be banned by law. Nor did the ships sail out empty from England. In 1618 Sir Thomas Roe, ambassador at the court of Jaohangir, advised the company to send "Imbrodred coates of Indian fashion, for our wastecoates they cannot use here—Gloves, hangars, scarfs; rounde cushions gathered like cloke bags to lean on. Any of theis in needleworke or embroiderie will sell cent per cent or not much less, all embroiderie being fallen in value, for they have learned by ours to do as well!" Perhaps the English embroideries did inspire the palampores, or hand-painted tree-of-life

LEFT AND ABOVE. Details from a 17th century coverlet. *Victoria and Albert Museum*

Waistcoat, multicolor embroidery on natural linen, English, 18th century. *Colonial Williamsburg*

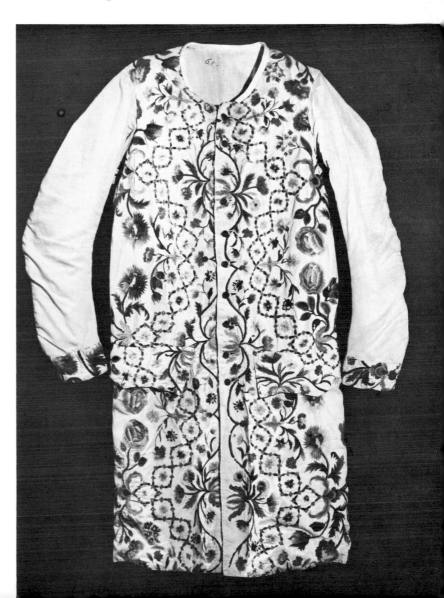

paintings, which became the prototype for crewel embroidery in the seventeenth century. Nothing quite like them had ever existed before in Indian art, so special requests from England may have made the interchange of ideas complete. But it was the excitement caused by these radiant hand-painted or "chaine"-stitched hangings from India which later influenced the English embroideress, and for the first time she realized the glorious freedom of surface decoration instead of surface covering.

In the New World, during the eighteenth century, the ladies were certainly not to be left behind by the current European fashions, and the busy Colonial housewives set to work to embroider "quilts, coverlids,

Detail from a 17th century Indian palampore. *Victoria and Albert Museum*

counterpins," and "bedticks" in crewel embroidery. As in England, the bed, curtained all round for warmth, was the most popular object for this decoration. The bed would generally have a "base" or dust ruffle, four curtains, and four "vallens" if the bed stood in the center of the room. If the bed stood against the wall, it would have four curtains, with a fifth flat against the wall at the head of the bed, and then only three valances were necessary.

The American embroideress was quite self-supporting—she spun her own yarn and dyed it—sometimes jealously guarding her methods.

Bedspread: an Indian printed cotton or palampore. *Cooper Hewitt Museum of Design, Smithsonian Institution*

There was a certain fast pink which was the secret of one ingenious Puritan woman, and she died without revealing it. "It was called *Wyndham* pink, and it made people sorry for her death, although she did not deserve it." Goldenrod, mayweed, and sumac were used for yellow; blackberries and pokeberries for purples and pinks. These last were very hard to make permanent even with the addition of alum and salt, and as madder gave only a brownish red, it was a great breakthrough when cochineal was finally imported.* A great deal of Colonial crewelwork was done all in blue and white, probably inspired by Canton china. The spare simplicity of this limited palette may have appealed to the Puritan mind, and the marvelous shadings which could be obtained by steeping the wool in indigo for various lengths of time certainly gave an effect which is both restrained and classic.

As in England, too, the embroidery was done on linen. These quotations from the New York *Gazette* of April 17, 1769, are revealing:

> This is to acquaint the Publik That George Robinson from England carries on the Flax-Dressing at his House next Door to the Sign of the Orange Tree near Golden Hill after the English manner and sells it either ruff, Heckled or hetcheled—and all possible care will be given to content all Persons that may be pleased to encourage this new branch of the business.

The following is a letter written by a gentleman in London to the Society of Manufacturers in New York in 1767.

> I received a piece of linen from the Society, it being brown I desired my Linen Draper to get it Bleach'd. He told me that during 45 years that he had been a Draper he had never seen such an excellent piece of linen, that as he had got a fortune out of North America, it gave him pleasure to hear it was manufactured there, but as a linen draper he was sorry for it. It has been six weeks on the grass and the Bleacher says it must be in his hands six more before it will be well whitened, for that he never saw a piece equal to it and desired to know of what Fabrick it was. Such are the praises of your Manufacture. I hope soon to see the day that we shall import great quantities of linen from New York into this Kingdom as well as from Ireland and Scotland and that Germany shall be excluded. (New York *Gazette*, Nov. 5th)

---

*Made from the dried, powdered bodies of the female *Dactylopius coccus* beetle from Mexico, this brilliant scarlet dye gave different colors if the beetles were crushed, or if boiling water were poured over them.

When we realize how many embroideries have been handed down to us from this period we can imagine how many more must have been done but have worn out because they were in everyday use. Because embroidery with worsted thread was so immensely popular at this time, the type of patterns then fashionable both in England in the seventeenth and in America in the eighteenth centuries have come to be synonymous with the name "crewelwork." Bed hangings, coverlets, pillows, and articles of clothing were all worked with an eye to the decorative nature of the design, rather than the realistic. The stylization and simple rendering of natural forms should be an inspiration to us when designing present-day embroidery.

Two things make crewel particularly suitable for an embroideress who has never done any needlework before but wishes to begin. One is that the freedom of crewel gives the possibility of individual artistry to the worker whether the design is completely her own or not. The second is that none of the stitches used in crewel embroidery are exclusively "crewel" stitches. Therefore it is easy to learn new techniques, experimenting with stitches used in many other forms of embroidery; yet working them easily, using the soft, pliable wool thread. The traditional textures and methods are just a springboard for contemporary effects with bold yarn and new approaches to the basic stitches.

TO BEGIN

Crewel embroidery is absolutely ideal for anything that is soft and supple, such as cushions, coverlets, curtains, or clothing. It is also magnificent in its variety of effects for pictures and wall hangings.

The texture of wool and the color and texture of the background fabric should be chosen carefully for items such as benches, chair seats, or handbags, where the fabric is stretched tight and the needlework will receive a lot of wear. But carpets can be done if rug wool or heavy crewel wool is used on a strong, close background fabric. You can also make bell pulls, slippers, eyeglass cases, room dividers, tabletops under glass, men's

Wall hanging with details opposite. *Worked by Mrs. Richard Robinson, designed by author*

ties, vests, or ladies' sweaters and dresses, blue jeans, belts, mirror frames—the list is endless and the variety whatever your imagination allows.

Just go ahead and start right out on anything that takes your fancy. Do not feel that your initial project should be small or timid. A crewel-embroidered sofa, wing chair, or curtain valance can be relatively quickly done since the stitching can be open and the background is already there. The rewards of seeing the results of your handiwork shown to its best advantage will be more satisfying than tucking a small eyeglass case into a handbag!

However, if you have never held a needle in your hand before, you may want to collect stitches on a sampler to serve as a sort of recipe book as you work on your grand project. Suggestions for these stitch samplers

Stool in contemporary design. *Designed and worked by Mrs. Laura Cadwallader*

are shown on pages 32, 46, 58, 74, 82, 92, and 100. Once you have decided how you would like to begin, your next step will be to choose the fabric.

FABRICS

Traditionally linen is the best material for crewel embroidery. It is still the best to begin on. Generally speaking, though, any material is good if it is firmly woven and the threads are easily separated as the needle passes between them. Do not choose lightweight cottons such as muslin or percale, as the material will pucker when you sew through it with heavy yarn. Surprisingly enough, closely woven cottons such as denim, sailcloth, ticking, and even organdy are excellent backgrounds for wool. This is because the fine threads part easily as the large needle passes through them, making a clear hole, and the wool can then lie flat. It is a good idea to soften certain fabrics like ticking or blue jean denim by laundering them before stitching.

In the eighteenth century, a linen and cotton twill weave fabric was found to be ideal for crewel embroidery. It was hard wearing, and its smooth surface with a faint diagonal rib was a pleasing contrast to the worsted thread. Sometimes this linen twill was brushed to form a raised nap, giving the fabric an attractive softness. This idea originated in Fustât in ancient times, where the twilled linen and cotton were brushed with teasels. The material became known as "fustian," and this was probably the origin of velvet. It is a fascinating fact that the same process is still used today and regular shipments of teasels are sent to American mills from the little town of Avallon in France! Contemporary brushed wool, acrylic, and nylon fabrics can be excellent for crewel embroidery, since they are easier to work on than velvet, and contrast well with the wool.

The photograph shows both traditional and contemporary fabrics. Whichever you use will be the deciding factor in your choice of wools and needles.

OPPOSITE, TOP TO BOTTOM, LEFT TO RIGHT. White linen twill, white fine linen, natural fine linen, natural coarse linen, white coarse linen, linen with natural and white weave, firm weave rug backing fabric, white steeped twill, blue linen, orange and gold weave acrylic fiber, natural linen twill, ticking, dull sheen rayon upholstery satin, blue brushed nylon, gold brushed nylon, brown Haitian hand woven cotton, natural bold weave wool

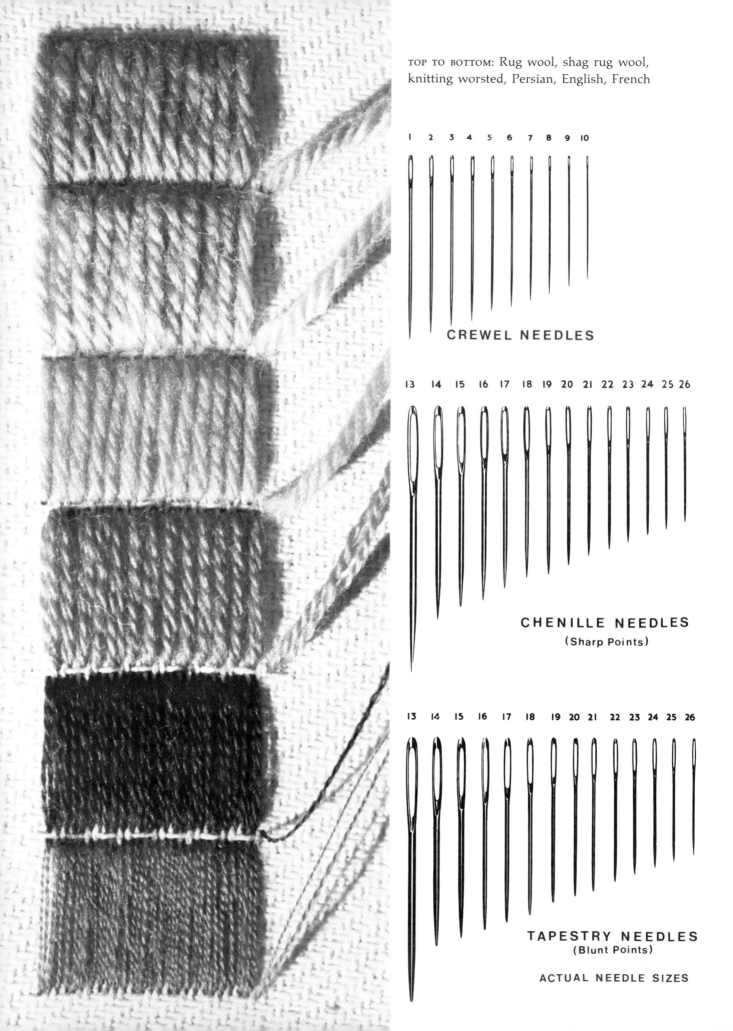

TOP TO BOTTOM: Rug wool, shag rug wool, knitting worsted, Persian, English, French

1 2 3 4 5 6 7 8 9 10

CREWEL NEEDLES

13 14 15 16 17 18 19 20 21 22 23 24 25 26

CHENILLE NEEDLES
(Sharp Points)

13 14 15 16 17 18 19 20 21 22 23 24 25 26

TAPESTRY NEEDLES
(Blunt Points)

ACTUAL NEEDLE SIZES

WOOLS

Besides the influence of the background fabric, the wool you choose will also depend on which textural effect you want as your end result. On the opposite page are some of the many kinds now available.

The Persian, English, and French wools are very flexible, as they may be used with several threads in the needle to obtain a bold effect, or singly for very fine stitching.

For Belgian or Irish linen (of fine, medium, or coarse weave), linen twill, antique satin, wool-backed satin (the kind used for upholstery with a dull sheen), or even a heavy weave silk, use English crewel wool, fine French wool or the three-stranded Persian wool. The fine texture of the wool is an attractive contrast with a coarse weave linen, if you use lacy stitches to give delicate light effects. Conversely, the soft yet raised look of the wool is effective in contrast with the flat sheen of silk or antique satin. On any of the fabrics you can use the thread singly or even up to six or more threads thick to give a contrast of texture in the same design.

If you are using coarse weave linens, burlap, coarse hand-woven wool, etc., you can work with rug wool or bulky knitting worsteds.

NEEDLES

The needle you use should make a clear opening for the thickness of the thread as it passes through the material. If the thread breaks, you are probably using too small a needle. If it seems difficult to keep your stitches even, and you are working with fairly fine thread, then your needle is probably too big. Many people prefer chenille needles, which have long eyes and sharp points and come in all sizes, because they are shorter and easier to turn as you "stab" up and down in a frame. Tapestry needles with blunt tips are useful for all stitches that are woven on the surface of the material, as they do not split or pick up unnecessary threads. If you want to weave a few stitches without bothering to change to a tapestry needle, push your sharp-pointed needle through, *eye* first, and it will have the same effect.

APPLYING THE DESIGN

Whether you draw your own design or whether you adapt a pattern (see page 359), it really takes no more skill to put your own design on fabric than it does to embroider the stitches. The following are some simple methods. You will be able to choose which method is best according to the texture of fabric you are working on. For smooth materials that are light in color the following is the quickest way of transferring the design.

APPLYING THE DESIGN WITH DRESSMAKERS' CARBON

Buy a packet of dressmakers' carbon from any notions department or sewing supply shop. (Ordinary carbon will smudge.) Fold the material in half and then in half again, and crease the folds so that they show clearly.

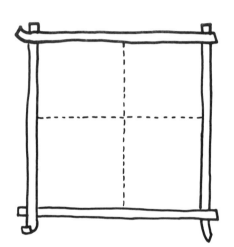

Then smooth the material flat on a table or board and hold it down evenly with masking tape on all four sides (as shown). A really smooth hard surface is necessary.

Fold the design, too, into four equal parts, open it up, and lay it down on top. Now slide a sheet of carbon paper, face downward, between paper and material. Use blue carbon for light materials, white for dark ones. Anchor the paper with some heavy weights (books, paperweights, etc.) and trace round the outline *very heavily* with a pencil. Using weights is a better idea than taping the design all round, because you can lift a corner occasionally to see how well the carbon is transferring. You really must *engrave* heavily to get good results, but you will soon find this out as you work.

Having folded the material, lay it out and fasten down with masking tape.

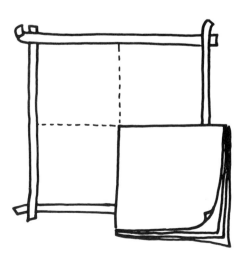

Fold the design into four parts and place it in position on one quarter of the fabric.

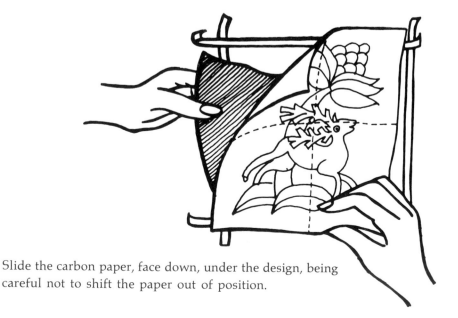

Slide the carbon paper, face down, under the design, being careful not to shift the paper out of position.

APPLYING THE DESIGN BY PERFORATION

(This method is best when design is to be used several times.)

1. Break a needle in half and set it into the eraser of an ordinary pencil. You will have to push the needle, blunt end first, into the eraser with a pair of pliers, then you will have a nice short pointed spike sticking out.

Set a needle into a pencil.

Prick the outlines of the design.

2. Trace the design onto a piece of layout or heavy tracing paper; lay this over a pad of felt, or any thick layer of material, placing a sheet of tissue between the two. Now prick holes with your spiked pencil all around the outlines, holding the pencil vertically—the holes should be fine and close, but as you practice your hand becomes like a machine, working fast and evenly.

3. First fold both fabric and perforation in four to find the center and hold it in place with weights (as in the carbon method). At a drugstore buy some *powdered* charcoal, and with a rolled and stitched pad of felt, or a blackboard eraser, rub the charcoal through the perforation you have made. Do this quite lightly, rubbing in a circular direction, without using too much charcoal. Lift a corner of the design to check, and if the line is not clear, rub through a little more "pounce" as the charcoal is called. If there is already too much, lift off the perforation and lightly blow off the surplus, leaving a clear line to follow with a brush.

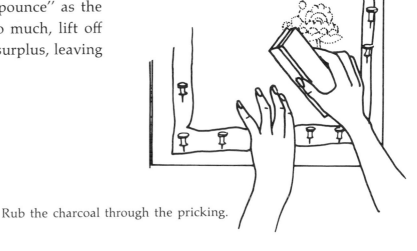

Rub the charcoal through the pricking.

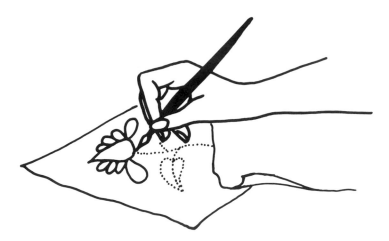

Paint around the outlines of the design.

4. Using a fine watercolor brush (#3 or #4) and a tube of blue watercolor paint, or gouache, paint around all the outlines. You will find the right mixture with practice—too much water, and the line will run, too much paint and it will not flow at all! Always begin at the edge nearest you, covering what you have done with a sheet of tissue paper, so that the pounce will not be smudged by your hand rubbing it. If you do not feel very much like an artist, use a fine, felt-tipped marker instead. Draw a line on the corner of the material first, to test the ink and see if it is fast. On dark material use white watercolor or gouache instead. Finally, bang the design hard with a clean cloth to remove the surplus charcoal. Rubbing will smudge it, so flick it until it is clean.

APPLYING THE DESIGN WITH A TRANSFER PENCIL

This product has arrived on the market lately and is a good short cut. Using the pink transferring pencil, outline the design on layout or tracing paper, then turn it face downward onto the material and iron like an ordinary commercial transfer, using a fairly warm iron. The one disadvantage is that it is apt to rub off and it does not provide a very clear, fine line. It is therefore most useful for larger, bold designs.

Certain fluffy materials, such as wool sweaters, for instance, will not take either paint or carbon well. In this case one satisfactory method is the one described next.

APPLYING THE DESIGN WITH BASTING STITCHES

Buy some batiste, organdy, or chiffon, and trace the design through the transparent material, using a hard pencil. (Of course the first two methods may also be used for this equally well, if desired.)

Pin the material with the design to the wrong side of the fabric. Then baste all around the outlines with small running stitches, using a contrasting color thread. The design will then be transferred onto the right side, and may be embroidered right over the running stitches to cover them.

Another method of transferring a design onto materials such as silk, velvets, and dark or delicate fabrics is:

APPLYING THE DESIGN WITH TRACING PAPER

This method is also excellent for ties and sweaters, or anything that you might be afraid of damaging if you put the design on incorrectly. With tracing or tissue paper any mistakes can be ripped out, leaving no sign of any unwanted design on the fabric!

First trace your design onto tracing paper or, even better, soft pliable tissue, using a felt-tipped pen which is soft and will not tear the paper. Center it, pin it, and then baste it into position on the material. Embroider the design, working through the paper and the fabric together. It is best to do the embroidery on a frame, or the paper may get damaged as you work. When you have finished, tear the tissue away, and, *voilà*—there is your design revealed on the cloth, looking beautiful! With your needle, stroke out any little pieces of paper left between the stitching.

Design on tracing paper basted in place on fabric.

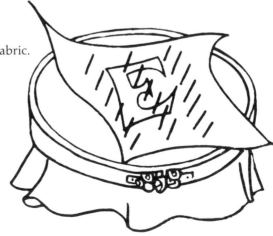

APPLYING THE DESIGN WITH NET

If your fabric is very "knubbly" and rough textured, and your design is bold in scale, use this method to transfer the pattern directly on the cloth. Trace the design onto regular net, using a rather heavy black permanent marker. Then pin the net in position on the cloth and trace it again, using the marking pen. The ink from the pen will pass through the holes of the net to the cloth, giving you a clear outline which is easy to follow. Adjust the thickness of your felt-tipped marking pen to the texture of the material.

Last but not least, perhaps you may want to let your stitches dictate your pattern, and not be regulated by any permanent lines on the cloth, yet need some guide lines to help you. In this case you can try the following method.

APPLYING THE DESIGN FREEHAND

Since you need only a rough suggestion of the pattern and not a detailed drawing, you have several choices. You can mark your design with blackboard or tailor's chalk, which will rub off whenever you want to remove it . . . and sometimes before, which is one of its disadvantages! To make more definite, clearer lines you could lightly mark the fabric with a watercolor felt-tipped pen, and then wash the fabric afterward if any unwanted lines are showing. (However, be sure first to test your fabric for washability.)

Another method you could try is to baste the lines with contrasting color thread, which can be removed afterward. Alternatively, and this is really freehand, you can *stroke* the fabric as it is held taut in the frame,

Seven dwarfs in red on grey knubbly linen. *Designed and worked by Bianca Artom*

using a blunt needle. This method is used by quilters who outline each shape of their pattern as they work. Let the needle follow your hand, holding it almost parallel to the surface of the stretched material as you stroke firmly. A clear groove or crease will be formed. If it is done carefully it will not tear the fabric, yet the creased lines will be clear enough to follow, and will fade away when not wanted.

TRANSFERRING A GEOMETRIC PATTERN TO FINE MATERIAL

If you want to work a cross stitch monogram on a denim shirt, or put a geometric border on a muslin blouse, you can do it in the following way:

To embroider cross stitch or any geometric design on fabric that does not have a clearly defined weave, baste a piece of single weave needlepoint canvas (mono) over the area where the pattern is to be. Stretch the whole thing in an embroidery frame and stitch the pattern through both thicknesses, keeping your stitches even by counting the threads of the canvas. When the design is finished, unravel the threads of the canvas at the edges and draw them right out, one by one. If your fabric is washable it may be easier to do this if you soak the embroidery in cold water. This softens the sizing in the canvas and loosens the threads enough to allow them to slip out easily.

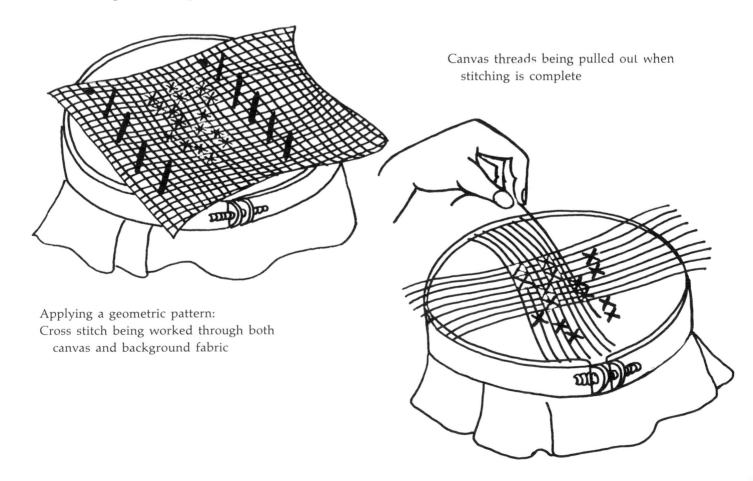

Canvas threads being pulled out when stitching is complete

Applying a geometric pattern:
Cross stitch being worked through both
canvas and background fabric

CHOOSING A FRAME

First of all, is a frame really necessary? The answer is yes! The stitches of any embroidery—crewel, silk, and needlepoint—are easier to keep neat and even as long as the background fabric is stretched taut. Hoops and ring frames are the most versatile way to stretch out the fabric because you can work on articles of any size. (If your design is on too small a piece of material, simply stitch strips of linen or sheeting to the four sides to extend the fabric.) A floor stand goes one step further because it allows you to have both hands free for working, which greatly increases your speed and skill. In fact once you are accustomed to using this type of frame, you will never want to be without it.

The only disadvantage of a standing frame is that you can't carry it around with you very easily, so a more portable variety is a lap frame, which has been nicknamed the "fanny frame" because you can sit on it! This makes it very firm and yet flexible to work on—and means you can do your embroidery almost anywhere—in the car, the plane, at the meeting, at the hairdresser's, the office, even in bed!

Linen or wool fabrics and needlepoint canvas are tough and resilient, and therefore never get damaged by having the hoops pushed over them. Certain delicate materials or raised stitches, however, might be marked by a hoop, so place layers of tissue paper over the design before pushing the frame down. Then tear the paper away from the surface of the work, leaving it protecting the fabric round the edge where the hoop would be liable to chafe it. Alternatively, you have four other choices. One is to mount a piece of linen into the ring frame, and then baste your fabric to the linen on top of the frame, just where the design area is. Work through both layers, and then cut the linen away on the reverse side, all around the design area.

The second choice is to use a large oval rug or quilting hoop (see illustration) so that the material that is marked by the hoop will only be at the outer edges, which will not show. (The oval hoop is also useful for large-scale embroidery of any kind.)

The third choice is to work on a stretcher frame. Artists' stretcher frames, used for oil painting, come in all sizes and are available from almost every art store. You should buy a larger size than the finished measurement of your work to allow you to work right up to the edge of the design

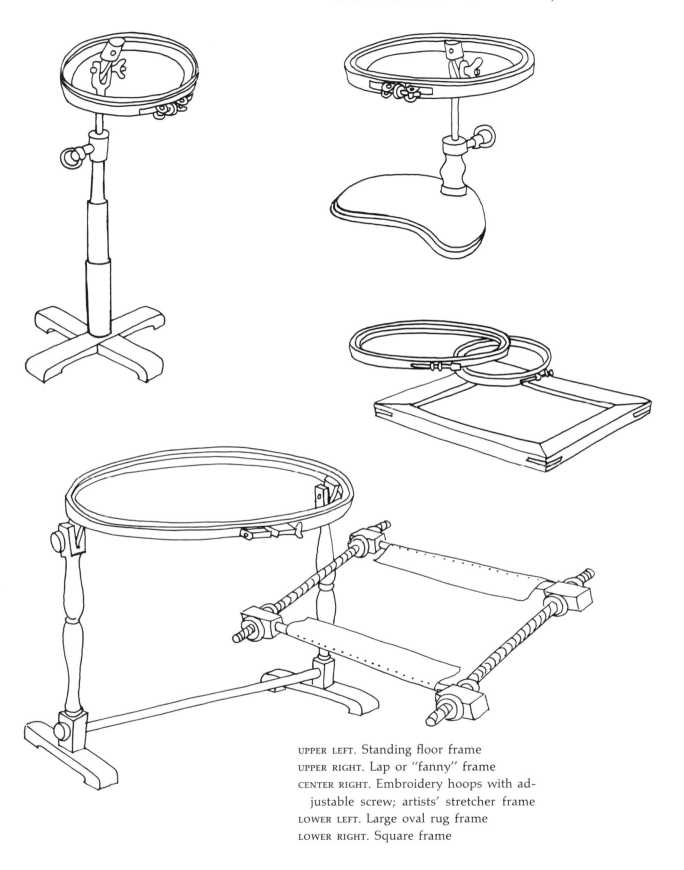

UPPER LEFT. Standing floor frame
UPPER RIGHT. Lap or "fanny" frame
CENTER RIGHT. Embroidery hoops with ad-
  justable screw; artists' stretcher frame
LOWER LEFT. Large oval rug frame
LOWER RIGHT. Square frame

without the wooden strips getting in your way. Assemble the four strips and stretch your material tightly over the frame, thumbtacking or stapling the fabric to the back. Then work exactly as you would on an embroidery hoop. When finished, if the design is to be a panel, you have an "instant picture" ready to hang on the wall! If the material becomes slack while you are working on it, push some thread or material into the sides to make it tight.

The fourth choice is to use a square frame. This is delightful to work on since the material is always beautifully taut. The main disadvantage of a square frame is that it is awkward to move about. Secondly, it will only take material of the same width as itself. The length may be rolled around the rollers, but the width can only be that of the frame, 18 inches, 24 inches, or 36 inches (average frame sizes). So it is impossible to work a large bedspread on a square frame without having the frame made up to a special size. This is where a hoop frame, which is used just to stretch the area on which you are working, is especially useful.

It is perfectly possible, of course, to do crewel embroidery in your hand. The only drawback is that certain stitches are eliminated from your repertoire. You cannot lay long threads across a surface, and tie them down afterward, for instance, unless you have a firm foundation to work on. A great many people do extremely neat work without using a frame at all, but for the average person a good effect is far more easily gained with its help. When using either a table or floor ring frame and both hands, the speed, dexterity, and ease with which you work will surprise you. *The stitches for which a frame is essential are marked with an asterisk on the stitch diagrams—all others can be worked without it.*

MOUNTING WORK IN A SQUARE FRAME

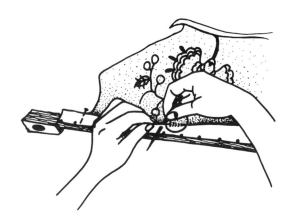

First stitch the fabric to the webbing of the square frame.

Then stretch tight, stitch webbing to either side and lace tightly with string as shown at right.

MOUNTING WORK IN A RING FRAME

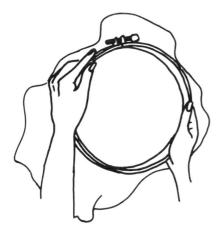

Before assembling the frame, adjust the screw so that the outer hoop fits snugly over the inner ring and the material. *Never* try to alter the screw when the frame is in place.

Pull the material taut; if the upper ring is tight enough the material will not slip back.

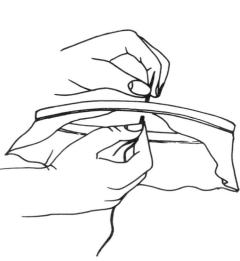

When the material is taut, push the upper ring down. To release the fabric do not unscrew the frame, but press thumbs down firmly into the fabric on the frame, at the same time lifting off the outer ring.

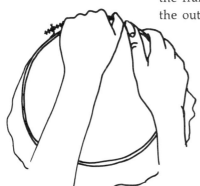

On any frame, always stab the needle up and down, never "sew." Work with both hands, keeping one *always* below the frame and the other above. This becomes much easier with practice and is essential for speed and dexterity.

Crewel is the first chapter of this book, because learning crewel embroidery is an ideal way to start doing any form of needlework, as the stitches can be used in *all media,* including needlepoint. There are no "crewel" stitches as such; they are all basic embroidery stitches which may be worked in silk, gold, or wool on any suitable fabric. Traditional crewel was done in two-ply yarn on linen, generally with very fine stitching, but today the almost unlimited varieties of texture and the dramatically quick results obtainable make working with wool like a more portable form of painting. To take wool brush strokes with the freedom of a painter is inspiring, and not the least of the fascination is the challenge of interpreting a design in stitches. These stitches, which may seem overwhelming in their many varieties at first, are really very simple.

Bedhangings, valances and window curtains worked for the Nantucket Historic Trust. *Designed by the author*

Tiger cat in satin stitch, laid work and long and short worked vertically for a tapestry
effect. *Designed by the author*

THE SEVEN STITCHES

There are only a handful of basic stitches which are the Adams and Eves of all the others, and however complicated and varied different techniques may seem they have all grown from these basic sources. The "ancestral" stitches, as we might call them, have been divided into seven different groups—stem, satin, chain, cross, back, weaving, and filling—upon which untold variations have been built. Each basic stitch has been worked into a "sampler" to illustrate how a simple change in texture and scale can make the same stitch almost unrecognizable. The sampler gives you freedom to experiment. Without having to fit stitches into any particular design you can work the main stitch in many different textures, try out its close cousins, develop your own techniques and ideas, and even, perhaps, by taking just another twist in the thread, invent your own original stitch!

So, take a piece of fabric and collect stitches on it in crewel wools, like the ones on the following pages. Once you have gained a knowledge of the simplest stitches you can add silk threads, mercerized cotton, and even metal threads of all varieties; and in studying each of the traditional techniques in this book you may find ideas for original creations in all media.

THREADING THE NEEDLE

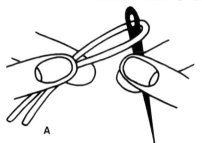
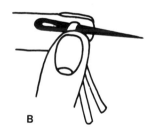
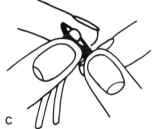

A. Wrap thread round the needle as shown. B. Hold thread tightly, close round needle; pull needle away. C. Squeeze thread *tightly* between finger and thumb, so that thread is almost buried. Press eye of needle flat down on to the thread, rather than attempting to push the thread through the needle. Pull through when amount of thread shown in diagram has appeared.

STARTING AND ENDING OFF

Put a knot in the thread and start on the wrong side of the material. As crewel work should always be backed, the wrong side is not of such tremendous importance, though care should be taken to keep the stitches flat, and not to jump too far from place to place without taking a small stitch in between.

End off with 2 small back stitches on an outline or inside the shape of a design which will later be covered. (The stitches in the diagram are enlarged to show clearly . . . . they should be very small.) Come up at A and pull through at B, then bring thread to front of work near by and cut off.

STEM STITCHES

Stem stitch is probably one of the oldest stitches in the world. Its ancestor, a twining stitch twisted into the weaving with the fingers, has been found in medallions used for clothing in Egyptian tombs, Coptic and Maori clothing, and remnants of antique fabrics all over the world, though in this early form it is scarcely distinguishable from weaving. Stem stitch is equally effective when it is used as a single outline or in rows used to fill an area solidly. It may be worked with the thread held either to the left or the right of the needle, but once a line has been started it should always be held to the same side.

The next logical development of stem stitch is split stitch, where, like its name, the needle *splits* through the thread instead of coming up to one side of it. Long and short stitch is really a collection of split stitches, arranged so that the colors blend softly. Therefore, these three basic stitches have been included together in this sampler.

Detail from an English 17th century bedhanging. *Colonial Williamsburg*

Stem Stitches

1   Stem, using rug wool alternately with 3 strands of Persian
2   Stem with 2 strands Persian
3   Split using 4 strands silk
4   Raised stem, using rug wool base, 3 strands Persian on top
5   Split, using knitting worsted
6   Whipped stem, heavy decorative yarn, whipped with 2 strands Persian
7   Satin, graduating to stem, 2 strands Persian
8   Split stitch circles, surrounded with lines of stem, worked with 2 strands of silk
9   Stem with 3 strands Persian
10 Long and short, fish scale pattern worked with 2 strands Persian
11 Long and short stitch in vertical bands worked with knitting worsted
12 Portuguese stitch worked in close vertical lines, alternating with whipped stem worked in lines spaced apart, using knitting worsted
13 Raised stem on a raised band. The band made of padded satin using 2 strands of Persian, the raised stem using 4 and 6 strands of mercerized cotton (embroidery floss)
14 Raised stem, worked in a chevron pattern, with 2 strands Persian

An excellent outline stitch, Stem Stitch may also be used as a solid filling. In this case, like Chain Stitch, the lines should all be worked in the same direction for smoothness. The thread may be held either to the right or left of the needle, but once a line or a block of stitches is begun it should be held always to the same side. When working an outline hold the thread away from the shape and towards the outside of curves. This will make the outline "roll" outwards instead of falling inwards and becoming "spiky."

When working stems and branches, work the main stem right through first, from top to bottom. Then, starting at the tips of the subsidiary stems, work them down to join the main stem, continuing the line alongside for several stitches to make a smooth join. Shorten the stitches slightly when working curves.

See Color Plate 1.

STEM STITCH

Needle comes up at A, goes in at B, and up again at C, exactly half way between A and B. Draw through, holding the thread to the left of the needle.

Needle goes in at D, up again at B, (in the same hole made by the thread going in previously at B). Draw through, still holding thread to left of needle.

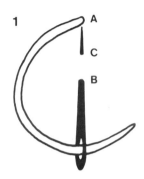

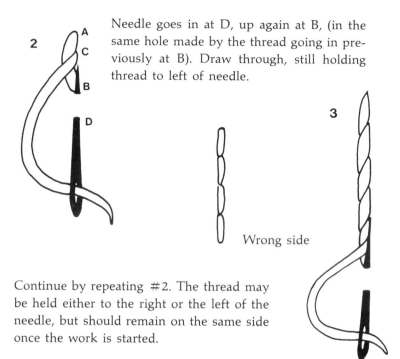

Wrong side

Continue by repeating #2. The thread may be held either to the right or the left of the needle, but should remain on the same side once the work is started.

✳ RAISED STEM STITCH

Though it is shown here as a banding stitch, Raised Stem may be used to fill whole areas. In this case the long basic stitches should be tacked down invisibly here and there, afterwards. The stitch may be shaded, working in vertical bands, or stripes of contrasting colors. When used to fill an uneven area it usually needs an outline of Stem Stitch.

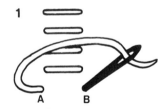

First work a series of parallel stitches (just under ¼" apart, as shown in diagram). *To work a wider area than the one shown, lay these lines across the whole width of the shape.*

Using a blunt (tapestry) needle, come up at A, and holding thread to left of needle slide under first thread from B to C. Do not go through material.

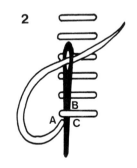

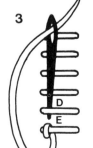

Repeat #2, sliding needle under thread from D to E, and work up to top of thread in this way.

Work several lines close side by side always beginning again at the bottom, working upwards until base threads are entirely covered. Do not pack too many rows in, however, or the effect will be lost.

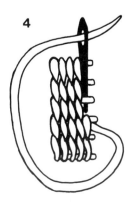

✱ RAISED STEM/CHEVRON PATTERN

1

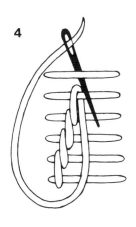

First work a series of parallel stitches just under each other, ¼″ apart.

Using a blunt tapestry needle come up at A, and, holding thread to left of needle, slide under the first thread from B to C. Do not go through material.

2

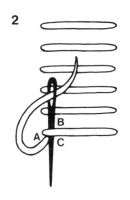

3

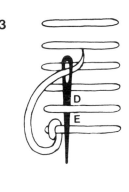

Repeat #2, sliding needle through the next thread from D to E.

Work up to the top thread in this way, to create a diagonal line as shown.

4

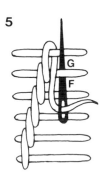

To reverse direction when the top thread is reached, slide the needle upwards from F to G keeping the thread to the left of the needle. Work down to the bottom thread in this way.

5

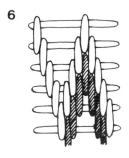

6

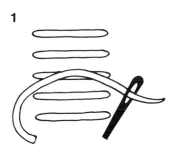

Several lines of different colors can be worked for the best effect.

✱ PORTUGUESE BORDER STITCH

First work a series of parallel stitches, just under ¼" apart.

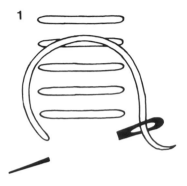

Starting at the base, using a blunt tapestry needle, wrap around the first two threads (A and B), four times. Do not go through the material. At the fourth stitch, pass only under *one* bar (at B), as shown in the diagram.

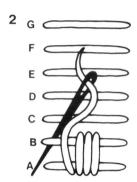

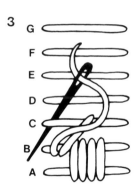

Wrap round bars B and C to make two slanting stitches as shown. On the second stitch pass only under *one* bar at C.

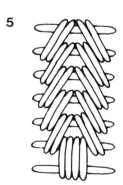

Continue to the top, repeating #3. End off the thread.

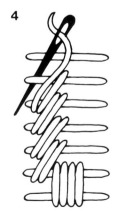

Go to the base again, and slanting the needle in the opposite direction, work up the other side as in the diagram.

PORTUGUESE KNOT

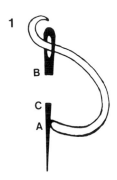

Using a blunt tapestry needle, begin with a stem stitch. Come up at A, go down at B and holding the thread to the right of the needle, come up at C, midway between A and B. Pull thread tight so the stitch lies flat.

Slide the needle under the first stitch at D, and bring it out on the other side just below C. Do not go through the material.

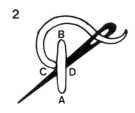

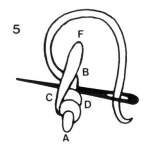

Pull thread tight, then slide the needle under the stem stitch again, so that it lies in place just below the first coil.

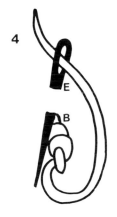

Pull thread tight and make another stem stitch, going down at E and coming up in the same hole formed by the stitch at B, holding the thread to the right of the needle.

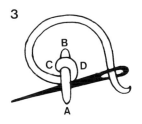

Pull thread tight. Now slide the needle through both the first and second stem stitch, where they overlap, just below B.

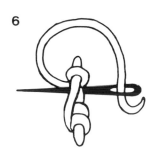

Repeat 2 and 3, sliding the needle under the second stem stitch to wrap it twice around as in #3. Continue, repeating 4, 5 and 6.

PALESTRINA KNOT STITCH

This stitch is very similar to Portuguese knot but has a looser effect.

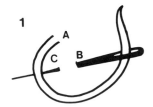

Come up at A, go down at B, slightly to the right and below A, and come up at C, level with B.

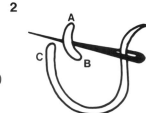

Slide through the bar just formed (A to B) and pull gently.

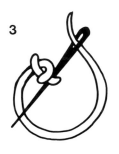

Holding the looped thread under the needle, slide through again, just to the right of the first stitch.

Now make a horizontal stitch into the material, from D to E, below the first stitch and about the distance of one knot away from it. Continue, repeating steps 2 and 3, to make a row of stitches as shown in diagram 5.

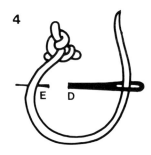

Shows a finished line. The effect can be entirely changed if the needle is slanted downwards instead of straight.

STEM STITCH/CHANGING TO SATIN

Start by working a row of stem stitch coming up at A, down at B and up again into the back of the previous stitch at C.

With each stitch, slant the needle a little more, so that instead of going back into the previous stitch (at C), it goes just to the right of it. Take up a little more fabric with each stitch, so that a widening band of satin stitch is formed as in the diagram.

By changing the slant of the needle the stitch can be graduated from wide to narrow or vice versa, as shown.

WHIPPED STEM STITCH

Whipped Stem Stitch makes a fine smooth line stitch when the Stem Stitch is whipped with the same color. (The Stem Stitches should not be too long.) An attractive candy cane effect is obtained if a contrasting color is used for the whipping. Generally it is best to use double thread in this case.

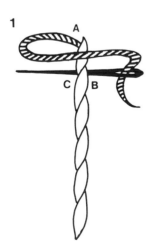

First work a line of Stem Stitch.

Then coming up at A change to a blunt tapestry needle and go through from B to C where stem stitches overlap one another. Pass only under the stitches, not through the material.

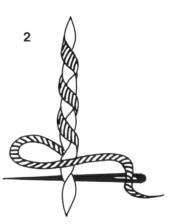

Continue, by repeating #2, until the whole line is whipped—finished effect should be like a raised cord.

∗ SPLIT STITCH

Like Stem and Chain Stitch, Split Stitch may be worked in close lines all in one direction. It is especially effective worked in one color when the only interest lies in the direction of line. It may be used as an outline stitch but it is more useful as an underlying padding on an edge which will later be covered with other stitching.

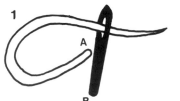

Needle comes up at A, goes down at B.

Needle comes up at C piercing through center of stitch from below, splitting it exactly in the middle.

Needle goes down at D, a little ahead of B—(the distance from C to D is the same as the length of the first stitch; from A to B). Repeat in this way, forming a smooth line of stitching slightly shortening the stitches when going around curves.

∗ LONG AND SHORT STITCH/ TAPESTRY SHADING

Whole designs, including the background, may be worked in Tapestry Shading. The effect will be like its name; the vertical shading of tapestry. This is a good stitch to practice before trying Long and Short—Soft Shading, since you can experiment with the size of the stitch and correct blending of the colors without having to bother about changing direction. Use double thread for practicing so that the stitches are clear. Though the colors should blend, it is better to have a clearly defined difference between them to show the stitch to its best advantage. An outline afterwards will spoil the effect of the raised edge obtained by the Split Stitch padding.

First work a row of Split Stitch along the outline. This stitch will be covered by Long and Short, but it is valuable as a firm padding and enables you to make a knife-sharp edge with the Long and Short. Come up at A and go down at B just *over* Split Stitch. Work a row of Long and Short Stitches side by side, as in diagram. (The short stitch is ¾ of the length of the long one.) Keep each long stitch alike and all the short stitches the same length.

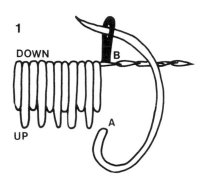

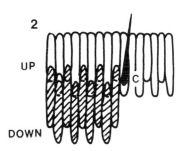

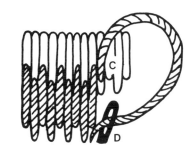

Next row. In another shade, *split up* through the first long and short stitches ¼ of the way back, at C. Go down into the material at D. NOTE: The stitches of this and all proceeding rows *are the same length.* Only the first row is long and short, then each following row fits back into the previous one in brick fashion. To give a smooth blend, split well back into these stitches. The dotted line on diagram shows how much of each previous stitch lies under the succeeding row.

In a third color, work a third line of stitches the same way (repeating #2), always coming up ¼ of the way back through the stitch. Be sure each row is long enough. Remember ¼ of the stitch will be obscured when the succeeding row is worked into it, and allow for this. Any number of rows may be worked in this way, using any number of colors, or only one. The best effect is obtained, however, if the rows are shaded gradually from dark to light, or light to dark, as in diagram.

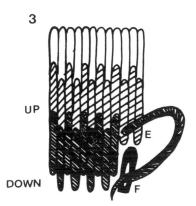

✳ LONG AND SHORT/SOFT SHADING

Long and Short—Soft Shading repeats the principle of Tapestry Shading exactly. Instead of running straight up and down, however, the stitches follow direction lines as indicated in the diagram, Direction of Stitches for Long and Short, page 44.

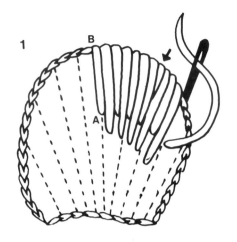

First draw guide lines in pencil on the material (as shown by dotted lines). Then outline the shape with Split Stitch, all around. Next work the first row of Long and Short, coming up at A and going down *over* the Split Stitch at B, starting in the center (or highest point) of each petal. It is easier to work downwards from the center on either side, since the angle of the stitch is straight to begin with, then gradually fans very slightly on each side. To achieve this, the stitches may be placed slightly wider apart on the outside edge and closer in the center, exactly like a fan. If this is not sufficient, a greater slant may be obtained by taking an extra short stitch over the upper edge occasionally (as indicated by the arrow in the diagram). This "wedge stitch" will not show, providing the next stitch is taken extremely close to it. On the shape illustrated, few wedge stitches are necessary since all the stitches gravitate to the center of the flower like the spokes of a wheel.

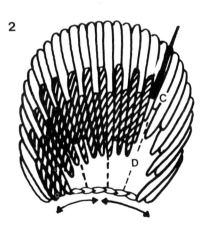

Work a second row of stitches in the next shade lighter or darker, coming up at C and down at D. Here again the stitches fan slightly as in the first row. They should not change direction abruptly, but should flow into one another smoothly. As in Tapestry Shading, be sure to split far enough back into the previous row and make the stitches long enough for the third row to split into them.

In the shape illustrated this second row of stitches comes right over the outline at the lowest point of the petals (as shown).

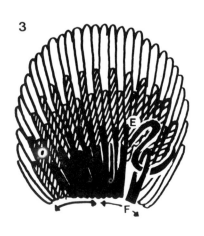

With the third color, fill the remaining space in the center of the petal. Come up at E and go down at F. Bring the stitches evenly down *over* the Split Stitch, making a smooth outline as at the beginning. On the third row it is impossible to fit each stitch *exactly* back through the previous stitch; every now and again miss one (as in the diagram). This is because there is less space in the center of the curve than on the outside. Still make the stitches look regular, keeping a long and short effect.

The first line (1) is a band of stitching following the outline exactly like Block Shading, (page 50) but with alternate long and short stitches. Follow this with the second line (2) in the same way, being certain to take the stitches high into the first stitches and echo the outline. The third row (3) repeats the second and makes a smooth row of outline stitches on the opposite side of the leaf (as shown).

1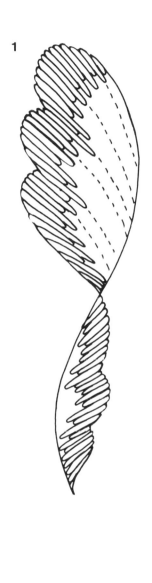

2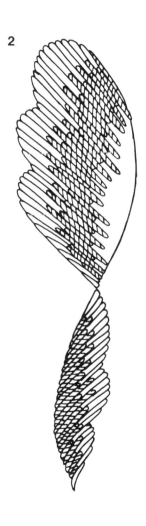

3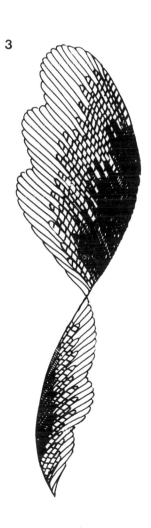

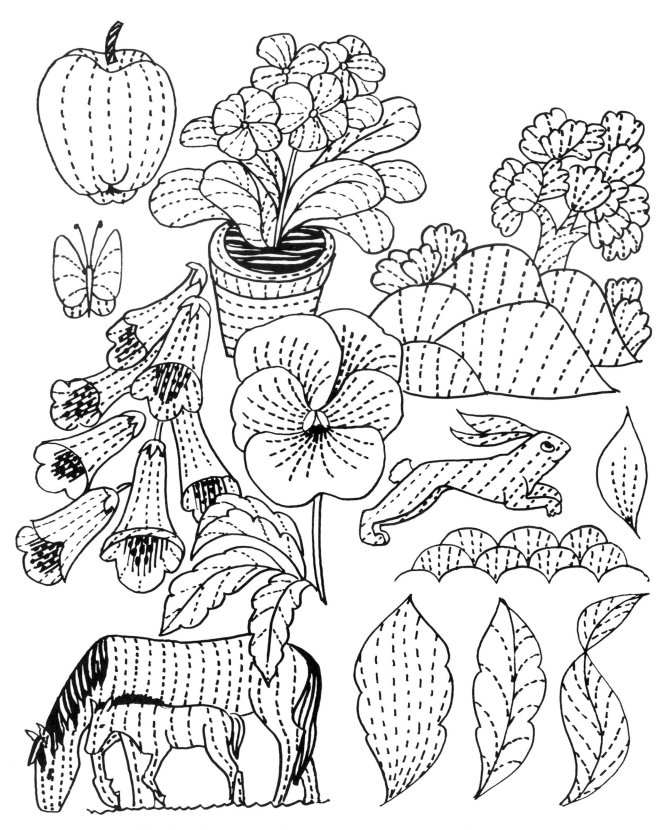

Direction of stitches for long and short shown by dotted guide lines

SATIN STITCHES

Satin stitch is really not a "stitch" at all in the true sense of the word. You simply "lay" threads side by side to closely cover an area, coming up at one edge of the shape and going down at the other. Nothing could be easier than laying in these straight stitches, yet nothing could be harder than keeping them meticulously even so that they appear smooth and "satiny." Of course sometimes a textured unevenness is intended, and then the effect is deliberately different. Since the stitch is so simple all the emphasis is on the thread you are using. The colors will be very dominant as there are no twists or loops to break up the light.

Since it is so basic, satin stitch has been a traditional stitch in needlework of all countries through the ages.

Closely akin to satin stitch is laid work, which from the front looks identical. But instead of the stitches being carried across on the back, they are worked only on the surface of the material, leaving very little thread on the reverse side, thus making laid work very economical with yarn. For this reason it is generally used in large areas which may be held flat by working other stitches on top afterward.

17th century English crewel work with chevrons of satin stitch. *Victoria & Albert Museum*

Satin Stitches

1   Satin worked in blocks, alternating direction, 2 threads Persian
2   Plate stitch worked with knitting worsted
3   Burden heavy yarn base 6 threads Persian on top rug
4   Laid work. 3 threads Persian, held flat with fly stitch, gold knitting lurex
5   Padded satin knitting worsted
6   Slanting satin. Alternating slant on each vertical band 3 threads Persian
7   Roumanian worked in bands, interlocking each row to blend colors. 3 strands Persian
8   Brick stitch. Heavy rug yarn
9   Laid work, English crewel yarn. Crisscross in 4 threads English yarn, tie down knitting worsted
10 Encroaching gobelin 2 threads Persian worked on canvas and applied
11 Chevron filling 3 strands Persian
12 Parisian stitch worked on canvas 3 strands Persian
13 Block shading 3 strands of English wool
14 Open burden worked on felt with gold knitting lurex held flat with 3 strands silk
15 Shaded laid work 3 strands Persian held flat with one strand
16 Bargello pattern worked on canvas knitting worsted
17 Burden worked vertically 3 strands Persian
18 Bargello pattern worked on canvas with 3 strands Persian

1	2	3
4	5	6
7	8	9
10	11	12
13	14	15
16	17	18

See Color Plate 2.

* SATIN STITCH

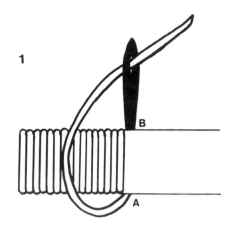

Come up at A and go down at B. Then come up again right next to A, and go down again next to B. Continue, coming up on one side and down on the other to form a smooth band of stitching. The stitches may be straight or slanting but they should always lie evenly side by side.

* SLANTING SATIN STITCH

Satin stitch needs practice in order to make it neat and even. A slant helps to make it smoother, and a Split Stitch padding makes it easier to keep the edge clean; both essential to the effect. It should never be used for large areas, because the threads could easily be pulled and disarranged when the embroidery is in use. On very small leaves it is easier to start at the tip and work downwards. To maintain the slant, come up close at the upper edge and go down with a slight space between the stitches on the lower edge. This tends to exaggerate the slant of each stitch but prevents them from flattening out.

First outline shape with Split Stitch.

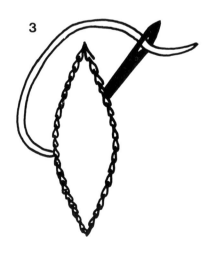

Starting in the center (to be certain of the exact angle), work slanting stitches close together across the shape, coming up and going down *outside* the Split Stitch. (Split Stitch forms a padding on the outline, giving a firm edge.)

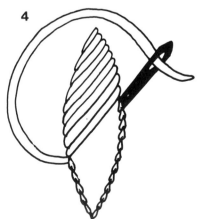

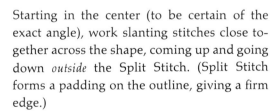

Work up to tip, then start at center again and finish working shape to the bottom. Stitches should lie evenly side by side, not crowded, but no material showing between. Do not pull too tightly.

* SATIN STITCH/TIED WITH BACK STITCH

This stitch may be used to fill a wider area, for unlike Slanting Satin Stitch, it has a row of stitching to hold it in the center. More than one row of Back Stitch may be worked if the area needs it. Do not pull the Back Stitch too tight for it will spoil the evenness of the Satin Stitch underneath it.

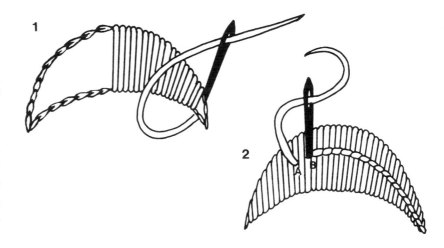

Having outlined shape with Split Stitch, Satin Stitch over it, starting in center to guide stitches at the correct angle. Keep stitches fairly upright at outside points (as shown). It is easier to work longer stitches instead of very short ones.

As stitches would be too long to leave untied, work a row of Back Stitch through the center of the shape, using the upper edge as a guide line. Needle comes up at A, and down at B, right into the hole made by the last stitch.

* PADDED SATIN STITCH

The top row of Padded Satin Stitch may be worked straight instead of slanting, but this is much harder to make even, especially when the stitches are small at the point of a leaf. It is therefore best to practice it on a slant first.

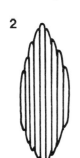

Starting in the center of the shape, come up at A, down at B.

Fill shape with stitches just side by side.

Go across with a few stitches to hold the long ones flat.

For the second padding, go up and down vertically again as in #2.

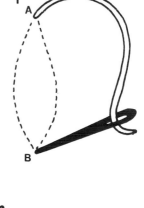

Come up at A, down at B, and cover the whole shape with slanting stitches as shown. To maintain the slant, A should always be a fraction ahead of the last stitch, and B should be pushed up very close to the previous stitches. (Otherwise the slant becomes flatter and flatter until it is almost straight.)

✳ BLOCK SHADING

Like Roumanian Stitch, bands of Block Shading should fit closely together, slightly overlapping the previous row, to prevent any material showing between them. When used to fill shapes, Block Shading should have the same direction of stitch as Long and Short. (See diagram page 44.) It is advisable to mark this direction in pencil on the material before working. Never outline Block Shading afterwards, the edge will be smooth and raised because of the Split Stitch padding.

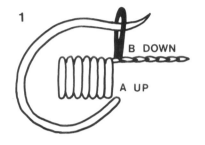

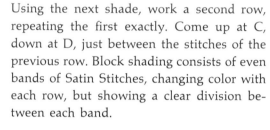

First outline shape to be worked with Split Stitch. Then work a row of Satin Stitches, bringing needle up at A, down at B, over Split Stitch. (This makes a firm, even edge.) Keep all the stitches close and even, side by side.

Using the next shade, work a second row, repeating the first exactly. Come up at C, down at D, just between the stitches of the previous row. Block shading consists of even bands of Satin Stitches, changing color with each row, but showing a clear division between each band.

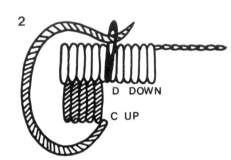

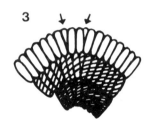

To work round a curve, place the stitches slightly wider apart on the edge, closer in the center to fan them, leaving no visible space between them, however. Occasionally slip in a shorter wedge stitch to help fan them (as shown in the diagram by the arrow).

✳ LAID WORK/TIED DIAGONALLY

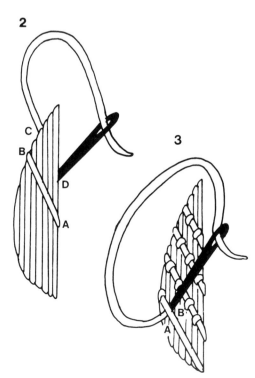

First read basic Laid Work, 1, 2 and 3, page 52. Having worked Laid Work over area (in direction shown), come up at A, down at B. This stitch lies across broadest area of the shape, to set the correct angle for the following stitches.

Come up at C, down at D, making a line parallel to A and B, about ¼″ above it. Then work from the center downwards until whole shape is laid with parallel slanting lines.

These lines must then be tied down with small stitches. Come up at A, down at B, going right through the material. These stitches should be placed alternately.

* SHADED LAID WORK

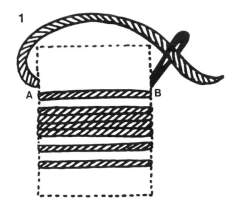

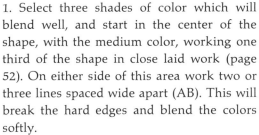

1. Select three shades of color which will blend well, and start in the center of the shape, with the medium color, working one third of the shape in close laid work (page 52). On either side of this area work two or three lines spaced wide apart (AB). This will break the hard edges and blend the colors softly.

2. Fill in the spaces between the medium stitches with light color, and continue to the top, filling the space closely with laid work.

3. Cover the lower half of the shape with the dark color, working in between the medium stitches, being careful not to stitch so closely with the dark color that the medium stitches are covered and lost.

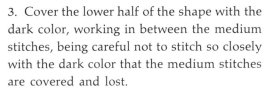

4. Finally, hold the laid work flat with parallel lines of split stitch worked in the opposite direction to the base stitching. Although any stitches may be used to hold the laid work flat, split stitch, using the medium shade, generally blends best with shaded background.

* PLATE STITCH

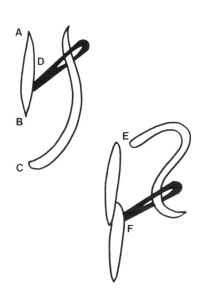

Come up at A, down at B, making a vertical stitch. Come up at C, down at D close to AB, making another vertical stitch below. Repeat, without packing the stitches too close together, yet allowing very little material to show in between. On the second row of stitches (at arrow) come up between those of previous row as shown.

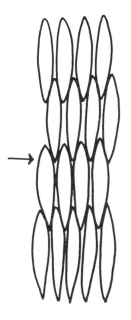

✳ LAID WORK/TIED WITH CROSS BARS

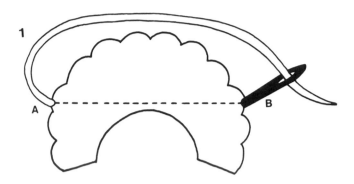

Laid Work may be used for large areas, since unlike satin stitch, no yarn is wasted on the reverse side. It may be held flat in many different ways by working other stitches on top in the opposite direction. Needle comes up at A, goes in at B right across widest point of shape, to establish desired direction. All subsequent stitches are parallel to this line.

Next stitch comes up at C close to B and goes down again at D close to A. When Laid Work is done correctly, very small stitches appear on the reverse side, while the right side is closely covered with long threads.

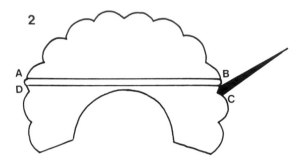

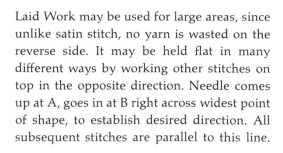

Continue working in this way, coming up close beneath previous stitch, on the same side as where you went down. (Stitches should lie evenly side by side with no material showing between them.) When lower half is completed go back to center and work upper half in same way.

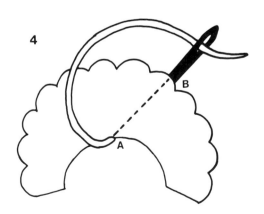

To hold Laid Work flat with Cross Bars, start in broadest part of shape and come up at A. Go down at B, laying a long thread diagonally across shape (angle is indicated by dotted line). This should cut across Laid Work threads at about 45°.

Come up at C, about ¼″ away from B, and go in at D, making a line parallel to A and B. Cover the whole shape in this way, and then work lines in the other direction to make perfect diamonds as shown in #6.

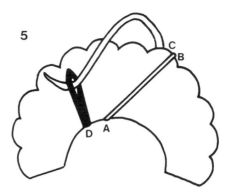

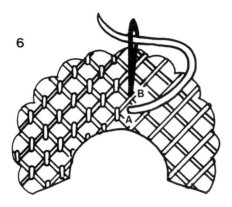

These threads are now tied down by a small stitch at each intersection. Come up at A, and go down at B, as shown, until all threads are tied down. At the edge make a little half stitch if necessary (as shown).

✻ BRICK STITCH

Using a blunt needle come up at A, go down at B. Up at C, then down at D, leaving the space of one thread between each stitch.

Work a second row so that the stitches overlap half way into the previous row, coming up at E, then down at F.

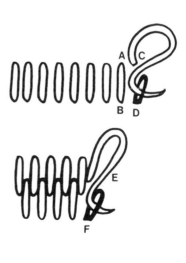

Work the third row so that the stitches come up into the lower hole formed by the first row of stitches. The blunt needle makes it easier to come up exactly into the holes. Finished effect is like a block of bricks.

ROUMANIAN STITCH

Roumanian Stitch is really a straight Satin Stitch tied down with a smaller slanting stitch in the center. If the small stitch maintains its slant well, the stitches will fit closely together with no separation between them, keeping the effect smooth. However, this small stitch may be worked on a greater slant if the area to be filled is wide. When several bands are worked side by side the stitches should just overlap one another at the edge. If each row fits into the *exact* holes of the previous one, the stitches are apt to pull away a little and leave material showing in between.

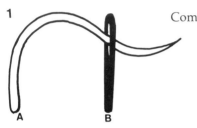

1 Come up at A, down at B; pull flat.

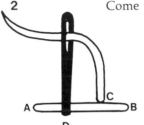

2 Come up at C and go over and down at D; pull flat.

Next, come up at E, below but touching A, go down at F, below but touching B; leave a loop.

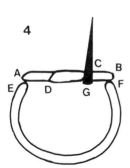

3

4 Then come up at G, close to and immediately below C, inside the loop; draw tight.

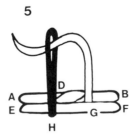

5 Go down over thread at H, directly below D, exactly as in #2, and continue; repeating #3, 4, 5. Keep center row of stitches G-H even (as shown in finished effect).

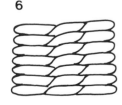

6 Finished effect

Plate 1.   Stem Stitch sampler

Plate 2.   Satin Stitch sampler

Plate 3. Chain Stitch sampler

Plate 4. Cross Stitch sampler

Plate 5. Weaving Stitch sampler

Plate 6. Embroidery in crewel and rug wools on hand-woven wool fabric. *Designed and worked by the author*

Plate 7.   "The Peaceable Kingdom", crewel wool on linen. *Designed and worked by the author*

Horses in split and stem stitch, adapted from a Chinese painting. *Designed and worked by the author*

Plate 8. Wool embroidery on antique satin. *Designed by the author and worked by Mrs. John Marsh*

* CHEVRON FILLING

This stitch is really borrowed from the Bargello Stitch of needlepoint or canvas work, but it makes an effective filling which may be carried out in as many colors as you please. It usually looks best if it is not outlined, so take care to keep the edge neat.

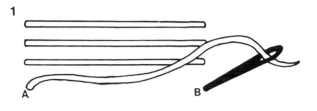

Lay parallel lines across shape to be worked, by coming up at A, going down at B. Lines are approximately ¼" apart. Always come up and go down on the same side of the outline, to avoid long threads on the back.

Start by coming up right underneath line #1, pass over line #2 and down close below line #3. Do four stitches in this way side by side. Now bring needle up right underneath line #2, pass over line #3, and down close below line #4. Do four stitches in this way side by side.

Now repeat this, coming up under #3, going over #4 and down just under #5. Continue these blocks of four stitches, going down three lines and up three lines until you have finished a complete row (as illustrated). Now, start over again, using a shade deeper color. Come up exactly in the hole made by the previous thread, underneath line #3, pass over line #4 and go down close below line #5. Continue in this manner across the complete row.

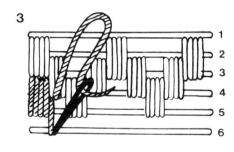

Now start your third row with a still deeper color. Then repeat the light shade, medium shade, and dark color over again (as shown in diagram). Always complete one row before beginning the next. Always start across the widest space to be filled, since the first row acts as a guide for all subsequent shorter rows.

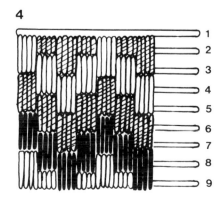

✳ BURDEN STITCH

This stitch may be used as a filling, or to cover large background spaces. It is attractive worked either very closely so that the basic threads hardly show, or quite wide apart to make an open lacy effect. It has the advantage of being an open filling, yet one where it is very easy to change color. The finished effect is almost like weaving. Generally it is best done in double thread, using the darkest color to underlay it and outlining the finished shape all round afterwards.

1

Coming up at A, going down at B, up at C, down at D, etc., lay parallel lines about ¼″ apart (coming up the same side as you go down).

2

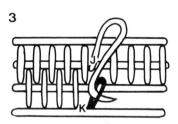

Work the complete line (as shown), coming up at G and going down at H. G is immediately below and *really touching* line A-B; H is immediately above and *really touching* line E-F. Keep all stitches at right angles to the original laid lines.

3

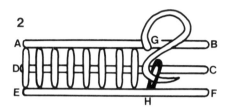

Coming up at J, just below the line, go down at K, just above the line as in #2. Come up in between the previous stitches, fitting them in like bricks. Again take care to make stitches touch the lines above and below. The finished effect is like weaving, as though the vertical stitches disappear under the horizontal ones.

4

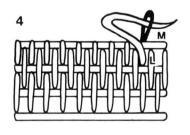

To finish the upper row, come up at L and go down at M, just over the top line. (It is easier to finish the top row of stitching after the scale has been set by the other rows.)

5

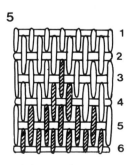

When shading use two needles and completely finish one row before going to the next. In row 3 for instance, work nearly to the center with light color, work one stitch of dark, change to light again and finish the row. In row 4 work the light stitches, then two stitches of dark and finish in light. (If all one color were worked first, insufficient space might be left for the other color, causing uneven spacing between stitches.)

CHAIN STITCHES

Who knows whether a thread was first looped through another in the air, or whether the first chain stitches were taken on cloth? The stitch is formed by loops of thread being drawn through one another to make a chain, and this may be stitched on fabric by using either a needle or a crochet hook. Many of the magnificent palampores or tree-of-life designs brought to Europe from India in the seventeenth century were done in fine silk chain stitches. These were the hangings that inspired the whole fashion for crewel. The stitches are so fine and the embroidery colors so cleverly blended that from a slight distance it is almost impossible to distinguish the embroideries from painting.

To work chain stitch smoothly you should always start at one end, go to the end of the row and stop. Start the second row at the beginning again. Working back and forth produces a different effect, rougher in texture. Once the thread is looped, the variations in stitches are endless. You may even invent your own!

Buttonhole, a well-known and basic stitch, is a close cousin of chain because the thread is simply looped to one side instead of returning to the same hole. Therefore, it has been incorporated with chain in this sampler.

Border detail, 17th century English crewelwork. *Colonial Williamsburg*

Chain Stitches

1 Cable chain, 2 threads English wool, interlaced with 1 thread

2 Raised chain, 3 threads Persian on base of heavy rug yarn

3 Chain knitting worsted

4 Fishbone knitting worsted

5 Ladder alternated with Vandyke, knitting worsted

6 Buttonhole in circles, 2 threads Persian

7 Whipped chain, base heavy rug yarn, whipped 6 threads Persian, alternated with lines of chain in knitting worsted

8 Trellis, knitting worsted

9 Open chain knitting worsted

10 Open buttonhole, each row worked into and alternating with previous row, knitting worsted

11 Rope, 3 strands Persian

12 Buttonhole scale pattern, alternate rows close and open. 6 strands embroidery floss

13 Ceylon stitch knitting worsted

14 Raised buttonhole on raised band—Padded satin stitch base, all knitting worsted

15 Detached buttonhole, worked two ways divided by lines braid stitch—2 strands Persian

16 2 strands of Persian for the following double chain

17 Detached worsted chain worked in gold lurex knitting thread on felt

18 Coral stitch 3 strands Persian

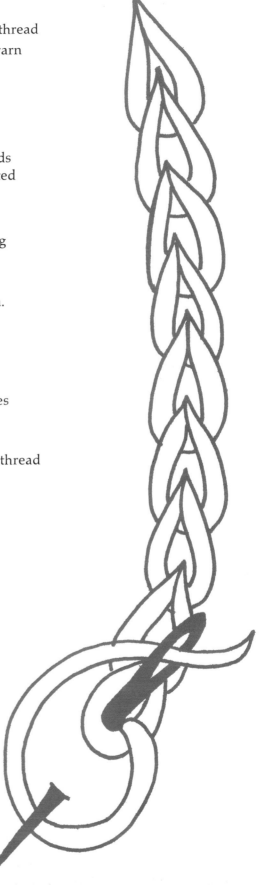

1	2	3
4	5	6
7	8	9
10	11	12
13	14	15
16	17	18

See Color Plate 3.

CHAIN STITCH

Chain Stitch may be used as a solid filling, working row upon row closely side by side. Do not pack the stitches *too* closely, however, or the effect will be lost. The filling is equally effective if the lines are shaded, or worked all in one color with contrasting outline. (The stitches should all begin at the same end and run in the same direction to make a smooth effect.) When extra lines have to be added to broaden the shape in one place, add them on the inside, allowing a continuous line to run along the edges. In this way the joining lines will not be obvious, especially if the first stitch of the joining line is tucked *underneath* the longer line.

Chain Stitch may also be used as an outline where a fairly broad dominant edge is needed.

Bring needle up at A. **1**

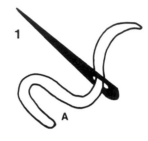

2

Form a loop, and put the needle in at A again, holding loop down with finger. Then come up at B, directly below A. Draw gently through, forming the first chain stitch.

3

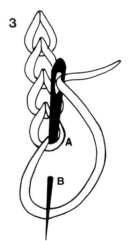

Repeat #2, always inserting needle exactly where the thread came out, *inside* the last loop—come up directly below, and draw through so chain stitches lie flat on material. When filling a shape by working rows of Chain Stitch, always work in same direction, beginning each new row at top and working down.

Wrong side

DETACHED CHAIN STITCH

Make a single Chain Stitch and anchor it down with a small stitch (as at the end of a row of Chain Stitch). This stitch may be used as a filling, combined with cross bars, or scattered over the ground as a "powdering" like seeding.

DETACHED TWISTED CHAIN

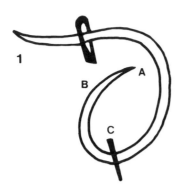

Come up at A, go down at B level with and to the left of A. Holding the thread across and then under the needle as shown, come up at C, in the center below A-B.

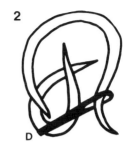

Anchor the stitch down outside the loop at D.

Finished effect

WHIPPED CHAIN STITCH

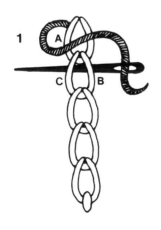

First work a row of chain stitch (see page 60). Then change to a blunt tapestry needle, come up at A, and slide needle through from B to C. Pick up the chain stitches only, do not go through the material.

Continue, sliding the needle lightly under each chain, without pulling the thread too tightly. The finished effect should be like a raised cord.

BACKSTITCHED CHAIN STITCH

Work a row of ordinary Chain Stitch. Then with a contrasting color, backstitch through it, coming up in the center of one Chain Stitch and going down in the center of the one before.

Finished effect. This stitch is equally effective when used as a solid filling with several rows side by side.

MAGIC CHAIN STITCH

Thread needle with two contrasting threads. Come up at A. Form a loop and put the needle in again at A holding loop down with finger. Come up again at B.

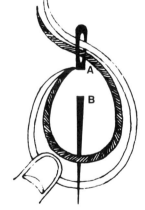

Keeping the light thread under the needle, allow the dark one to go above it. Pull the threads through and the light one will form a single chain stitch while the dark one will disappear behind the material.

Repeat the process, this time holding the dark under the needle and allowing the light to slip through. Continue to work in this way alternating dark with light or, if you wish, take two light stitches and two dark.

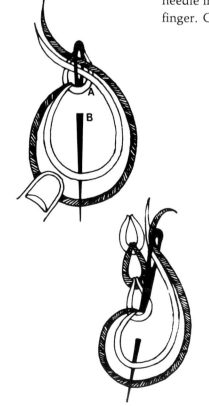

Finished effect

ZIGZAG CHAIN STITCH

Like Interlaced Running, this stitch needs space to show it to its best advantage.

This stitch is exactly like Chain Stitch, except that every stitch is worked at an angle to the previous one, as shown. The angle may be increased or decreased according to the effect required.

OPEN CHAIN STITCH

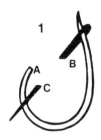

Make a chain stitch, coming up at A, going in at B, and coming up again at C, directly below A. Loop the thread under the needle as in the diagram and pull gently through.

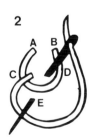

Repeat, going in at D *inside* the first chain stitch to the right and level with C, and up at E directly below C. Loop the thread under the needle and draw through gently. Note that the needle is always slanted instead of straight, as in regular chain stitch (page 60).

Finished effect shows a line of open loops.

INTERLACED CABLE CHAIN STITCH

This stitch is useful as a single line, or it may be worked in rows and interlaced to make a light open filling as shown. When used as the latter it is more effective to use double thread for the cable and single for the interlacing.

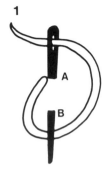

Work a Chain Stitch, coming up at A and going down again at A, holding the loop open—come up inside this loop at B and draw flat.

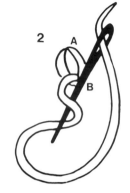

Holding the needle as shown, twist the thread once around it (as in French Knots).

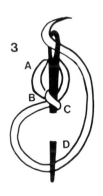

Draw the twist tight and put the needle in at C, (outside the Chain Stitch loop). Now form another loop, and with the thread under the needle, come up at D and draw flat (as shown). This makes another Chain Stitch.

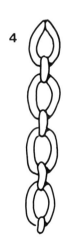

Repeat #2 again and continue making a Chain Stitch and a French Knot alternately so that the finished effect is like the diagram.

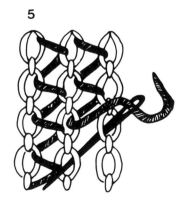

Using a blunt needle and a contrasting colored thread, lace the "cables" together (as shown). Do not draw the interlacing thread too tight.

* BRAID STITCH

Braid stitch is strictly an outline stitch, as it would be difficult to work rows close together without the needle interfering with the previous row. Single thread may be used, but double thread will show the stitch to its best advantage.

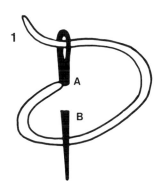

Make a small Chain Stitch. Come up at A, and go down again at A, holding the loop open—come up inside this loop at B and draw flat.

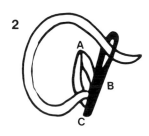

Anchor this Chain Stitch by going down outside the loop at C.

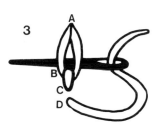

Using a blunt needle, come up at D and slide through the Chain Stitch (not through the material) from right to left (as shown).

Then go down at D through the material.

Next come up at E, just below D. Slide the needle from right to left under the anchoring stitch B-C, as well as the last chain just completed (diagram #4). Do not go through material.

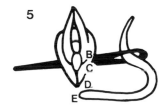

Go down through the material at E.

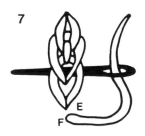

Come up at F and going back two stitches, slide the needle from right to left under both of them (as shown).

Continue in this way, sliding the needle from right to left under the two previous stitches together. Go down into the material where the thread came up, and come up again below ready to repeat.

The finished effect, drawn closely, is like a braid on top of the fabric.

ROPE STITCH/NARROW

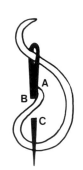

This stitch may be used as an outline, or as a solid filling, working the rows close together, all in the same direction. It is difficult to make this stitch smooth without practicing a little first, but it helps if the stitches are fairly long. Use double thread.

Come up at A and go down at B, immediately below A. Form a loop and come up at C, directly below B and inside the loop; draw flat. This stitch is like Chain, except that the thread is crossed in front of the needle before looping under it, and exactly like Rope Stitch-Broad, except that the needle is almost straight, instead of slanting.

Go down at D, pushing the needle very close up into the waist formed by the twisted chain. Looping the thread under the needle, come up at E on a straight line below A; draw flat.

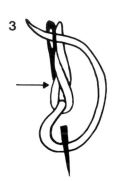

Repeat #2, and continue along the line. A smooth effect will be gained only if the needle is pushed very close, almost under the stitches (at arrow). The stitch must also be pulled down toward you to tighten it, or the loop will not lie flat.

Finished effect

ROSETTE CHAIN STITCH

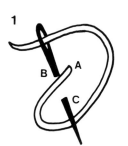

It is best worked fairly small and closely, too large a stitch can easily become caught and pull when in use. It is most effective as a single line or edging.

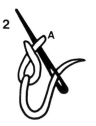

Working on a line from right to left, using a blunt needle, come up at A, go down at B, a little to the left and below A, and come up at C, slightly to the right and below B. Hold the thread across in front of the needle, then twist it under the needle, as shown. Pull through, keeping the stitch lying flat on the material.

Now slide needle under the stitch at A, as shown. Do not pass through the material.

Then repeat #1, a little distance away from the stitch just made, but level with it.

Repeat along the line. The effect of this stitch can be varied by placing the "rosettes" near one another or further apart.

ROPE STITCH/BROAD

This stitch is really exactly like Narrow Rope Stitch, except that the position of the needle is different. Used for a stem, Broad Rope appears rather like a Slanting Satin Stitch band, flat on one side and raised on the other. It may be worked as a solid filling, or a line of rope may be worked sometimes broad and sometimes narrow in one continuous line.

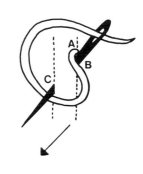

Come up at A and go down at B, tucking the needle just under A (as shown). Bring the needle out at C, twisting the thread first over and across the needle, then under it (as shown). Draw flat, pulling the thread taut in the direction of the arrow. The slant of the needle from B to C is about 45°.

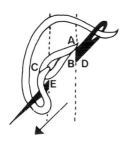

Go in at D, and come up at E, parallel with, and just touching A-C. Twist the thread over and then under the needle as before, and draw it flat, taking care not to let the loop rise up before the thread is tight. It is very easy to lose the slant and flatten out when working this stitch. To maintain the 45° angle keep the needle at D very close and touching A. Come up at E a *slight* distance below C; and again draw flat in the direction of the arrow to keep the loops lying smooth.

If the angle is maintained, a smooth Satin Stitch effect will result (as in diagram).

CORAL STITCH

The knots may be spaced closely or far apart, but should always be at right angles to the line. When several rows are worked close together the stitches should be fitted into the spaces between the knots on the previous lines. The effect of the stitching when it is solid is almost like rows of fat French Knots. To make it effective it is best to use double thread.

Wrong side

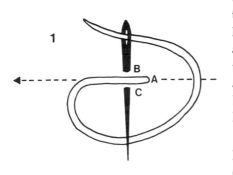

Bring needle up at A, lay thread flat in direction of working (indicated by dotted line). Needle then goes in at B, and up at C at right angles to the thread. Holding the thread under needle (as in diagram), draw through and pull gently up to form a knot. The space between B and C determines the size of the knot.

Next stitch repeats #1 a little distance away. (The stitch is more effective if the knots are fairly close together.)

CRESTED CHAIN STITCH

Make a horizontal chain stitch. Bring needle up at A, form a loop, return needle to the same hole at A again, and come up at B inside the loop. Draw gently through.

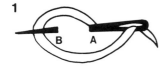

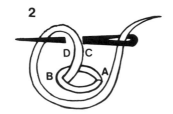

Immediately above the chain, make a coral stitch. Go in at C and up at D. (C to D is about half the length of A to B.) Take the thread over, then under needle as in the diagram. (It may be held in this position by your thumb as you take stitch DC.) Pull gently through.

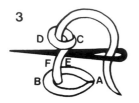

Now slide the needle *under* the connecting thread between the chain and coral stitches, from E to F. Do not go through the material, pass only under the thread, being careful not to split it, and once again gently through.

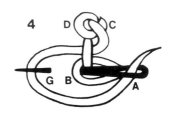

Finally return to the base to make another horizontal chain stitch, going into the same hole at B and coming up at G, inside the loop.

The upper and lower stitches should be parallel to make a wide, even band. The stitch is more effective with slight spacing between the coral stitches as shown.

DOUBLE CHAIN STITCH

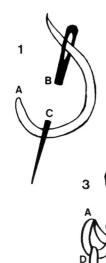

Come up at A, go down at B and up again at C, midway between and below A and B. Loop the thread to the right, under the needle, as in the diagram, and draw gently through. Hold thread flat with your thumb to keep the loop firm until you take the next stitch which secures it.

Go in at A again and come up at D, immediately below it. Loop the thread to the left, under the needle, and draw gently through.

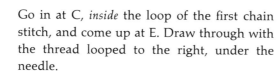

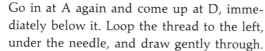

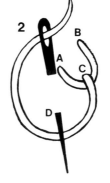

Go in at C, *inside* the loop of the first chain stitch, and come up at E. Draw through with the thread looped to the right, under the needle.

Continue, looping the thread alternately to left and right to make a double row of chain stitches as in the diagram.

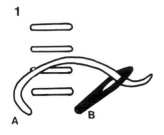

1

* RAISED CHAIN STITCH

See notes on Raised Stem Stitch (page 34).

First work a series of parallel stitches (just under ¼" apart) as shown in diagram. (As for Raised Stem Stitch.)

Then bring thread up at B and slide under thread from C to D (do not go through material). This stitch is best worked with a blunt needle. Draw through and hold thread upwards keeping it rather taut.

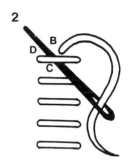

2

3

Next slide needle downwards under same thread, but to the right of first stitch, from E to F, draw through, holding thread under needle; do not pull too tightly so the appearance of the stitch is as in #4.

Continue stitch by repeating #2 and #3. Several rows may be worked side by side to fill a space (as in Raised Stem Stitch) instead of single row shown. In this case end off row at base and start again at the top, ready to work downwards.

4

FLY STITCH

These stitches may be scattered over an area, or worked in regular rows. They are useful for holding flat other stitching such as laid work. In this case they may be worked right on top of the first layer of stitching.

Come up at A, go down at B, and come up at C. Loop the thread under the needle as shown and draw gently through.

Go down at D, over the loop to secure it.

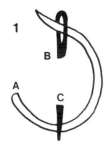

1

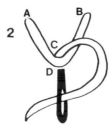

2

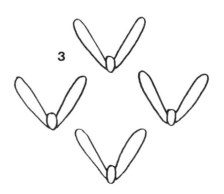

3

✳ FISHBONE STITCH

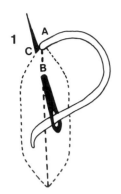

The first stitch (A to B) should be at least ¼″ long to start the stitch off on a good slant. To maintain this slant, bring the needle up and go down on the edge, almost in the same holes as the previous stitches, and keep the center stitch (B to E) a good length. The stitch looks best if a smooth edge is made which does not need outlining afterwards. Like Cretan, Fishbone may also be worked with spaces between the stitches for an open effect.

1. Come up at A in the center of point. Go down at B directly below it (draw line down center as guide line). Come up at C to left and slightly below A, but touching it, on outline of shape.

2. Go in at D to right and slightly below A, but touching it. Come up at B, and form a loop by holding thread under needle.

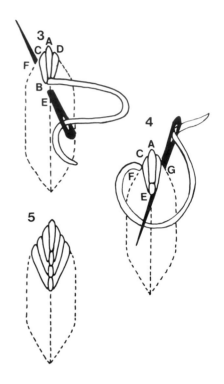

3. Draw through and insert needle at E a short space directly below B, come up at F—again to the left and slightly below C, but touching it.

4. Now repeat #2 again; come up at F, go in at G (touching previous threads). Come up at E with thread under the needle. Anchor it down as in #3, and continue in this way.

5. Finished effect

BUTTONHOLE STITCH

This is one of the most versatile of stitches. It may be worked in solid rows, or radiating from one central point to form a circle, in scallops, or with the spokes outwards as an outline around a shape. (This was frequently used in Jacobean embroidery to soften the edge of large leaves.) Always space the stitches just far enough apart to allow the loops at the edge to lie smoothly. Like Chain Stitch, Buttonhole Stitch is the basis for many other stitches, notably Coral Stitch.

Needle comes up at A, goes in at B, and up at C directly below B, and level with A. Thread is held under needle as in diagram. Draw through downwards.

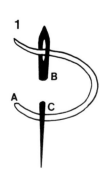

Next stitch repeats #1 at an even distance apart. Stitching may be spaced as shown, or worked closely as in #3.

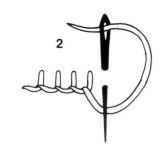

Diagram shows angle of needle when working curved shapes.

CRETAN STITCH

This stitch may be worked very close and slanting, as shown, or flatter and with spaces between the stitches. In this way two completely different effects may be obtained, just as in Fishbone Stitch.

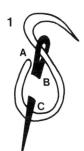

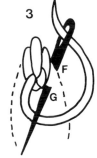

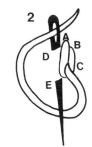

Come up at A. Go down at B a fraction below and to the right of A. Form a loop and come up at C inside the loop.

Go down at D, a fraction to the left and below A. Form a loop and come up at E, inside the loop. E is a little to the left and below C.

Repeat #1, going down at F and up at G, inside the loop as shown. F and G are a fraction to the right and below the previous stitches.

Repeat #2. Needle goes down and comes up a fraction to the left and below other stitches, coming up inside the loop each time.

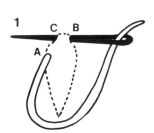

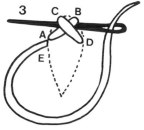

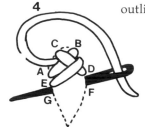

Finished effect

Continue in this way so that a plait is formed down the center of the shape. Keep the stitches very close together on the edge to maintain the slant, and the center stitches on an even line below one another, as shown.

VANDYKE STITCH

Using a blunt needle, come up at A and take a small stitch from B to C at top of shape to be worked (as shown).

Go down at D and up at E, a needle's width below A on the outline.

Slide needle from right to left under the Cross Stitch formed by A-B, and C-D. Do not go through the material.

Go down at F on the outline, a needle's width below D. Come up at G below E on the outline.

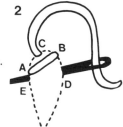

Repeat #3 and #4 until shape is filled. If you space the stitches well, keep the tension even and do not pull too tightly, a smooth raised braid will be formed down the center.

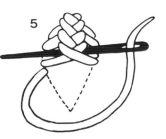

✳ KNOTTED PEARL STITCH

The Buttonhole Stitches should not be pulled too tightly, and should always be drawn up into the center of the band, to make a row of raised knots down the middle of the stitch. Do not attempt to work too wide a band with this stitch.

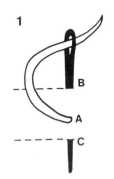

Come up at A, go down at B, and up again at C. A-B-C are all on a straight line (as shown).

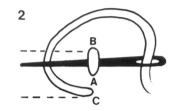

Using a blunt needle, slide under stitch B-A from right to left without going through material. Holding loop under the needle (as shown), pull flat. This forms one Buttonhole Stitch on bar B-A.

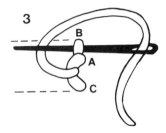

Now work a second Buttonhole Stitch by going under the bar B-A again, exactly as in #2.

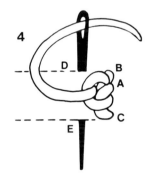

Go down through the material at D, come up at E. D and E are level with B and C (as shown).

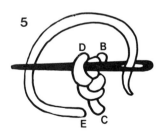

Now repeat procedure of #2 again . . . this time the Buttonhole Stitches are worked into the bar at D (as shown). Be very careful to pick up only the bar at D and not the other stitches.

Finished effect. To complete row, go down outside last Buttonhole loop to anchor it.

CROSS STITCHES

Simple cross stitch is probably one of the easiest stitches of all. It may be worked separately, as an open "powdering," or close together to fill an area. It is essentially geometric and therefore looks best if all the stitches are counted evenly on the background linen. The "half" cross stitch or "tent" stitch, as one variation is called, is the same stitch used to cover the geometric mesh of needlepoint canvas. Some of the oldest embroideries in the world have been found in the Greek Islands. These were most often done in cross stitch, and its next logical development was herringbone (which is really a horizontal line of overlapping cross stitches).

Cross stitch should be worked so that the second stitch, which forms the X, is always slanted in the same direction. This makes the stitch beautifully smooth and even.

THE MOST WASTED DAY OF ALL

IS THAT ON WHICH YOU HAVE NOT LAUGHED

Cross Stitches

1. Herringbone, 2 strands knitting worsted, on laid work base worked horizontally in 2 threads of knitting wool

2. Cross stitch. Heavy acrylic wool

3. Interlaced herringbone 3 strands Persian on base of laid work, done vertically in 2 strands knitting worsted

4. Herringbone in heavy acrylic wool, worked on a base of laid work worked horizontally

5. Tent stitch on needlepoint canvas, knitting worsted

6. Rice stitch on needlepoint canvas, knitting worsted

7. Herringbone ladder stitch worked in 3 strands Persian on a base of laid work in knitting worsted worked horizontally

8. Interlaced band 6 strands Persian interlaced heavy acrylic

9. Double herringbone 6 strands Persian

10. Chessboard filling heavy acrylic, knitting worsted

11. Tied herringbone 6 strands Persian

12. Threaded herringbone, heavy acrylic wool threaded 6 strands Persian

13. Herringbone, 6 strands Persian, 11, 12, 13 worked on base of laid work done vertically in knitting worsted

14. Double back stitch 2 strands knitting worsted

15. Rice stitch on canvas, knitting worsted and Persian

Between each area a band of close herringbone (where solid black lines are indicated) worked with 6 strands Persian.

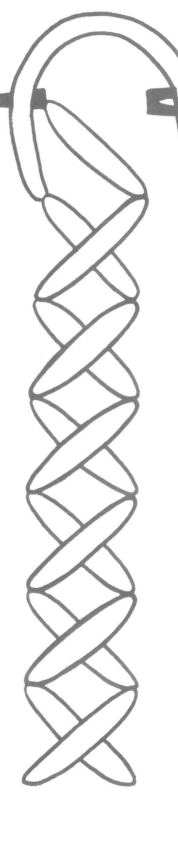

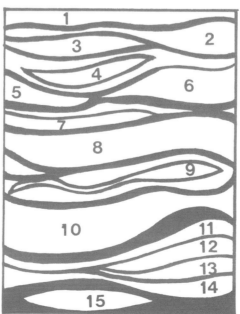

See Color Plate 4.

CROSS STITCH

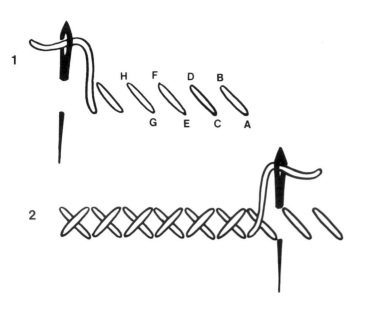

Working from right to left, come up at A, go down at B, up at C, and down at D, making a row of slanting stitches. If the needle is always kept vertical and the stitches are spaced evenly apart, the slant of each stitch will always remain the same.

Working from left to right, return along the line, again keeping the needle vertical, and going into the exact holes of the first row of slanting stitches. This forms a continuous line of cross stitches as in the diagram. It is important to always keep the final stitch of the cross slanting in the same direction. When blocks of stitches are worked this has a much tidier effect than if some stitches slant from right to left, others from left to right.

HERRINGBONE STITCH

This stitch is the simple foundation for many variations. It may be worked as broad or narrow as desired and may require a little practice at first to keep it regularly spaced and even.

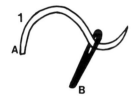

Come up at A, go down at B, diagonally below A.

Come up at C, a little to the left, and level with B, and go down at D, level with A, making a diagonal stitch in the other direction.

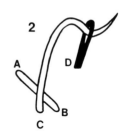

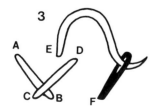

Come up at E, a little to the left and level with D, go down at F. E to F is another diagonal stitch parallel with A-B. Repeat from #2 again.

Continue repeating #2 and #3, spacing the stitches evenly so that the diagonals are parallel.

* CLOSE HERRINGBONE STITCH

This stitch is smoothest if kept slanting. Space the stitches a little apart when the needle goes down, and keep them close together (almost touching) when the needle comes up on the edge. This will help maintain the slant, and make a sharp V in the center. It is attractive when used on small leaves.

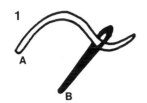

Come up at A, go down at B, diagonally below A.

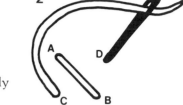

Come up at C, go down at D (C is directly below A; D is directly above B).

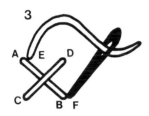

Come up at E, close to A, go down at F, close to B.

Come up at G, close to C, go down at H close to D.

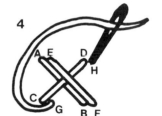

Continue in this way along the line, forming a solid band of stitching.

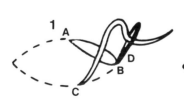
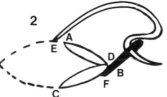

To work a shape as above: 1. Come up at A, about ¼″ away from point. Go down at point B. Repeat on opposite side (C to D) making 2 closely crossed stitches. 2. Continue working first one side then the other. Maintain a steep slant by leaving a space each time you come up (between E & A) and go in close at B. 3. Shows finished effect

INTERLACED HERRINGBONE STITCH

First work a row of Herringbone. Beginning on the right, with a blunt needle and contrasting thread pick up the first bar of the Herringbone, slanting the needle downwards. Pick up the next bar slanting the needle upwards (direction of needle is indicated by arrows). Continue to the end of the line.

TIED HERRINGBONE STITCH

First work a line of plain Herringbone. With a blunt needle and contrasting thread, slide the needle under the Herringbone cross, pointing the needle towards the center of the line. While needle is held in position, twist thread over and under the needle, as shown. Draw tight to knot it. Work this Coral Knot on each cross along the line, always pointing the needle toward the center of the Herringbone band.

HERRINGBONE LADDER STITCH

Work two lines of backstitch parallel to one another as shown.

Using a blunt needle, slip under the first backstitch, and holding the thread under the needle, pull through lightly.

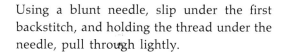

Now repeat this on the opposite side, remembering to still loop the thread under the needle as in a buttonhole stitch.

Continue along the line, working first on one side, then on the other, always sliding the needle from the outside towards the center of the band, and holding the thread under the needle with each stitch.

THREADED HERRINGBONE STITCH

First work a row of Herringbone. With a blunt needle and contrasting color, pick up the under thread of the Herringbone cross, and weave along first the upper, then the lower edge in this way, as shown.

DOUBLE HERRINGBONE STITCH

Begin a row of Herringbone as on page 76, taking small stitches on either side (from A to B).

After taking each *upper* stitch (B to C), slide the needle under the stitch you have just taken, (AB), and continue the line of Herringbone, spacing the stitches wide apart. One stitch will then always lie completely on top, and one completely underneath, as shown.

With contrasting color thread work another line of Herringbone in the same way, weaving the thread over and under as shown, to form an interlaced line of stitching. To make the second line a correct weave, the thread must always go *under* at D and E.

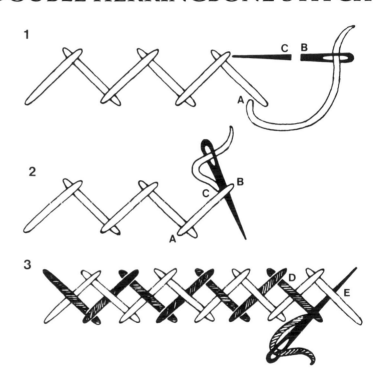

* CHESSBOARD FILLING

Because of its geometric nature, this stitch is best done on fabric with a clear weave, so that the background threads can guide the stitches evenly. Begin by making a block of four stitches, all the same size, coming up at A and down at B, and up at C, etc.

With the same thread, or a contrast, work a cross stitch on top of these stitches, from corner to corner (I to J, K to L).

Hold the cross in place with a small vertical stitch in the center, on top of all the stitches.

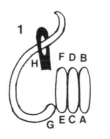

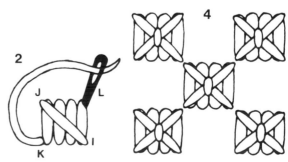

To make a checkerboard pattern, work the blocks of four stitches first, letting them touch at the corners. Then work all the cross stitches on top afterwards.

* INTERLACED BAND

Practice this stitch first with bold wool (such as knitting worsted or rug wool) working in large scale so that you can easily follow the weaving pattern.

1. Begin by making a band of Double Herringbone, using only one color (see page 79).

2. Using a blunt needle and a contrasting color, weave under and over the upper half of this foundation as shown in the diagram. Note that in this first step, starting at A, the needle goes over, under, over, under, over, and finally under *both* the working thread and the foundation bar.

3. In this second step, continuing from B where diagram 2 ended, the needle goes over, under, over, and under the foundation bars.

4. Continue weaving to the end of the line, repeating 2 and 3, and pulling the thread snugly but not too tightly, as shown. At the end of the line turn the corner. Starting from C the needle goes over, under, over, and under *both* the working thread and the foundation bar.

5. Now weave over the foundation bar, and under both the working thread and foundation bar. Continue, repeating 5 and 6, to the end of the line.

6. Continuing from D the needle goes over, under, over, under the working thread, over the working thread, and finally under the foundation bar.

7. Shows finished effect—well worth the trouble of figuring it out!

BACK STITCHES

Back stitch probably has its origin as the very strongest way of holding two pieces of cloth together. Since this is the stitch the sewing machine duplicates, it might almost be synonymous with the word "stitch." But its decorative use in embroidery is found in geometric patterns and in oriental needlework often interlaced with gold thread (Pekinese stitch, page 89).

Surprisingly enough two close cousins of back stitch have no visual similarity. Turkey work, the stitch which imitates oriental knotted rugs with a needle, is really a series of back stitches with raised loops in between. These loops may be left as they are, giving the effect of close tufts, or clipped to form a velvet pile.

The other cousin, couching, is simply a means of sewing down threads on the surface of the material, using a single "back" stitch at right angles to the direction of the main threads.

All kinds of patterns can be built up with these small stitches as row after row of couching is laid down, side by side. For example, the stitches may be worked in a brick pattern, alternating them on each row, or into a chevron, straight, or diagonal linear design. Alternatively, a single line of "random" couching may be worked, where the threads meander freely over an area to form an open rather than a solid effect. Couching may also be worked simply as an outline, as well as a solid or open filler. It may be worked flat, or raised by padding underneath, using felt or string.

Though couching is eminently suitable for fragile gold threads which cannot be stitched through the background fabric, wool or silk couching can be equally successful and effective.

18th century silk embroidery with backstitched background. *Colonial Williamsburg*

Back Stitches

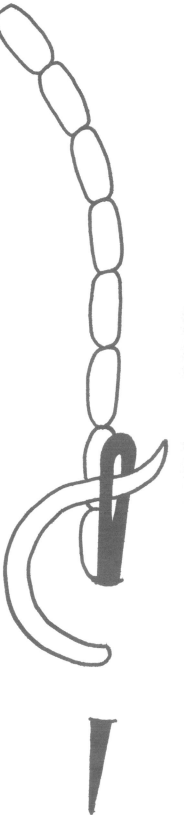

1   Threaded running stitch 6 strands Persian

2   Circular couching Japanese gold thread held flat with waxed silk, couched with radiating spiral and brick pattern

3   Circular couching with radiating lines heavy acrylic yarn

4   Fancy couching #1, 3 strands Persian over 6

5   Fancy couching #2, 2 strands Persian over 3

6   Brick pattern couching over string. 4 threads imitation Japanese gold, 12 threads of silk

7   Pekinese stitch (6 strands Persian) alternated with back stitch, heavy acrylic yarn

8   Cut Turkey work, 6 strands Persian

9   Scroll couching on laid work. 6 threads Persian couched with 2. Laid work 4 threads English

10   Guilloche stitch. Heavy acrylic yarn threaded through 6 strands Persian. Heavy acrylic french knot in center of each loop. Outline either side stem stitch, knitting worsted

11   Bokhara couching 12 threads English wool held flat with 2

12   Brick pattern on string. 2 strands knitting worsted

13   Uncut Turkey work

14   Cut Turkey work

15   Threaded running—3 strands knitting worsted

16   Scale couching on laid work. 6 threads Persian couched with 2 on laid work in base 6 strands English

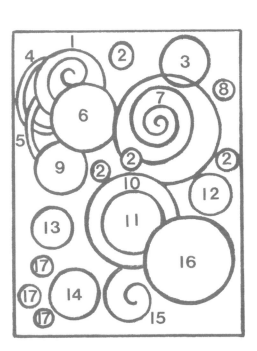

See jacket front.

BACKSTITCH

Come up at A, go down at B, then up ahead at C. Repeat, going back into same hole as the previous stitch. Keep all stitches the same size.

THREADED BACKSTITCH

Work a line of Back Stitch, and using a blunt needle and contrasting color, thread it through as shown. The needle passes under the first Back Stitch from right to left (not into the material), through the second Back Stitch from left to right, and so on. Do not draw the interlacing thread too tightly or the effect will be lost.

* BOKHARA COUCHING

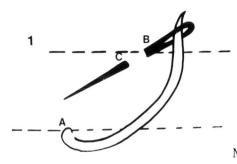

Come up at A, and take a long stitch, right across the shape to be filled, going down at B, diagonally above A. Come up at C, slightly to the left and below B.

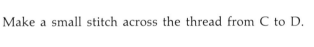

Make a small stitch across the thread from C to D.

Continue, making small stitches across the long stitch at regular intervals until the end of the line.

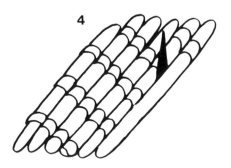

Repeat #1, making another long stitch close to the first one. Then repeat 2 and 3, again making small stitches, close to the previous ones, but a little below them. The final effect will be close slanting lines held firm by stitches worked diagonally across them, as shown.

* COUCHING

Couching may be worked as a plain outline, having the couching threads the same color as those underneath. Either one or two threads may be used in the needle and any number of threads may be couched down. Or two contrasting colors may be used, and the top stitches worked to form patterns. Couching may be used as a solid filling, working the threads back and forth or round in circles, or following the shape of the motif being filled. It may also be used as an open filling, called Random Couching, and is worked in any direction until the ground is evenly but lightly filled.

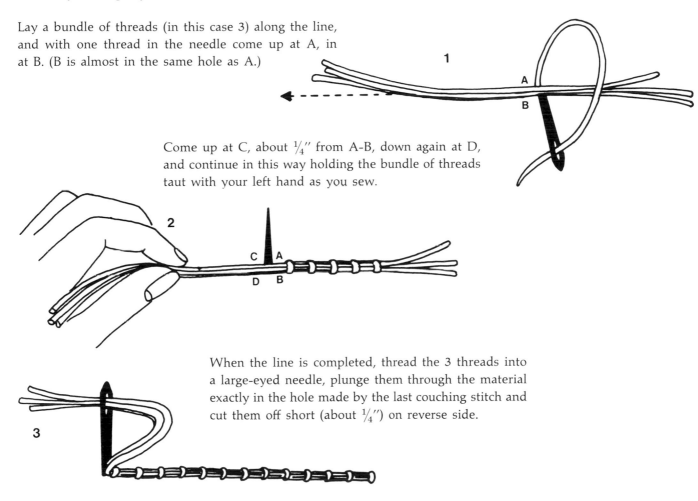

Lay a bundle of threads (in this case 3) along the line, and with one thread in the needle come up at A, in at B. (B is almost in the same hole as A.)

Come up at C, about ¼″ from A-B, down again at D, and continue in this way holding the bundle of threads taut with your left hand as you sew.

When the line is completed, thread the 3 threads into a large-eyed needle, plunge them through the material exactly in the hole made by the last couching stitch and cut them off short (about ¼″) on reverse side.

Patterns may be made with the couching stitches (brick stitch shown). Always bring needle up on the outside, and go down close to the line already worked, so that no material shows between lines of couching. At the corners work couching stitch at the angle shown to make a sharp corner without having to plunge threads at the end of each line.

* FANCY COUCHING

The couching illustrated here shows what a great variety of effects can be obtained from this simple stitch.

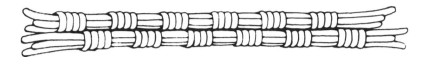

Fancy couching #1. Sew down one bundle of threads, grouping the stitches in blocks of four. Sew down the next bundle, close to the first, with the blocks of stitches placed alternately, as shown.

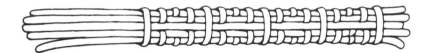

Fancy couching #2. Sew down a heavy bundle of at least six threads, working over them with contrasting thread in the pattern shown.

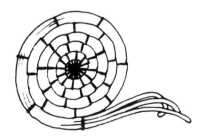 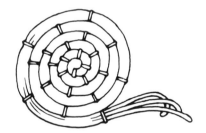 

Couching wheels. Begin in the center and work round and round to the outer edge (see page 196).

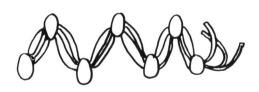

Zigzag couching

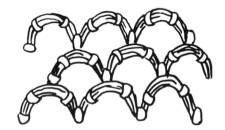

Scale couching

Bokhara couching. The bold wool is laid straight up and down, and a finer texture is couched diagonally over each thread, line by line (see page 84).

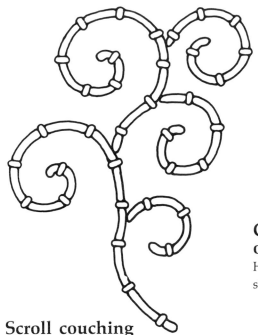

Scroll couching

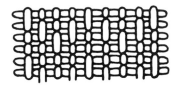

Couching with wool over lines of wool or string (see page 203)
Here the lines are spaced slightly apart to show the base threads.

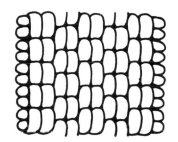

Brick pattern worked with wool over string (see page 203)

GUILLOCHE STITCH

Clear, even weave fabric is the best background for this attractive geometric border. Begin by working two lines of stem stitch the desired distance apart (it is difficult to reduce the scale much beyond half an inch). Next work small blocks of three stitches each, horizontally through the center, spacing them as far from each other as the width between the lines of stem stitch. Then, using a blunt needle, slide through these blocks as shown. Leave the thread loose so that it curves instead of forming a sharp Vee. Finally, work one French knot in the center of each circle.

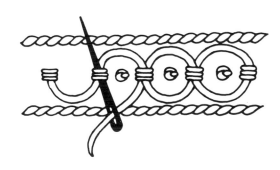

∗ TURKEY WORK

Turkey work is a series of loops cut to form a pile like a Turkey rug. For a different effect the loops may be left un-cut.

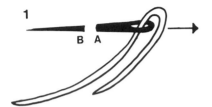

Go down at A, come up at B. Do not knot the thread, but leave about 1″ hanging on top, (as shown in diagram #2). Arrow indicates direction of working.

With thread *below* the needle, on a line with A and B, go down at C, and come up in same hole as A. Draw this stitch tight, holding on to the loose end of thread (so that it does not pull right through the material).

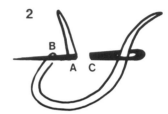

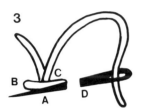

With the thread *above* the needle, go down at D, come up in the same hole as C. *Do not* draw tight, but leave a loop, (as shown). In this stitch, the needle should always be horizontal. (In order to show the stitch clearly in the diagram, it has been drawn on a slant.)

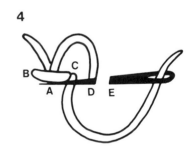

With the thread once more *below* the needle, go in at E, and up in the same hole as D; pull tight.

Continue along the line, coming up each time into the hole made by the previous stitch. The thread is alternately above the needle, leaving a loop, and below the needle drawing it tight.

Finished effect of single line. Work this stitch in lines one after the other. To achieve a thick velvety effect at the end, take small stitches and work the lines very close together. (This working diagram is much enlarged.)

Having filled the shape, cut all the loops along dotted line (as shown in diagram). Do not cut each line individually; trim the whole shape to the desired length (a full ⅛″ long).

Cut turkey work has a smoother pile if it is worked in lines, regardless of the shape to be filled. Do not be afraid to cut the loops down low in the end, the result is neater if the effect is like a piece of thick velvet. Uncut turkey work, where the loops are left as in #6, may be worked round in circles, or in lines following a simple shape. To keep them even, the loops may be worked over your finger. If the loops get in your way while working either cut or uncut Turkey work, pin them down to the material.

8

Finished effect

PEKINESE STITCH

This is a decorative stitch best worked as a single line, several close together are difficult to do. Keep the first back stitching small and even, and do not leave the loops too long. The finished result should be like a neat braided edging.

1

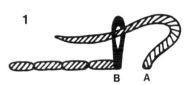

Work a line of Back Stitch, coming up at A and going down at B, into the same hole as the previous stitch (as shown).

With a contrasting color, using a blunt needle, come up at C (just below the first Back Stitch). Slide the needle upwards through the second Back Stitch (not through material), from D to E (as shown). Leave a loop.

2

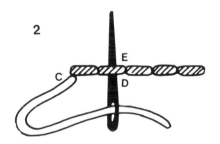

Then slide downwards through the first Back Stitch from F to G. Bring the needle out on top of loop made by the first stitch; pull flat, but not too taut.

3

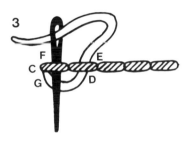

Now slide the needle upwards through the third Back Stitch from H to J; leave a loop as in #2.

4

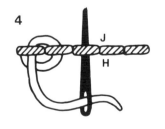

Slide the needle downwards through the second Back Stitch from E to D. Bring needle out on top of loop made by the previous stitch; draw flat.

5

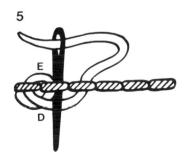

Repeat #2, 3, 4, 5, making a row of inter-lacing stitches into the Back Stitches. The low edge has a series of even loops, while the upper edge is flat (as shown).

RUNNING STITCH

Come up at A, go down at B and up at C, making a straight line of even stitches. The length of the stitches should equal the space between them. Several stitches can be taken up on the needle at one time, if the work is being done in the hand and not on a frame.

INTERLACED RUNNING STITCH

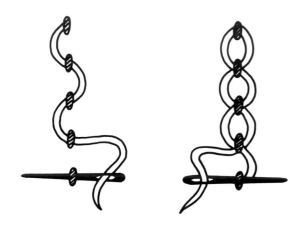

With a heavy thread work a row of Running Stitches, then with a blunt needle and contrasting color, thread it through as in Threaded Back Stitch. Finally thread it back in the other direction, to make ovals of equal tension, as shown.

Spring orchard with nesting cardinals using a variety of stitches to give a realistic effect. *Designed and worked by Wilanna Bristow*

WEAVING STITCHES

Weaving stitches are as old as fabric itself, for the needle simply takes the place of the shuttle.

A block of weaving, like sock darning, may be done entirely on the surface of the background material. Or horizontal rows of running stitches in contrasting color may be woven through the existing fabric to form geometric patterns, used largely in black work (page 237). For instance, a checkerboard pattern may be formed by running the needle over four and under four threads for several rows, and then reversing it so that the needle goes under four and over four to alternate these blocks formed by the stitching.

Still a third method is to draw out threads from the background material, leaving a warp, which is then rewoven with the needle into new patterns to make bands and borders. This last method of drawn thread work is called needle weaving. All weaving is done with a blunt needle to avoid splitting the threads. Just as in weaving on a loom, all kinds of variations in texture and color can make the effect very exciting.

Coptic panel. *Victoria and Albert Museum*

Weaving Stitches

1   Surface darning ½ strand knitting worsted

2   Weaving, 1 strand knitting worsted with 2 strands French wool, woven with 2 strands Persian

3   Weaving, 2 strands knitting worsted in both directions

4   Honeycomb filling 2 strands Persian

5   Surface darning 2 strands Persian

6   Surface darning 2 strands English

7   Cloud filling 3 strands English

8   Weaving 6 strands Persian, both directions

9   Wave stitch worked closely 2 strands Persian

10 Surface darning 2 strands English

11 Surface darning 2 strands English

12 Surface darning 2 strands English with raised needleweaving 2 Persian on top

13 Squared filling #00 6 Persian, woven with 6 English

14 Surface darning, 2 Persian, with raised whipped spider webs, 3 English on top

15 Surface darning 2 strands Persian

16 Honeycomb filling 2 strands Persian

17 Surface darning 2 Persian

18 Surface darning knitting worsted. Woven and whipped spider's webs, 2 strands knitting worsted, on top

19 Squared filling #00 6 strands Persian

20 Wave stitch worked openly knitting worsted

21 Knotted ground 2 strands knitting worsted

22 Needleweaving 2 strands Persian

23 Knotted ground 2 strands Persian

24 Needleweaving 2 strands Persian

25 Knotted ground 2 strands Persian

See Color Plate 5.

* WEAVING STITCH

This is really exactly like sock darning! It may be done with at least two or three threads in both directions. Then when the weaving is completed evenly the result is a series of perfect squares in contrasting colors. It is also possible to use three or four threads for laying the first row of stitching, then to darn through with only one or two in the other direction. (This is useful to give a seeded effect on a strawberry, for instance.) Try to keep the outline even, for this stitch usually looks best if it is not outlined.

Come up at A, down at B, up at C, down at D, etc., laying threads side by side (the width of one thread apart).

Change to a blunt tapestry needle, and using a contrasting color, come up at M. Weave under and over the threads, starting through the center (or the widest part). Go down through the material at N.

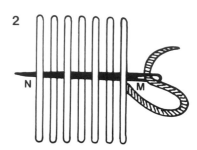

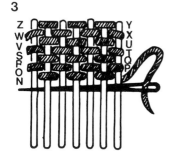

Come up through the material at O, and weave through the threads, go down at P, up at Q, continue to Z, pushing threads together so that even squares of each color are obtained. Go back to the center (A), and finish weaving the lower part.

* CLOUD FILLING

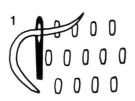

Work a series of straight stitches over the ground to be covered, using a double thread and spacing them evenly, checkerboard fashion, as shown.

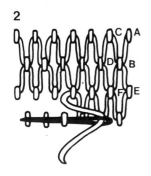

Using a contrasting color, a single thread, and a blunt needle, thread through these straight stitches from right to left. Begin at A, go down to B, up to C, down to D, and so on to the end of the line.

Then start again at E on the right, go up to B, down to F, and so on. This stitch is more effective when there is a strong contrast either in thickness or color, or both, between the straight foundation stitches and the interlacing thread.

* WAVE STITCH

Coming up at A, and going down at B, make a row of straight stitches along the top of the shape to be covered. For clarity the spacing is shown wider in the diagram than it should be when worked.

Using a blunt needle, come up at C in a direct line below A and slide the needle through the stitch A-B. Do not pass through the material.

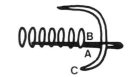

Go down through material at D, close to and on a line with C, and come up at E, close to D and on a line with it. Slide through the next straight stitch above (as in 2), and repeat to the end of line.

Starting on the right again, come up at F, the same distance below C as C was from A. Slide the needle under C. Do not go through the material.

Go down at G, come up close to it at H, and slide through D and E together (not through the material).

Continue sliding through two stitches together to the end of the row.

Finished effect. The stitches should be placed fairly closely, as shown, for this stitch to be really effective.

* HONEYCOMB

Start with a block of squares as in Squared Filling #1 (see page 102). Do not tie them down. With a blunt needle and contrasting thread, weave diagonally across the squares, picking up the *under* thread of the foundation, as shown.

* RAISED HONEYCOMB

Lay basic squares as in Squared Filling #1 (see page 102). Do not tie them down. Starting at the top, using a blunt needle and contrasting color, whip over each thread from right to left, working down to the bottom. At the bottom of the line go down through the material to anchor the thread, come up again a fraction away, and whip up to the top on the same thread again weaving the needle under from right to left.

Whip over all the upright bars in this way, and then repeat exactly the same thing on the horizontal ones.

Finished effect. Because the thread crosses four times at the intersections, the cross effect shown in the diagram does not appear clearly. The bars simply become raised bumps where they cross.

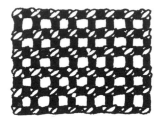

* TWISTED LATTICE STITCH

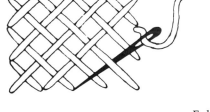

Using a blunt needle, make a ground work of parallel diagonal lines. Then weave under and over in the opposite direction to make diamonds. As in laid work, carry the thread across the shortest possible distance on the reverse side to avoid wasting thread, and keep the mesh flat.

Following the needle position in diagrams 2 and 3 weave a series of identical horizontal lines across this lattice as shown.

NOTE: When the needle slants upward the thread is below. When the needle slants downwards the thread is above.

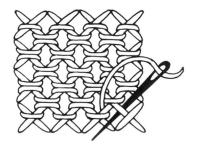

Now repeat, weaving a second series of horizontal lines to fill in between the previous ones.

NOTE: Where the thread was below on the previous line it must now be above, so that each stitch of the second series coincides with the first. This forms a network of double stitches, as shown.

LADDER STITCH

Using a blunt tapestry needle, come up at A, go in at B and come up again at C, a little above and to the left of B. Go in at D immediately below B. Come up on the left at E, immediately below A.

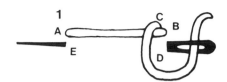

Without going through the material, slip the needle downwards under the first stitch from F to G.

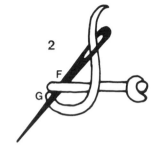

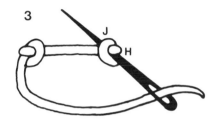

Pull the thread firmly. Now slip the needle upwards from H to J through the center of the cross formed by the first 2 stitches.

Go in at J just below D and come up at K, just below E.

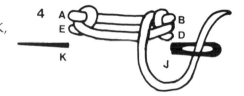

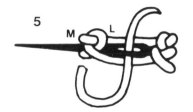

Without going through the material slip the needle from L to M under the cross made by the stitch above.

Repeat the procedure on the right, slipping the needle under the cross from N to O. Repeat #4, 5 and 6, working down until the shape is filled.

Finished effect

∗ SPIDER'S WEB/WHIPPED/WOVEN

Both Whipped and Woven Spider's Webs should be worked very tightly in the center to show the spokes clearly, loosening the threads slightly toward the outer edge. The spokes may be covered completely and the Spider's Web outlined, or just the center may be worked, leaving the spokes showing all round. One or several colors may be used for each web, and one or more threads, depending on the size.

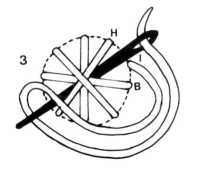

Using a blunt (tapestry) needle, come up at A, down at B, across center of circle.

Then come up at C, and down at D, (C to D should be slightly off center as shown). Come up at E, down at F, up at G and down at H. (H goes in quite close to D.)

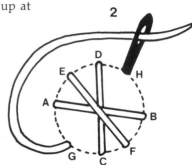

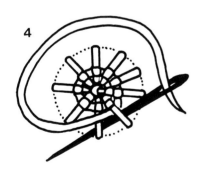

This leaves a space for the needle to come up finally at I, a point midway between H and B. Then slide the needle under all the threads at their intersection. Take the thread and loop it across the needle and then under it as shown. Draw through and pull upwards to knot threads together in center.

Whipped

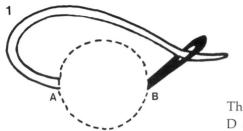

With the same thread, starting in the center, slide under 2 threads. Then place needle behind the thread just taken, slide under it, plus a new one. Progress in this way, back one and under two, till the spokes are all covered. Then either outline circle with Stem Stitch or leave plain.

Woven

Starting in center, weave under and over spokes, round and round, till whole circle is filled. Outline circle with Stem Stitch or leave plain.

FILLING STITCHES

Filling stitches are all those delightful decorative stitches which add zest and individuality to embroidery, giving even the most traditional needlework an abstract, often three-dimensional, quality. For instance, the squared filling patterns of Jacobean embroidery are totally unrelated to the leaf shapes they fill, and similarly the myriad filigreed stitches of black work bear no relation to the silhouettes in which they are worked. In both, it is the surprise contrast of pattern within pattern which makes the stylized designs so marvelously effective.

Most filling stitches cover an area with geometric patterns. Although they are formed from combinations of cross, running, back stitches, and others, it seemed most suitable to include them in this sampler so that they could be grouped for their effect as fillings.

If you want to work geometric patterns on fabric which does not have a "countable" mesh, such as satin, twill, or rough uneven weave linen, you can put in a crisscross pattern by eye, and then work other stitches on top of this grid. These are the squared fillings of crewel embroidery.

On regular weave fabric you can work all kinds of geometric patterns by counting the threads, either to cover the material entirely or to fill silhouette shapes, as in Elizabethan black work. Added to these geometrics are the "frosting" stitches such as French or bullion knots which may be stitched individually or embroidered closely to fill a whole area. These give embroidery that irresistible tactile quality and add to its three-dimensional effect.

Spider's webs, french knots and buttonhole used as geometric fillings. *Wilanna Bristow*

Filling Stitches

1   Squared filling #1 2 strands Persian
2   Tête de boeuf 2 strands Persian, gold lurex
3   Squared filling, 2 threads English wool, gold lurex, knitting worsted
4, 5   Black work fillings 2 ply fingering knitting wool, gold lurex
6   Top to bottom: French knots on stalks knitting worsted
    Bullion knots 2 strands Persian
    French knots 2 strands Persian
    Seeding 2 strands Persian
7   Black work filling 3 strands English
8   Black work filling 3 strands English
9   Squared filling 3 strands English and knitting worsted
10   Black work fillings 2 strands English
11   Black work fillings 1 strand English, fine lurex
12   French knots on stalks radiating from center, 3 strands Persian
13   Black work filling, 2 ply fingering
14   Squared filling #8 knitting worsted, 2 strands English
15   Squared filling #5 knitting worsted 2 English, 3 Persian
16   Black work pattern 2 strands English
17   Bullion knot roses, flowers, 6 strands silk leaves 3 strands English
18   Black work pattern 2 strands English

1	2	3
5 4 X 4 5	6	7
8 12	9	11 10 X 10 11
13	14	15
16	17	18

See jacket back.

* SQUARED FILLING #1

The following are just a few of the many variations of Squared Fillings. Once you have grasped the basic idea, it is a simple matter to invent your own, and so add more to the collection. Squared Fillings are useful for breaking up plain areas, and it is possible to achieve unlimited color combinations with them. Squared Filling #3 may be shaded by changing the color in the blocks of Satin Stitch. All of them look best when used to fill stylized shapes and when combined with simple flat areas such as Laid Work in one color. They are so variegated in themselves that they need plain surroundings to set them off.

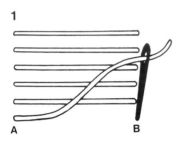

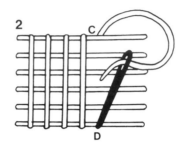

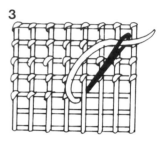

1. Coming up on one side of shape, make a long stitch right across, going down on other side. Fill the whole shape with exact parallel lines about ¼" apart.

2. Then lay threads in the opposite direction, making perfect squares.

4. Using a contrasting color, diagonally crisscross whole design with long lines, first in one direction across the center of every other square, then in the other direction so that the threads cross in the center of the basic squares.

5. With another contrasting color, tie down these diagonal lines where they cross in the center of the squares. This stitch should touch the basic squares at the top and bottom.

3. Tie down these squares at the corners with small stitches, all slanting in the same direction, as shown.

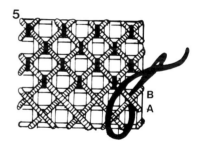

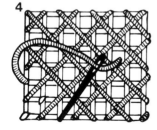

* SQUARED FILLING #2

Use a blunt (tapestry) needle for this stitch. Having laid long, parallel lines in one direction, go across in the other direction, but instead of laying the lines on top (as in squared filling #1), weave under and over like darning, making squares as shown.

Starting across broadest part of shape, with contrasting color, pick up the first threads diagonally at intersection slipping needle through from A to B as shown. (Do not sew through the material.)

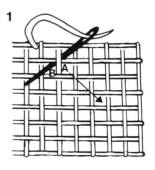

Work diagonally across as in diagram. Go through the material at C, and up at D, and start working upwards; take up threads at intersection exactly as when working downwards. Do not pull too tightly.

Now repeat #2 using another contrasting color, leaving one intersection clear between the lines of stitching. Cover the entire shape in this way, alternating lines of color and leaving one intersection clear between each line.

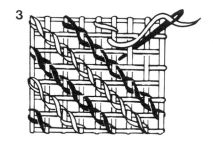

* SQUARED FILLING #3

Lay parallel lines diagonally across the space to be filled, two lines close together though not touching, then a wider space, then two closer again, and so on (as shown).

Using the same color, repeat #1 in the opposite direction to make diamonds.

Using another color, fill each large diamond with Satin Stitch. To start the stitches evenly, put one stitch across the center, then two or three small stitches on either side.

With a third contrasting color, tie down the crisscross lines with four stitches coming up in the Satin Stitch and going down in the center, thus forming a star. When you tie down with these four stitches, be certain to maintain the space between the diagonal lines so a little material shows through (as shown).

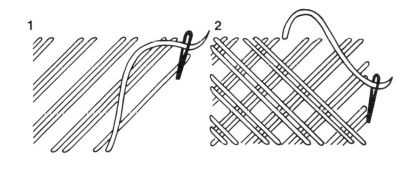

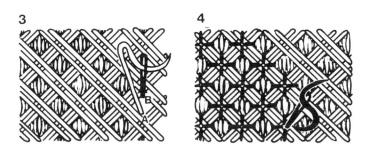

Squared Filling #3 may be shaded by changing the color of the Satin Stitches in the diamond.

* SQUARED FILLINGS #4/#5

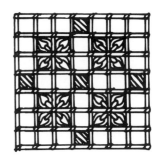

#4. Both patterns have a base of squares tied down at the corners as in Squared Filling #8. For Filling #4 work four Detached Chain Stitches converging at one point, as shown. Place them in checkerboard fashion, leaving four empty squares between each block. Then work four French Knots close together in the corners of the empty squares, using a contrasting color.

#5. Work exactly the same way as #4 but leave a clear line of squares around the blocks of Detached Chain Stitches. Then work five Slanting Satin Stitches in the blank square connecting the corners of the blocks, as shown.

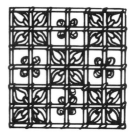

* SQUARED FILLINGS #6/#7

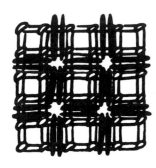

#6 and 7. First lay a foundation of squares and tie them down as in Squared Filling #8. For #6, work two stitches side by side (not touching) right over the squares, radiating them from a central square, as shown.

For #7, work a cross right over every other square, checkerboard fashion, but do not allow the crosses to touch one another.

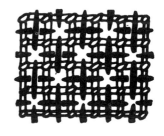

* SQUARED FILLING #8

1

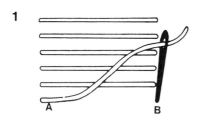

Coming up on one side of shape, make a long stitch right across, going down on other side. Fill the whole shape with exact parallel lines about ¼" apart.

Then lay threads in the opposite direction, making perfect squares.

2

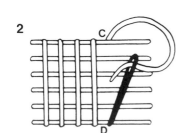

Tie down these squares at the corners with small stitches, all slanting in the same direction, as shown.

3

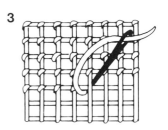

Using a contrasting color diagonally crisscross the whole design with long lines, first in one direction across the center of every other square, then in the other direction, so that the threads cross exactly where the basic square threads crossed. In this way a series of stars is formed, each with eight bars radiating from the center.

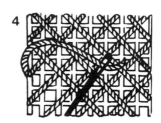

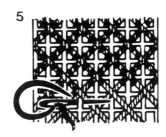

Using a blunt needle and with another contrasting color, tie down these diagonal lines where they cross and converge with the basic squares. To do this, come up on the left of one of the "square" lines and weave round in a circle, passing over the diagonal and picking up the "square" lines as you go round. Go down through the material just on the right of where you came up. Do not pull the circle too tight or it will disappear. A strong contrast in color is needed to make it show up well.

FRENCH KNOTS

French Knots may be scattered like seeding, to fill an area lightly, or they may be arranged in rows to fill a space solidly. The latter is most effective if each row is clearly defined and the knots lie evenly side by side. Alternatively they may be sprinkled closely but unevenly to produce an intentionally rough surface.

Bring needle up at A, twist thread once round needle as shown.

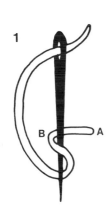

Put needle in at A, or just beside it, pull the thread until it fits *closely* round the needle (not too tightly). Pull needle through.

The finished knot. The thread should only be twisted once round the needle, as this makes a neat knot; *never* two or three times. The size of the knot is determined by the number of threads and size of the needle used.

✶ FRENCH KNOTS ON STALKS

Come up at A, and twist the thread once around the needle as in the diagram. Pull gently, so that the thread fits round the needle, and still holding the thread so it does not loosen, go down at B, about ¼" away from A. Pull gently through, to form the effect shown at 2.

The knots may be used singly, or may be worked to overlap each other. They can be very effective radiating from the center of a circle, as shown here.

TÊTE DE BOEUF

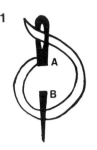
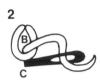

Work a single detached chain stitch, coming up at A, going back at A again, looping thread around needle and drawing it through at B.

Go down at C outside the loop to hold it flat.

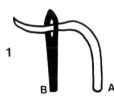

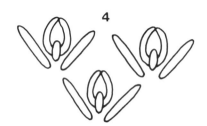

Make a pair of slanting stitches on either side of the detached chain, from E to F, and from G to H.

The completed stitches may be scattered freely, or arranged in a checkerboard fashion as shown.

BULLION KNOTS

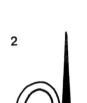

Double thread is usually best for this stitch. The knots may be used individually, or worked side by side. They should not be too long, or they will curl instead of lying flat on the material.

1. Bring needle up at A, go down at B, but do not pull thread through.

2. Stab needle up at A again but bring it only *halfway* through material.

3. Holding needle from below, twist thread round needle at A, until number of twists equals the distance between A and B.

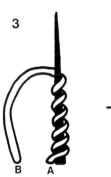

4. Holding top of needle and threads firmly with finger and thumb of left hand, draw needle through with right hand, loosening coil of threads with left hand as you do so, to allow needle to pass through freely.

5. Then place needle against end of twist, at the same time pulling on the thread, as shown, until the knot lies flat on the material. If any "bumps" appear in the knot, flatten these by stroking the underneath of twist with the needle, at the same time pulling on the thread.

6. Put needle in close, at the end of the twist and pull through firmly.

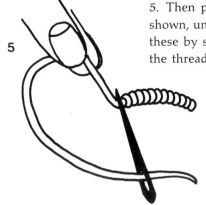

✳ BULLION KNOT ROSES

To make roses, work three bullion knots to form a triangle, as shown. Then work one bullion knot to wrap around one corner of the triangle, putting a few extra twists on the needle so that the knot curls around instead of lying straight. Next, add another bullion, overlapping half way over the previous one. Work round the triangle in this way, until the rose is formed as shown in the lower drawing. Stem and detached chain make the leaves and stem. Adding a second ring of knots makes a larger rose, which is effective with a darker color in the center shading to light on the outside.

✳ SEEDING

1

Come up at A, and go down at B a small distance away. Pull through, lightly.

Come up at C and go down at D, across the first stitch, diagonally. Pull through, so that the stitch forms a firm, round, slightly raised "bump" on the fabric.

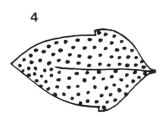

2

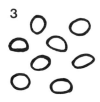

3

The finished effect appears as one raised stitch instead of two. When worked with thread which matches the background fabric in color seeding gives an attractive textured effect.

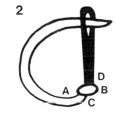

4

Stitches scattered evenly, each slanting in a different direction.

Stitches massed closely to form a shaded effect.

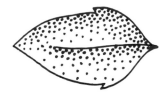

STRETCHING AND BLOCKING

When the sampler is finished it may be pressed or blocked. The latter is preferable, for pressing never brings out the very fine creases in heavy material like twill, and pressing is also inclined to pull the article out of shape. If, however, you wish to press an article such as a sweater which cannot be blocked, iron it on the wrong side into three or four thicknesses of toweling, using a damp cloth or steam iron. To block the finished work, first soak the embroidery in cold water, and lay it, dripping wet, on a board or old table which has been first covered with a sheet. If the embroidery is raised, lay it out right side uppermost; if it is flat and a smooth finished result is needed, put it right side down. Then, with carpet tacks, nail down the four corners first, measuring the opposite sides to see that they are even and making sure the corners are true right angles. You may have to pull the material out with pliers to make sure it is really taut. Then nail down four more tacks, one in the center of each side, and then eight more in the spaces between. Continue round and round, adding in this way more tacks until they are about $\frac{1}{4}$ inch apart. Allow the fabric to dry. When it is thoroughly dry, take it up, and if it is not being mounted immediately, roll it round a cardboard tube with the embroidery outward (so that the stitches are not crushed against one another). (See illustration, page 165.)

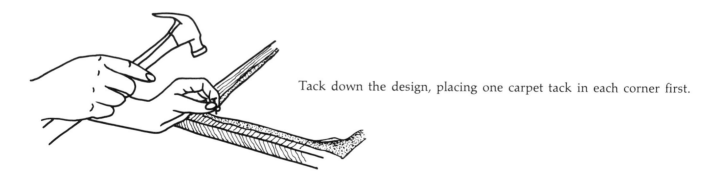

Tack down the design, placing one carpet tack in each corner first.

Tack the fabric all around, pulling it out flat with pliers so that it is really taut.

WHERE TO USE THE STITCHES

One of the dilemmas that often confronts the beginner is which stitch goes where. Of course, there are no rules, and the enjoyment of finding your own perfect stitch for a particular shape is part of the fascination of the whole thing. However, here are a few of my own suggestions which are by no means arbitrary or complete, but which may be useful as a starting guide in helping you to reach your own decisions.

Centers and Circles: Buttonhole worked into a center hole, spiders' webs, padded satin stitch, bullion knots worked side by side across the circle, French knots close together, Turkey work cut and uncut, couching spiraling from the center, French knots on stalks radiating from the center.

Leaves: Fishbone, close herringbone, cretan, laid work, long and short, chain, stem stitch worked closely, or as an outline around seeding, slanting satin, burden stitch.

Stems and outlines: Chain, rope, stem, coral, back stitch, herringbone, composite stitches, e.g., whipped stem, Pekinese.

Petals: Laid work, long and short, buttonhole, satin, seeding, cretan, fishbone, close herringbone, trellis, weaving.

Fruits and vegetables: Split, long and short, brick, burden, French knots, spiders' webs, laid, stem, chain, coral, fishbone, close herringbone.

Baskets: Raised chain, stem, buttonhole, split, chain, stem, flat buttonhole, weaving, burden.

Birds: Satin, all kinds of laid work, buttonhole, bullions, close herringbone, fishbone, Turkey work (for chicks).

Animals: Stem, chain, split, Turkey work, long and short, straight stitch, satin, split, French knots.

Faces: Split, stem, satin, French knots (eyes), back stitch.

Trees: French knots on stalks, satin stitch, burden, fishbone, close herringbone, cretan, laid work, raised seeding.

Sky: Long and short, long lines of split stitch (open), cloud filling, laid work, running stitches, straight stitches, seeding.

Sea: Lines of split, lines of stem, burden, chevron filling, couching, straight stitches, French knots, French knots on stalks.

Houses: Brick stitch, burden, laid work, satin, squared fillings, couching, buttonhole, raised stem, chain, split, and back stitch.

The stitches have been listed here under descriptive headings to help you find the right stitch for certain areas. But there is no reason why you can't take a line or banding stitch and use it as a solid filling, for instance, or take a detached stitch and make it into a line or banding. The following groupings are just guides to help you with your stitch selection until you start experimenting on your own.

BAND STITCHES	LINE STITCHES	SOLID FILLING STITCHES	OPEN PATTERNED STITCHES
Raised stem	Stem	Long and short	Burden
Raised stem chevron pattern	Portuguese Knot	Satin	Cross stitch
Portuguese border	Whipped Stem	Slanting Satin	Chessboard filling
Roumanian	Split	Backstitched Satin	Wave stitch
Double chain	Chain	Block shading	Squared fillings
Rosette chain	(all varieties)	Laid work	(all varieties)
Crested chain	Narrow rope	(all varieties)	Cloud filling
Raised chain	Coral	Plate stitch	
Interlaced	Knotted pearl	Chevron filling	DETACHED STITCHES
Cable chain	Braid	Bokhara	
Fishbone	Back stitch	Couching	Detached Twisted chain
Cretan	Back stitch threaded	Brick stitch	Fly stitch
Vandyke	Couching	Turkey work	Spider's webs
Broad rope	Fancy couching	(cut and uncut)	(whipped woven)
Open buttonhole	Pekinese	Weaving	French knots
Open herringbone	Running stitch		French knots
Close herringbone	Running stitch interlaced		on a long stitch
(all variations)			
Interlaced band			
Guilloche stitch			

NEEDLEPOINT

"Home to my poor wife, who works all day like a horse,
at the making of her hangings for our chamber and bed."—SAMUEL PEPYS

A carpet of needle worke of sundrye coloured silks, the ground sad green,
with a border of roses, and sundrie posies about it, the ground of the borders
orange tawnie, 6 yds long, 1¾ wide—KENILWORTH CASTLE INVENTORY, 1588

Tapestry "La Vie Seigneuriale." Note the lady working on her embroidery. *Musée de Cluny*

No one who has been intrigued by the romance of medieval history can help imagining long galleries hung with woven tapestries, or mullioned castle windows surrounded by the rich glow of the "arras." These images have been intensified by literature and poetry. Who can forget Keats's "The Eve of St. Agnes," for instance, when in the icy cold of the castle "a chain-droop'd lamp was flickering by each door; The arras, rich with horseman, hawk, and hound, Flutter'd in the besieging wind's uproar. . . ." Or Stevenson's hero of *The Black Arrow*, who stands transfixed when, as a prisoner in the long gallery, he sees the gleam of a real eye which stares down at him from the woven face in the tapestry lining the walls. Because the little town of Arras in France became famous for its magnificent woven hangings, tapestry from early times became equally well known by that name. The tapestries were done on an upright loom, and the weaver, his cartoon sketched out on a sheet which hung on the wall behind him, would weave from the wrong side so that he could more easily leave his working ends of threads hanging, and could watch his design progressing by looking through the threads of the tapestry into a mirror.

Tapestry, of course, is not embroidery at all for it is woven over vertical threads and has no background other than these. (True embroidery always presupposes a background fabric.) But it is easy to imagine that early embroiderers would have found it quite simple to imitate these tapestries with a needle on an evenly woven linen. It was some time during the sixteenth and seventeenth centuries that embroidery on canvas, or needlepoint as we know it today, began to develop.

But it was not only from the background of tapestry that needlepoint originated. During the thirteenth century in Germany and what is now Switzerland (then called Saxony), beautiful altar frontals were embroidered on linen in silk. (See White Work, page 249.) The stitches were geometric, and done by counting the threads of the linen, which was quite coarse and not unlike our present-day canvas. The most beautiful though blood-   / *113*

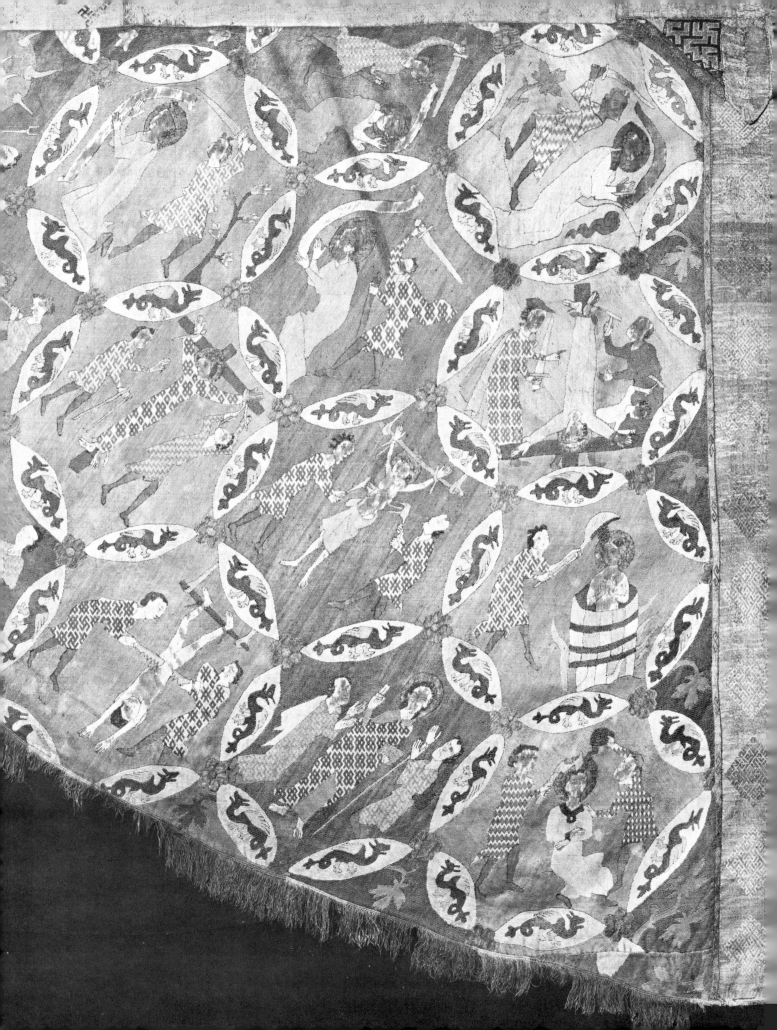

The Hildesheim Cope and detail. *Victoria and Albert Museum*

curdling example of this is the Hildesheim Cope, which illustrates the martyrdom of the saints as only a medieval mind could portray it. The whole linen is covered with design which is worked in brick stitch, using silken thread of earth reds and dull golden green.

Peasant costumes, which have remained unchanged in technique and design for hundreds of years, also show that geometric stitching was not a new idea for the sixteenth-century embroideress who wished to imitate tapestry. Cross stitch from the Greek Islands is one of the earliest forms of embroidery known to us, and Yugoslavian linen shirts often had deep bands of stitching at the neck and cuffs done in the same tent stitch used on canvas today. Tent stitch, or petit point, which covers the whole canvas with tiny slanting stitches, seems to have always been the most popular for needlepoint from ancient times until the present day. The stitch is worked across each intersection of the canvas and does closely resemble tapestry.

Demi point (medium size) and gros point (large stitch) were used later as terms to designate the scale of the stitch. The Countess of Shrewsbury's inventory of her furniture at Hardwick Hall in the sixteenth century mentions "a long quition of pete point" and a list of Lady Morton's possessions from her castle in the Orkneys in 1650 includes "I Gryt Sweet Bagg soad with pitty point."

The stitch that petit point describes is half a cross stitch, or tent

Yugoslavian peasant embroidery. *Author's Collection*

stitch, worked diagonally over the intersections of each of the threads of the fabric. The background fabric, canvas, got its name from the Latin *cannabis*, meaning hempen cloth.

Hemp probably originated in India or Persia, but became naturalized all over the world. Although it is today a universal weed, it grew particularly well in Turkey, where since time immemorial the Turks have known of the intoxicating properties of the smoke from its dried leaves, for it is none other than the versatile marijuana, whose oils have been used for centuries to make soap and whose strong fibers, when separated by water from its inner bark, have been used throughout history for making rope, sailcloth, and tents. Perhaps this is where tent stitch, the basic stitch in needlepoint, got its name.

In case we imagine a rough textured cloth, however, we should take note of Herodotus, who wrote: "Hemp grows in the country of the Scythians, which except in the thickness and height of the stalk, very much resembles Flax; in the qualities mentioned, however, the Hemp is much superior. The Thracians make clothing of it very like linen; nor could any person without being very well acquainted with the substance, say whether this clothing be made of Hemp or Flax." Therefore we can imagine that "Poldavie" canvas from Brittany, a sailcloth used for tents and beds, which was among the fabrics available for embroidery in Edinburgh in 1562, might have appeared to be an evenly woven linen.

This was at the time of Mary Queen of Scots' marriage to Lord Darnley, when Edinburgh must have been humming with activity in all the arts, for Mary encouraged and may have even inspired the fashion in Scotland for bed valances, while wall and window hangings, table and cupboard carpets, all embroidered or appliquéd with petit point, were the fashion in France and England as well. The richness of the numerous beds the Queen brought with her from France is shown by the description of the one she gave to Darnley, which had belonged to her mother, Mary of Guise. It was hung with violet-brown velvet, embroidered with ciphers and flowers, and trimmed with cloth of gold and silver.

Indeed, a description of the canvas work of the sixteenth century is not complete without mention of Mary Queen of Scots and the effect of her life on the fashion and the embroidery of her time. She herself was an embroideress perhaps superior in skill to her cousin Queen Elizabeth, having spent the halcyon days of her short childhood in France. There, the court, under the Queen, Catherine de Medici, and the influence of the King's mistress, Diane de Poitiers, had all the pomp and splendor, brilliance and wit, that the combined backgrounds of Italy and France could bring to it. The young Queen Mary (whose mother, as Regent, was on the Scottish throne) was tutored in music, painting and, of course, embroidery, and she was evidently a good pupil although, being tall and athletic, horseback riding was her chief delight.

Her skill with the needle was later to stand her in good stead, for from the moment she set foot on Scottish soil, then only nineteen, having been widowed at the age of sixteen, her life as Queen of Scotland was a series of tragedies. Used as a pawn by scheming Scottish and English nobles, she was finally considered too dangerous to remain alive by Queen Elizabeth, who had her executed in 1587 at the age of forty-four. Half her life was spent, if not in actual prison in close confinement either in Scottish castles or in England as the "guest" of Lord Shrewsbury. It was with the Shrewsburys at their estates at Sheffield and Chatsworth that most of her embroidery was done. It must have greatly soothed her mind to sit stitching while plotting to regain her rightful place as Queen of Scotland and, perhaps in her mind, of England, too. Many of the designs she stitched had double meanings, and with their hidden aspirations they expressed well the fugitive, frustrated nature of her life. This "emblem" embroidery (page 119) which the Queen enjoyed was done in tent stitch in small motifs, which were then cut out and applied to large velvet panels, for use as hangings or bed curtains, coverlets or cushions. The tent stitch appliqués were bordered with metal thread to neaten the edges, and an interlacing design of gold or silver embroidered right on the velvet often linked them together. (See Stump Work, page 299.)

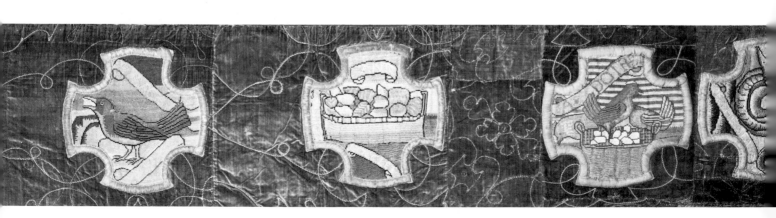

Emblem panels mounted on velvet. Several are signed with the ES monogram of Elizabeth, Countess of Shrewsbury (Bess of Hardwick). *Victoria and Albert Museum*

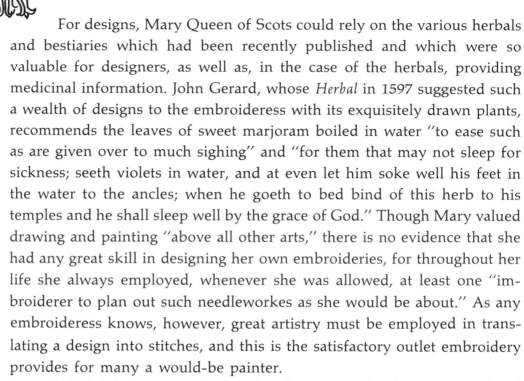

For designs, Mary Queen of Scots could rely on the various herbals and bestiaries which had been recently published and which were so valuable for designers, as well as, in the case of the herbals, providing medicinal information. John Gerard, whose *Herbal* in 1597 suggested such a wealth of designs to the embroideress with its exquisitely drawn plants, recommends the leaves of sweet marjoram boiled in water "to ease such as are given over to much sighing" and "for them that may not sleep for sickness; seeth violets in water, and at even let him soke well his feet in the water to the ancles; when he goeth to bed bind of this herb to his temples and he shall sleep well by the grace of God." Though Mary valued drawing and painting "above all other arts," there is no evidence that she had any great skill in designing her own embroideries, for throughout her life she always employed, whenever she was allowed, at least one "imbroiderer to plan out such needleworkes as she would be about." As any embroideress knows, however, great artistry must be employed in translating a design into stitches, and this is the satisfactory outlet embroidery provides for many a would-be painter.

While Mary was at Sheffield and Chatsworth, she spent much of her time stitching with Elizabeth, Countess of Shrewsbury, since Queen Elizabeth had appointed both Shrewsburys to act as Mary's custodians. The Countess was a remarkable woman, masculine in the management of her affairs, who had been described as "a sharp and bitter shrewe, and therefore lieke enough to shorten your life if she should kepe you company." This she surely did for, married first at the age of twelve, she was betrothed to her fourth husband, George Talbot, Earl of Shrewsbury, when she was forty-eight, and outlived him by seventeen years. Having acquired an accumulation of wealth and estates each time she was widowed, she became an inveterate builder and interior designer and delighted in planning and executing numerous large hangings and embroideries for her manor houses.

Once the Earl of Shrewsbury dared to write complaining of her extravagances, particularly her costly needlework projects, and she retorted that her "grooms, women and some boys she kept, wrought on them. His lordship never gave the worth of £5 towards the making of them." In this case, however, she could have been correct, for in the big households no

one was permitted to be idle at any time. A room where embroidery would be set up with frames (also called "tents," and perhaps yet another reason for the name tent stitch) would always be occupied by one member of the house busily embroidering. All through the day, sewing women or helpers who had nothing else to do would be dispatched to this room; so that one can imagine how large pieces of needlework would be finished with the work of many hands.

It was also in the sixteenth century that Cardinal Wolsey started the fashion of importing Turkey and Caucasian rugs. Being rather rare and special, these rugs were used to cover tables, sideboards, or cupboards, and were seldom used on the floor, where skins or sweet-smelling herbs were strewn. The latter were most necessary, for all the rubbish and food

Spanish canvas embroidery, using silk, wool and metal threads. Late 16th—early 17th century. *The Metropolitan Museum of Art, Gift of Charles Zadok, 1948*

of the great halls were allowed to lie underfoot month after month. It was said that Cardinal Wolsey could not cross the courtyard of his own house without holding his nose! Thus, it was customary in noble households for the entire family and its retainers to move out every so often, lock, stock and barrel, to one of their other manor houses or castles, while the one they had left could be thoroughly cleaned. The Dutchman who visited England in 1560 must have fortunately timed his arrival with the moving to a newly cleaned house, for he reports: "The chambers and parlors strewed over with fresh herbes refreshed me, their nosegays finely intermingled with sundry of fragrant flowers . . . in their bed-chambers and privy-rooms with comfortable smell cheered me up and entirely delighted all my senses."

Because the oriental carpets were expensive and hard to come by, it was only natural that their pattern and effect should be imitated. This was done sometimes on a loom, with the knots twisted in with the fingers in the traditional manner of making carpets, but it was also done with a needle on canvas. Both originals and copies were used on tables, and over cupboards and doors, where they must have been most useful for keeping out icy draughts of air during inclement winters, particularly when they were made of Turkey work. When this stitch was carried out in needlework to imitate the oriental knot, it was done by making a series of loops, securing each one as you went along, with a form of back stitch, and then clipping the whole thing afterward to form a velvet pile. (See page 152, Turkey work.) The popularity of this type of work is shown by some brief extracts from the will of Dame Anne Sherley in 1623.

A long cushion and a chaire of needleworke of apples, my carpet of needleworke of gilly flores and woodbyns [honeysuckle]

My Turkey carpet of cowcumbers [carnations]

My cabbage carpet of Turkey worke

My carpett of hawthornes and other flowers with a black ground.

My Turkey worke carpett on the longest table in the dyning roome at London

A cupbord of thistles.

17th century chair done in Turkey work
Victoria and Albert Museum

OPPOSITE
Detail from the Bradford table carpet. Tent stitches on canvas. *Victoria and Albert Museum* (See title page.)

Although Turkey work was obviously so popular, all kinds of other stitches were collected on a "sampler," or long strip of linen, for future reference by the seventeenth-century embroideress (see Chapter 6, Stump Work). The favorites seemed to be cross stitch, rococo, eyelet holes, and "Irish" stitch. The latter is an upright stitch made to interlock like bricks and is identical with our present day Florentine, Bargello, or flame stitch.

One of the earliest examples of this style of stitching is on a thirteenth century altar curtain from Lower Saxony, p. 249 (and also see the Hildesheim Cope, page 113) and the interesting thing about the design of this and many others done in the same stitches is that their patterns are often reminiscent of the Book of Kells, the ninth-century Celtic illuminated manuscript, which influenced ecclesiastical design throughout the Christian world for centuries. This makes the word "Irish" for brick stitch seem logical. At any rate it is fascinating to conjecture about the possible connection. Being such a simple stitch, its beauty lies in the juxtaposition of vibrant or blended colors, and the variety of patterns obtainable by counting threads of the background canvas. Many magnificent altar hangings were made in flame stitch in silk in Italy—hence the name Florentine. Bargello was used to describe the patterns made by introducing a shorter stitch with the regular brick filling, and designs using this were found in the Bargello Palace in Florence—hence the name. This type of needlework was brought to America, where it was very popular with early settlers, who covered sofas, chairs, and even made entire four-poster bed-hangings with it. Very little wool—or silk—is wasted on the reverse side of Bargello stitching so economy and speed of working no doubt influenced its popularity.

Above all, though, the basic tent stitch and Turkey work seem to have had universal appeal throughout the ages, and if they fell out of fashion for a time they were soon reinstated again. This amusing letter was written in 1758 to the New York *Mercury* by a disconsolate husband who obviously had no love for "fancy work," as it was called.

> But my wife's notion of education differs widely from mine. She is an irreconcilable enemy to idleness and considers every state of life as idleness in which the hands are not employed or some art acquired by which she thinks money may be got or saved. In pursuance of this principle she calls up her daughters at a certain hour and appoints them a task of needlework to be performed before breakfast.

Early Bargello work in silk on hemp, Italian, 18th century.
Cooper Hewitt Museum of Design, The Smithsonian Institution

Sampler of needlepoint stitches worked on linen, 17th century
with animals and flowers in shaded tent stitch and some geometric patterns worked in rococo stitch (see page 148)
Victoria and Albert Museum

By this continual exercise of their diligence she has obtained a very considerable number of laborious performances. We have twice as many fire screens as chimneys and flourished quilts for every bed. Half the rooms are adorned with kinds of futile pictures which imitate tapestry. But all their work is not set out to show; she has boxes filled with knit garters and braided shoes.

About a month ago, Tent or Turkey stitch seemed at a stand; my wife knew not of what new work to introduce. I ventured to propose that the girls should now learn to read and write; but unhappily my wife has discovered that linen wears out and has bought the girls little wheels, that they may spin hukkaback for the servants' table. With these she alowes no doubt that the three girls if they are kept close, will spin as much cloth every year as would cost £5 if one was to buy it!

However, all young girls were evidently not so docile, as this letter written to the *Spectator* in 1714 shows:

Those hours which in this age are thrown away in dress, play, visits and the like were employed in my time in writing out receipts, or working beds, chairs and hangings for the family. For my part I have plied the needle these fifty years, and by my good will would never have it out of my hand. It grieves my heart to see a couple of proud idle flirts sipping their tea for a whole afternoon, in a room hung round with the industry of their great grandmothers. Pray, sir, take the laudable mystery of embroidery into your serious consideration.

Which the *Spectator* duly did, replying:

What a delightful entertainment must it be to the fair sex . . . to pass their hours in imitating fruits and flowers and transplanting all the beauties of nature into their own dress. Your pastoral poetesses may vent their fancy in rural landscapes, and place despairing shepherds under silken willows, or drown them in a stream of mohair . . .

I humbly submit the following proposal to all mothers of Great Britain.

1. That no young Virgin whatsoever be allowed to receive the addresses of her first lover but in a suit of her own embroidery—
2. That before every fresh humble servant she be obliged to appear with a new stomacher at the least—
3. That no one be actually married until she hath the child-bed pillows, etc. ready stitched as likewise the mantle for the boy quite finished.

These laws if I mistake not, would effectually restore the decayed art of needlework and make the virgins of Great Britain exceedingly nimble fingered in their business.

This advice must have been taken to heart for the eighteenth century has left us a great legacy of tent-stitch pictures, pole screens, settee coverings, and furnishings of all kinds, both in England and in America. Just as crewel was transplanted from England to America, early settlers brought over designs which were then fashionable for needlepoint in England.

Designs were taken from engravings and many variations of shepherdesses, pastoral landscapes, and hunting scenes were worked with charming naïveté. Especially interesting are the Fishing Lady series, over fifty of which have been found in New England. These may all have been provided by the same source, a finishing school owned by a Mrs. Condy in Boston, who advertised "Patterns of all sorts, especially Pocket Books, House-Wifes Screens, Pictures, Chimney Pieces, Escrutoires, etc. for Tent Stich in a plainer manner and cheaper than those which come from London." The Fishing Lady designs were often framed as "chimney pieces" and the walnut frame which exactly fitted above the mantel would scroll outward at the two lower corners to form sconces for candles.

During the Victorian era a prodigious amount of canvas embroidery was done in the form of Berlin wool work. A Berlin printer and his wife invented a method of printing colored charts whereby, with little skill,

A "Fishing Lady" picture, worked by Sarah Warren, 1748, in silk and wool, showing Boston Common. *Courtesy, Museum of Fine Arts, Boston*

Berlin design done in Turkey work and beads
Mrs. Harley Tracey

A typical piece of 19th century Berlin work
Author's Collection

Needlepoint rug, early 19th century

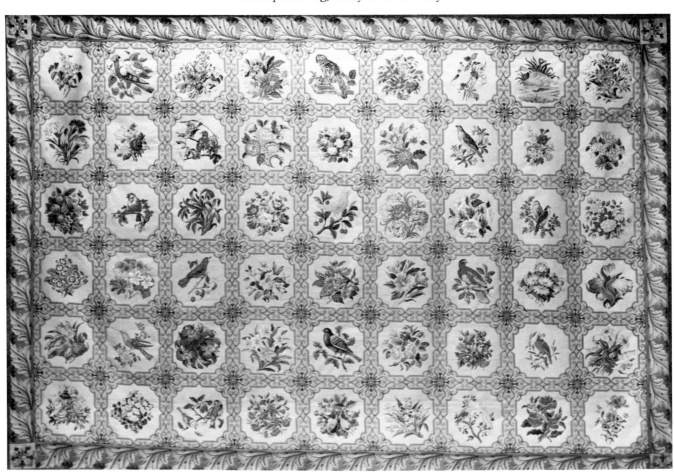

designs could be counted out onto the canvas. Special merino sheep were bred in Saxony to provide a very soft wool for this needlework (which the moths adore!) and it became so much the rage that an embroidery encyclopedia, published at that time, says about "Canvas Work": "Before the introduction of Berlin patterns in 1835, all wool work upon canvas was called by this name, which, has now, however, become almost obsolete!" In other words canvas work, or needlepoint as we know it, was at that time known only as "Berlin Work."

The type of design was "completely in harmony with contemporary fancy work—with the making of feather flowers, the plaited hair ornaments, with gilding and bronzing of plaster casts, the fabrication of pictures in sand, waxen fruit and flowers and sea-weed pictures." A great many of the Berlin designs were done in cross stitch, but some were done in a form of Turkey work known as plush stitch. This was very popular and was done on canvas, closely working row after row of Turkey work loops over a knitting needle. When the knitting needle was pulled out the loops were cut to form a velvet pile. The background of silk canvas was sometimes left bare, and the raised pile was often cut to give a modeled effect. Sometimes, if the subject was an animal or bird, glass eyes were added to give the final touch of realism. It has been customary to dismiss all these Victorian embroideries as "monuments of misplaced activity." But tastes change, and who knows when fashion may love to escape once more to the peaceful world of beribboned nosegays, cabbage roses, King Charles spaniels, and brilliantly plumed parrots?

In the 1930's in England, a needlewoman named Louisa Pesel designed some beautiful kneeling cushions and choir stall cushions for Winchester Cathedral. This started a great deal of interest in church needlepoint both in England and in America, and in 1956 a similar project was started for the National Cathedral in Washington. Although needlepoint, or embroidery on canvas, has had its periods of "creative slump" it has never really gone out of fashion since its early popularity in the sixteenth century.

Today the rich effects of covering an entire surface with the mellow shadings and glowing colors of wool are being explored by contemporary designers who have inspired embroiderers with the realization that the field is as unlimited as painting.

TO BEGIN

You can really take off in any direction you wish, and make almost any article you can think of—cushions, carpets, chair seats, wall hangings, handbags, belts, vests, slippers, even a coat! Curtains may be beautiful but they are apt to be too laborious an undertaking, though Mary Queen of Scots' idea of applying small motifs in petit point to a fabric background might be an inspiring idea to try. (See page 118.)

As needlepoint, being so closely stitched, is extremely hard wearing, it is ideally suited to things like rugs, carpets, chair seats, benches, and footstools. Its close tapestry-like finish means that it does not have to have much stiffening or interlining so it is also perfect for pocket books, eyeglass cases, or anything that should remain stiff, yet be flexible.

The most versatile and basic stitch used for needlepoint has a great many names to describe it. It is variously known as tent stitch, continental stitch, basket weave, gros point, demi point, and petit point. Tent stitch is really the only correct name since all the others describe the different ways of working it; "continental" means tent stitch worked in horizontal and vertical lines, and basket weave is tent stitch worked diagonally. Gros, demi, and petit point describe large, medium, and small size tent stitches in that order. The smooth-shading tapestry effect of tent stitch has made this stitch synonymous with needlepoint. But there are many other stitches which can give needlepoint variety and excitement. One of the simplest and perhaps most effective of these is the brick stitch used for flame stitch, Florentine, or bargello patterns, also known as Hungarian point.

A contemporary variation of canvas work is the concept of "crewel point" which combines the textural effects of crewel with the velvety smoothness of needlepoint. This new and exciting technique can be done either by filling in the ground with tapestry-like needlepoint stitches and accentuating the design with crewel textures (Turkey work, fishbone stitch, satin or French knots, for instance) or by reversing the process, working the background with rows of chain or buttonhole stitch and the design in smooth shading of tent stitch.

If you've never done any needlepoint before and you are wondering how to start, the best way would be to begin by making a sampler, or collection of some of the many different stitches, on a long strip of canvas. This can make a most attractive wall hanging, just like the beautiful samplers made in the 1500's when this was the only way to record the stitches.

Crewelpoint sampler—using crewel and needlepoint stitches—adapted by the author from an embroidery by Natasha Josefowitz

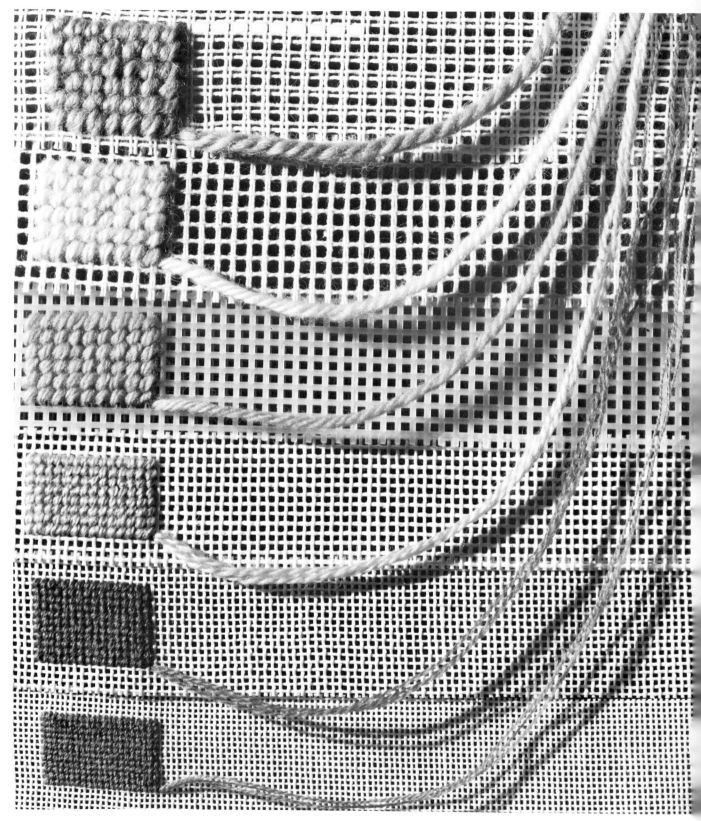

TOP TO BOTTOM:

Rug canvas (Penelope), 5 to inch, with rug wool   Monocanvas, 10 to inch, with 2 strands Persian wool

Rug canvas, 7 to inch, with shag rug wool   Monocanvas, 12 to inch, with 2 strands English wool

Plastic canvas, with knitting worsted (10 to inch)   Monocanvas, 14 to inch, with 3 strands French wool

CANVAS—WOOL AND NEEDLES

Suit your wool to the canvas and your needle to the wool! Of course, the first thing to decide is which size canvas to buy, and that will be determined by your design and what you want to make.

There are two basic types of needlepoint canvas; double thread, usually called penelope, and single thread, known as mono. Both come in a variety of sizes of mesh from very fine to very coarse. Both are made of linen or cotton (nowadays mostly the latter) or even of acrylic fiber. There is also a plastic canvas which simulates mono, and comes only in one size. How do you decide which to use? First you have to know the differences between them, so that you can see which effects you like best. On the whole, single thread or mono canvas is probably the most versatile to start with but all three types are equally easy to work on.

Double thread canvas:
1. Firm, interlocked weave is excellent for bold mesh canvas. (Rug canvas is generally double thread.)
2. Half cross instead of tent stitch may be used (taking half as much yarn).
3. Tramé may be used (a method of applying the design to canvas with long horizontal stitches, page 153).
4. Petit point (fine) and gros point (bold) may be combined in the same design, working over the single mesh for the fine and over the double thread for coarse stitching. (See rug canvas opposite.)

Single thread canvas:
1. The stitches tend to blend together. They are not "square" as when worked on double thread canvas. This makes shading and curves easier.
2. Tent stitch is worked with long slanting stitches on the reverse (instead of half cross with its small straight stitches on the wrong side). This makes the stitching firm and hard wearing.
3. Geometric stitching is easier, as double thread canvas might interfere with the pattern.

Plastic canvas: This canvas is flexible yet rigid enough to be used without backing for such articles as handbags, belts, book covers, and boxes. It comes in sheets, 11 by 14 inches, and as it is plastic may be cut to size and edged and joined without any turnings.

You can readily see that all three canvases have characteristics which are valuable and individual, so experiment and use the one that suits your purpose best. The illustrations and descriptions on page 132 may help you decide which kind of canvas you may need for specific projects.

Wools range from rug yarn to the very finest English or French crewel wool, with cotton, silk, or gold threads to be added at will, for variety. The most versatile, adaptable, and useful wool is Persian. It comes in three strands which can be easily separated and may be used in as many thicknesses as required to cover the canvas. Tapestry yarn, which is a rounded thread made especially for penelope canvas, is easy to work with but will only fit certain mesh sizes, and as it is hard to separate it is wise to use it only when it fits the scale of the canvas perfectly.

English crewel yarn may be used like Persian, with as many threads as you need to fit the canvas, and it is really just as versatile, but finer.

French wool is very fine, but blends into one, even if you are using as many as six strands in the needle and, as it wears, the needlepoint develops a beautiful silky sheen. The colors are interesting, too, since the range is limited and the shades appear quite separate, yet when they are worked together they blend beautifully without ever appearing too dull or muted (which is apt to happen if you try to shade with too many closely blended colors).

Needles must always be blunt "tapestry" needles, since the wool must pass smoothly between the threads of the canvas, never splitting them. The sizes are as shown on page 16. As the numbers increase, the size of the needle decreases. If the needle is too big, you have to force it through the canvas; if it is too small, you have to drag it too hard, as it sticks where the yarn is doubled at the eye, making it difficult to pull through.

A Victorian strip sampler. *Author's Collection*

BEGINNING THE DESIGN

There are two distinctly different ways of working needlepoint. The first is done by outlining or painting a design on the canvas, and then following it with stitching. The second is done by stitching the design onto a blank canvas by counting the mesh, working from an existing embroidery or a pattern on graph paper. (See illustration, page 138.)

The first, generally a "free" design (i.e., not a repeating geometric pattern), must be outlined on the canvas, and then the design coloring can be done in several ways. It can be painted directly on the canvas by using oil paints, or paints or markers which are not water soluble. Then the pattern can be worked over this, matching the colors to the paint exactly. Alternatively, a colored painting or "cartoon" can be made on paper, and the design outlined on the canvas with a permanent black marking pen. The design can then be embroidered, working with the cartoon or color sketch constantly beside the canvas as a guide. Another method, tramé, can be done only on penelope or double thread canvas. The design is outlined on the canvas in the permanent ink, then the colors are put in with wool, working with long horizontal or traméed lines between each double thread of the canvas. Afterward these lines are stitched over with half cross stitch in wools exactly matching the traméed lines.

The second method of working needlepoint is counting the design out stitch by stitch onto the blank canvas. This method is really the most practical and accurate if the design is geometric, but it can be used for a "free" design, too. To work geometric patterns, first mark off one or two repeats on graph paper with marking pens (page 329). A difference in scale can make a pattern almost unrecognizable. To get an idea of the finished design you want, buy graph paper of the same size or close to the size of the canvas you are going to work on.

A third method is to find your design—a photograph, a painting, or a book illustration—which is the right size and which seems suitable in design. Trace round its outlines with a black permanent marker on tracing paper or acetate (that marvelous plastic material which is clear as glass, enabling you to trace your design perfectly). Then transfer this outline to the canvas shown at top left on page 138. Now comes the clever part! Overlay your original colored design with a plastic sheet, which has a grid printed on it. This clear plastic "graph paper" is available in art stores and comes in the same sizes as the mesh of the canvas. You will then be able to count out your colored stitches within the outlines you have already marked, and thus transfer your pattern very accurately to the canvas. Sometimes the grid will show half a stitch in one color and half in another. Since it is impossible to work half stitches, you will just have to decide which stitch is to be which color, but this skill will develop with practice and you may ultimately find you are getting so good at it that you can dispense with the grid altogether!

These last two methods are ideal for plastic canvas, since you can only mark the plastic with permanent markers and the design is best counted out within a traced black outline.

Once you have decided the type of needlepoint you would like to begin on, you will be ready to apply your pattern.

APPLYING THE PATTERN

Your first step is to cut the canvas the proper size. Always plan your work so that the selvage runs up and down both sides of the design, not across; the needlepoint is stronger when worked this way.

Allow plenty of turnings! You can always cut the canvas smaller, but you cannot add more quite so easily! Besides, you need enough canvas at the edge to work with when you finish and block the embroidery. It is best to bind the edges with masking tape to prevent them from fraying.

To prepare your canvas for accurate placing of the design, fold it in half vertically right down the center and repeat this horizontally. Mark these crease lines by running a pencil lightly between the threads of the

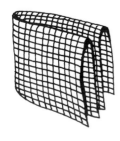

canvas, allowing them to guide you in keeping the lines straight. *Pull* the pencil across the canvas rather than push it. Then you will find it will easily stay between the threads without running off the line. Run a pencil border around the design in the same way, marking the size and shape you want your finished article to be. Be generous with this line, too. A few lines of stitching can always be taken into the turnings, but if white canvas shows, you will have to add more stitching after you thought you had finished—a very boring thing to have to do!

Draw your design on paper with India ink or with a permanent black felt-tipped pen. Lay it on a table or firm surface and hold it in position with masking tape. If you used tracing paper, or acetate, place several layers of white paper under the drawing. This will make your black lines more distinct, so that you can see them easily through the canvas.

Then put the canvas over the design with the selvage running down both sides. Mark the top of the design on the canvas, so that you will not forget which edge should be uppermost when you start stitching later. Then match up the center lines on the canvas with those on the drawing. At this point you may find that the center lines on the canvas, although they were drawn by the thread, are not entirely straight. This is because the canvas may sometimes be pulled a little out of shape by being stored in a large roll. Just pull the opposite corners and stretch it a little until the center lines are at true right angles again. Then when you lay it on top of your design it will lie flat and your mesh will be square.

Trace the design on the canvas, using a black waterproof felt-tipped pen, or a fine paint brush and India ink. Test the pen to make sure it will not run when the canvas is made wet for blocking. Then draw the design with a fine light line because a heavy black line may be hard to cover with light colored wools. Draw the design as you would on paper, ignoring the mesh of the canvas, and make the lines smooth and flowing. For example, a curve should be a curve and not a series of steps following the square mesh. You will find that you will better interpret a circle with your needle if you draw it smoothly on the canvas, instead of anticipating the stitches with a zigzag drawing which follows the canvas.

If you want to paint your design in color on the canvas, use oil

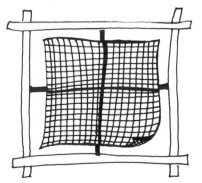

TOP LEFT. Design outlined with permanent marking pen
TOP RIGHT. Design painted with oil paints
BOTTOM LEFT. Tramé design on Penelope canvas
BOTTOM RIGHT. Design on graph paper, to be counted onto canvas

paints. These together with the waterproof marking pens are the best permanent colors to use. Though some acrylics are quite satisfactory, some have been known to run on occasion. Watercolors will run into your wool when the work is blocked and be hard to eradicate. (If this should happen, see page 166 for cleaning and blocking.) Oil paint is easy to work with if you mix every color with some turpentine in a small jar and shake well. Then you will have a series of ready-to-use colors which will not be so heavy they clog the canvas or so thin they go pale. Working with them can be just like filling in a children's coloring book, and equally as much fun! Just be patient and allow the paint to dry thoroughly before you start the stitching—up to three days.

Geometric designs do not have to be applied; they are counted direct from your graph onto the plain canvas. Do this in the following way:

1. Fold your canvas in four, open it up, and mark these creased lines with pencil through the center in vertical and horizontal lines.
2. This will indicate the center of your design. Always begin in the middle and work out to the edges, then your repeat pattern will be balanced and identical on both sides.
3. Always count the *threads* of the canvas, never the holes. This makes it much less confusing when you are deciding on the size of each stitch and means your counting will be consistent.
4. Mark the outside edges of the design, drawing a pencil between the threads of the canvas, (as shown on page 136).
5. For some patterns it may be helpful to mark the true diagonal of the canvas. To do this, place a square of canvas flat on the table with one of the corners toward you. Kneel, so that you are at eye level with it. Shift the canvas a little until you can see the *clear ridges* formed by the mesh, running diagonally across the canvas. Place a ruler beside the one you need to mark and draw the line with a pencil.
6. To start a geometric design, pick the predominant pattern and work all of this "framework" first. Keep checking by running your needle along the threads of the canvas to make sure that the repeats are lined up correctly. Then if you have made a mistake in the count of this "framework" you will not have so much to unpick as if you had filled in an entire section. Also once the "framework" is made you do not have to count threads; you can fill in the areas within the pattern using the outlines as a guide.

Bargello designs with predominating
pattern worked first (6 and 7)

A contemporary chair with an all-over geometric pattern. *Designed and worked by the
author*

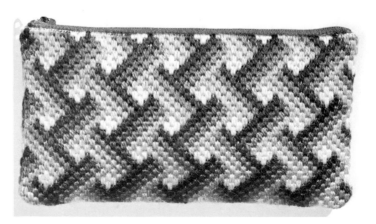

Zippered pouch in bargello pattern, worked in soft blues and
greens. *Elinor Parker*

7. Start bargello patterns by working the first zigzag lines horizontally across the center of your canvas, starting at the right-hand side and working toward the left. Then you can follow this exactly above and below, just repeating the pattern without counting threads.

8. To decide on the color scheme for bargello, first work your line across the canvas as above. Then put in a small section of all the colors on the right-hand side of the design. From this you can visualize the finished color scheme and change any of the colors, if necessary, without having too much to unpick.

Sampler showing various stitches in geometric patterns. *Worked by the author*

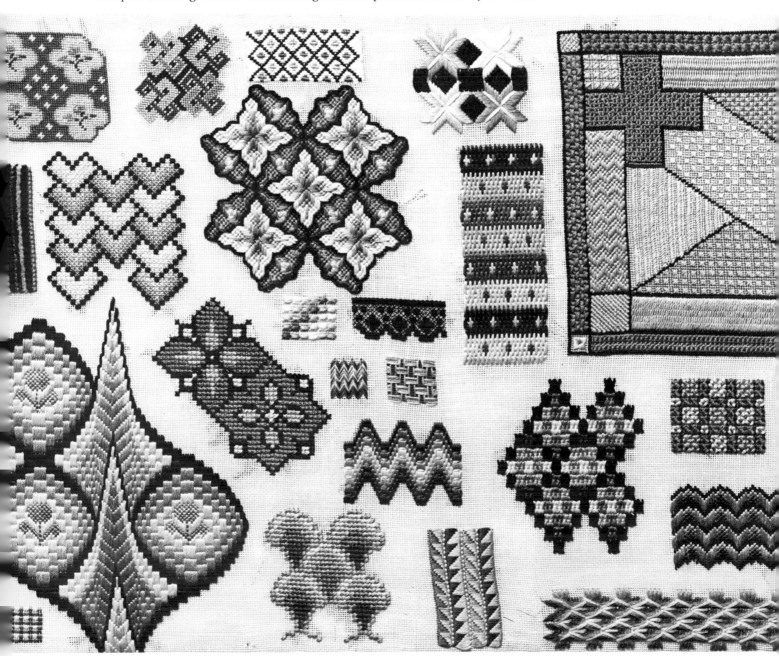

FRAMES

Once again comes the question, should you use a frame? The answer is that frames have been used since medieval days by professionals and in workshops, because they make the needlepoint faster and smoother, and the outlines and shading more flowing. The work is also flatter and the stitches more regular, so the piece hardly needs blocking afterward.

Because the canvas is stretched out flat like a board, in using geometric designs you can count the threads more easily when the work is in a frame. As you work, you can see how the stitches line up with one another, and can run the needle along the threads of the canvas to check this. You can also work with several needles threaded with different colors and leave them hanging on the front of the frame to use as you need them.

When you are working a large rug, a square frame in which the canvas can be rolled up on one side and unrolled on the other as the work progresses is a tremendous help. Even if you are using a large ring frame, the rest of the rug could be rolled up and kept clean and out of the way by tying it up in a pillow case.

If you have worked successfully all your life without using a frame, it will probably be very frustrating to change. Most people's complaint is that it is annoying to take a frame around with them: they love a piece of needlepoint to just pick up and carry anywhere. The answer to this is,

do all the complicated shading at home on the frame and fill in the background in your hand wherever you happen to be. Alternatively, the portable hoop on a lap stand was specially designed for the traveling needlepointer. If you are first starting out you will find that using a frame is a really good habit to establish right away. The types of frames and how you can use them are discussed on page 25.

WOOL THICKNESS—REPAIRS AND JOINS

Now you have your canvas and wools and you have chosen your first stitches. The next question is, how many threads of wool to use? This depends on what your stitch is going to be, and on the size of your canvas—and, of course, on what type of wool you are working with, see page 132.

Sometimes it is impossible to tell the right amount until you have tried a small block of stitches on the edge. Work with fewer threads rather than too many. You can always work over the stitches again, adding another thread if the canvas is not covered sufficiently, but if you have used too many threads of yarn the stitches will be thick and uneven, the canvas threads will pack tightly together, and you will hardly be able to force the needle between them. Then you will have to cut out all your stitches and begin again.

If you *do* have to cut out stitches, clip them from the back. On the reverse side there are longer stitches to cut and more wool to get hold of. Cut as much wool as possible at the back, then rub your scissors over the front to loosen up the stitches, pull out what you can, cut more again at the back and continue until you have removed everything you want.

Should you cut a few threads of the canvas during this operation, don't faint! It can be easily repaired. First fill the canvas with stitches all around the hole, leaving an open space of at least ½ inch all around the cut. Ease the loose broken threads to the back and weave them into the stitches on the reverse side. To do this first push the needle into position and *then* thread it, since the ends of canvas will probably be very short. Unravel two or three long threads from the edge of your canvas and, still working on the reverse side, darn these into the hole so that the mesh

OPPOSITE
Geometric design worked entirely in cross stitch over two threads of canvas. Black lace effect obtained by working outlines in bold wool thread, filling in with a single thread of DMC floss, allowing the canvas to show through

Repairing a cut canvas

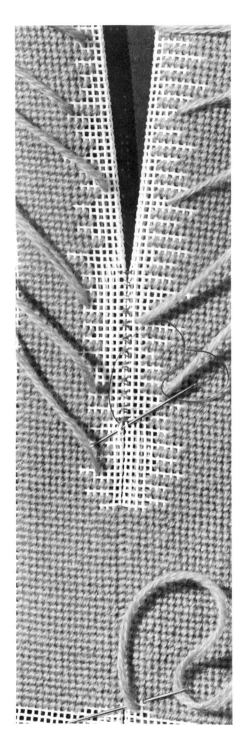 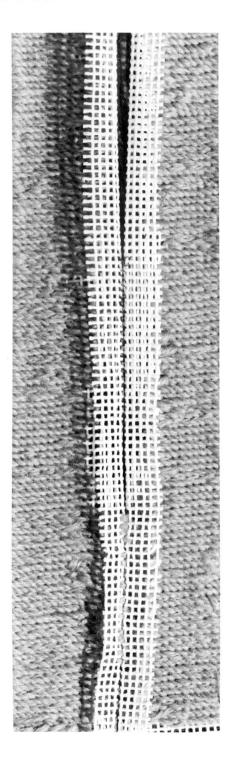

Joining canvas:

LEFT. Shows canvas with irregular lines of stitching, and working threads left hanging, to be sewn across join later. In the center the needle is shown oversewing join with strong button thread. Contrasting color was used here only to show stitching; the thread should match canvas. In lower section join is being covered using threads which were left hanging, so that the join is invisible.

RIGHT. Reverse side, with raw edges turned back

is perfectly and invisibly repaired. Once this has been embroidered you will never know that the cut was there.

If you know you are going to have to join two pieces of needlepoint, you should first embroider the canvas, leaving about $\frac{1}{2}$ inch of unworked canvas at each edge. You can leave the working threads hanging so that these threads may be used to continue the stitching right across the join, once the canvas is stitched together. Now crease back the unworked edgings and lay the two pieces of canvas side by side, lining up the mesh so that it runs true. Pin them flat side by side and, starting at the top, oversew or whip the threads together, using fine linen or button thread. Join the two pieces as though they were one, taking a stitch into each mesh and pulling tightly so that the two vertical threads of canvas merge completely together. Hold the two turnbacks together on the reverse side and embroider the canvas right across the join, being careful not to stitch through the turnbacks as this would cause an unnecessary ridge.

A few dos and don'ts on needlepoint and crewel point:

1. When doing needlepoint with tent stitch, outline the shapes first and then fill them in afterwards. Work a little of several colors to see how they blend together before you fill in the whole area, so that not too much is worked, in case you decide to change anything.
2. Hold up your finished work in front of a strong light and you will see where you have to fill in any missed stitches.
3. Always thread your needle, put a knot on one end and leave the other hanging—never knot both ends together. This leaves the thread free to untwist as you work and makes for smoother stitching.
4. Begin by placing a knot on top of the canvas, go through to the back and start about $1\frac{1}{2}$ inches away. The thread lying at the back will then be "locked in" by your subsequent stitching and you can cut the knot off. End off in the same way, securing the short end of thread hanging on the front until the thread is covered, then it may be cut off.
5. Never end off darker colors into a light background—they will show through on the front and make it look dirty.
6. If you are working a large area of background horizontally or vertically, but are finishing only a small section at a time, always leave the edges

Determine dark and light areas first when shading with tent stitch, and work them, then fill in intermediate shades.

irregular so that the next piece of background will blend into it invisibly. If you leave straight lines, hard edges will be formed which will show where each section joins.

7. Start basket weave tent stitch (worked diagonally for background) in the top right-hand corner (or bottom left if you are left-handed) and continue across the design, working rows back and forth until it is finished. This forms a basket weave pattern on the back of the canvas. Working two rows in the same direction (instead of going back and forth) will interrupt this pattern, causing a break which will show on the front.

8. In tent stitch always work the design first and the background later, so that smooth shapes will be clear cut around the design. Then the background can be filled in afterward.

9. Never start the background in a second place when you are working it with a geometric stitch. The count will probably not come out correctly when the two areas come together.

THE STITCHES

Since needlepoint is really a "stitched" tapestry, the canvas is usually embroidered with tent stitch (page 154). This gives a lovely, smooth, flat effect, with rich glowing colors. Another stitch that makes horizontal ridges across the canvas so closely resembles tapestry that it is called Gobelin, a name famous for tapestry weaving in France since the Middle Ages. Entire designs worked in this stitch have a bold stylized effect, but it is also attractive when used for backgrounds.

"Encroaching Gobelin" is a close cousin, with a smooth look, since, as the name suggests, each row of stitches projects into the previous row, giving a more blended effect.

Another upright straight stitch is brick stitch, which is used for flame stitch or bargello patterns, but which can be most effective when combined with other stitches in a regular piece of needlepoint.

After the upright stitches, cross stitches make another separate group with a different effect. Apart from simple cross stitch there is rice stitch—a

Bolster of Algerian eyelets with tent stitch. *Designed and worked by the author. Photo by Martin Blumenthal*

marvelously hard-wearing geometric stitch ideal for rugs worked on a giant scale. Long-armed cross stitch will make borders and rug edgings as well as being effective when worked within a design. Turkey work can be cut to form a velvet pile; or left in loops to fill a whole design; or be worked in a small area to contrast with other stitches.

A beautiful stitch called rococo was most popular in the eighteenth century for small geometric designs. It leaves a pattern of small holes over the canvas and is especially effective when worked in silk or cotton.

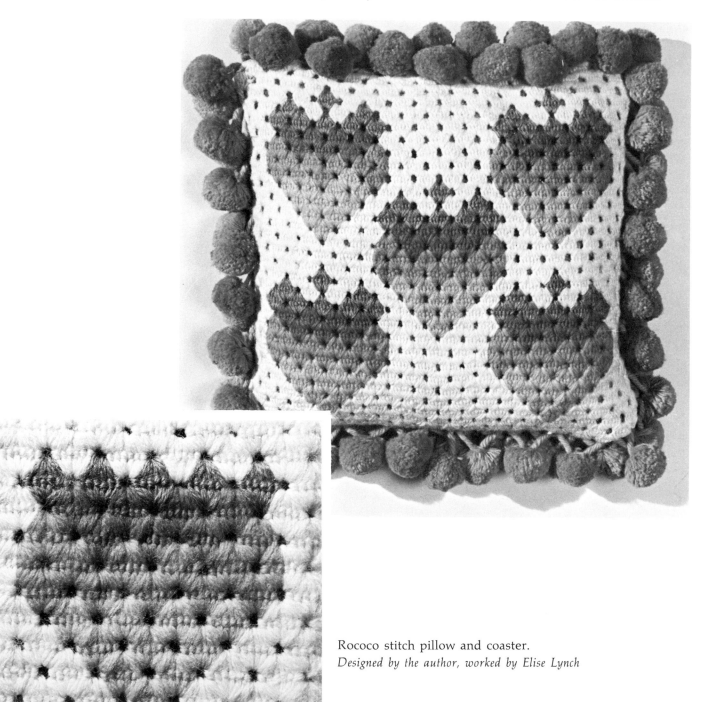

Rococo stitch pillow and coaster.
Designed by the author, worked by Elise Lynch

ROCOCO STITCH

Begin by forcing open two holes in the canvas (at A and B), six threads apart. To do this, twist a closed pair of scissors or a stiletto several times around in the canvas to part the threads without breaking them (see page 157).

1

2

Come up at A, (in the lower hole) and go down at B, 6 threads above A. With the thread to the left of the needle, come up at C, 3 threads below B (half way between A and B). Pull *tightly.*

Make a small horizontal stitch across this first stitch by going down at D, one thread away from and level with C. Bring the needle out at A again.

3

Go down at B again, and then come up exactly in the same hole made by the small horizontal stitch (at D).

Repeat #2 and 3, to make three stitches, side by side, each going into the same holes at the top and bottom of each stitch. Pull firmly.

4

With the thread to the right of the needle come up in the center again at C, and repeat 2, 3 and 4, to make three identical stitches to the right, working from the center out.

5

This completes one whole stitch shown here at the upper left. Come up next at the arrow (having first forced the hole open) and complete the stitch in the center of diagram, then the one at the lower right. (Working diagonally means you will avoid covering the open holes with your working threads.)

6

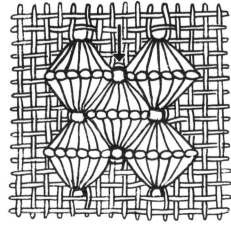

Always begin by opening a hole in the canvas at the top and bottom of each stitch, and pull tightly to keep the holes open as you work. Be sure your working thread does not cross behind these holes, or it will spoil the effect.

CREWEL POINT

The varieties are endless, and are even further extended when crewel point is added. Here the regular needlepoint stitches should be worked first, then the crewel stitches worked to slightly overlap these flatter needlepoint ones. You can treat the canvas as though it were embroidery linen, and without counting threads simply work the crewel stitches in whatever direction you wish. The combination of smooth tent stitch with stitches such as Turkey work, spiders' webs, fishbone, chain, padded satin, buttonhole, raised stem or French knots are possibly the most effective. If you experiment you will find each new idea brings out another.

Starting crewel point: complete tent stitch areas up to outlines; then work crewel stitches freely as if the canvas were linen, overlapping slightly at the edges.

Owl bell pull using satin, stem, fishbone and bullion knots on a tent stitch background.

Crewel point. *Beatrix Potter's Hunca Munca adapted and worked by the author*

Crewel point on plastic canvas, for a doorstop or workbox. The roof hinges at the back. *Designed and worked by the author*

CREWEL POINT STITCHES

Crewel stitches may be worked in combination with needlepoint stitches quite freely on the canvas, treating the mesh as though it was linen. Alternatively, the stitches may be worked geometrically, by counting the threads, as shown here. The stitches may be worked over any number of threads, as long as the canvas is closely covered. The six stitches shown here are only a beginning; any of the crewel, stump work, silk and gold, black or white work stitches may be experimented with on canvas, working either freely or geometrically.

Chain

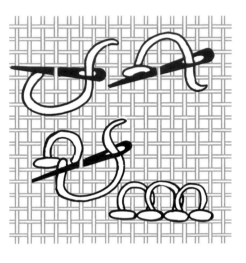

Turkey work

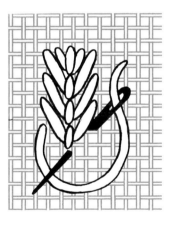

Fishbone

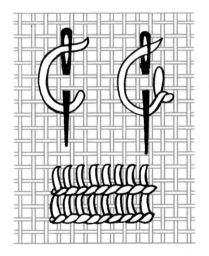

Buttonhole

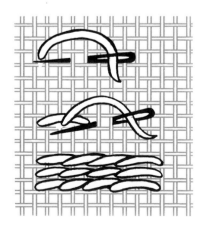

Close Herringbone

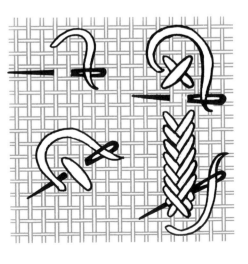

Stem

NEEDLEPOINT STITCHES

HALF CROSS STITCH

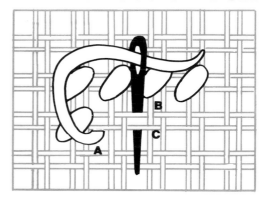

Come up at A, count one double thread up and one double thread over to the right, and go in at B. Come up at C, one thread immediately below B. The needle is therefore always vertical, as shown. Work to the end of the line, then turn the canvas completely upside down, and make another identical row below, fitting the new stitches into the holes made by the previous ones. Continue, turning the canvas at the end of each row.

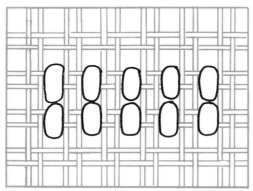

This shows the small upright stitches formed on the reverse side.

Half cross stitch should always be worked on double thread (penelope) canvas. Because the canvas has such a firm weave, the upright stitches formed on the reverse side, cannot slip between the mesh, as they might on single or mono canvas.

CROSS STITCH

Work a row of half cross stitches (as shown above). Then complete the cross by working back in the opposite direction, repeating the first row of stitching, and going into exactly the same holes as the previous stitches, as shown.

TRAMÉ

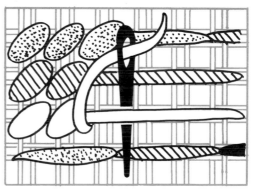

Between the double threads of the canvas, stitch long lines of thread in the colors required to form the pattern.*

Join new colors in the same way, bringing the needle up through the end of the previous stitch, splitting the thread. When the tramé lines have been laid in, work half cross stitch on top (see right) in matching color. This completely covers the traméd threads, as shown.

* If the required line of color is too long to lie smoothly (more than an inch), complete the stitch by going down into the canvas between the double threads. Then start a new stitch by passing back under one thread on the reverse side, and coming up, splitting right through the thread of the stitch you have just laid in.

TENT STITCH

Tent Stitch, the basic stitch used for needlepoint, has long slanting stitches covering the canvas, on the reverse side, while the Half Cross has short straight ones with canvas between. Therefore, Tent Stitch is firmer, smoother and wears better than Half Cross Stitch when worked on single thread canvas.

STARTING AND ENDING OFF

Having knotted your thread, take the needle down through the canvas, 6 or 7 threads away from where you intend to begin stitching, leaving the knot on top. Work toward the knot, covering the long thread on the reverse side. When you have worked up to the knot, cut it off—the end of the thread will be held securely under the canvas by the stitches on top.

When you are finished with a thread, bring it to the top of the canvas some distance from your last stitch. Leave the thread there until, as with the knot, the long thread on the back has been covered by more stitching. Cut off the end of the thread.

TENT STITCH/worked horizontally (Continental Stitch)

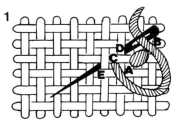

Starting at lower right of area to be filled, come up at A. Go down at B, (*one* thread above and *one* thread to the right of A). Come up at C, one thread to the left, and level with A. Repeat, going in at D, up at E, making a horizontal row of slanting stitches, working from right to left across the canvas.

At the end of the line, turn canvas and work a second row of identical stitches above the first. Bring needle up in the same holes as the previous line of stitches, so that no canvas shows between. By turning the canvas completely around at the end of each line, the rows may *always* be worked from right to left, making it easier to the right handed to 'sew' each stitch with the needle slanted as in diagram 1 & 2. Left handed people should simply turn these diagrams upside down to follow them, beginning each area to be filled at the top left hand corner.

For effect on reverse side, see opposite.

TENT STITCH/worked vertically (Continental Stitch)

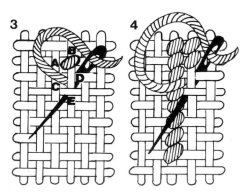

Tent Stitch may also be worked in vertical rows, turning the canvas so that you always work from top to bottom. Begin at the top left of the area to be filled. When worked in straight lines, Tent Stitch is often called the Continental Stitch.

For effect on reverse side, see opposite.

TENT STITCH/worked diagonally (Basket Weave)

Tent Stitch may also be worked in diagonal lines. When working from top to bottom, the needle is placed vertically so that the next stitch may be taken on the true diagonal of the mesh.

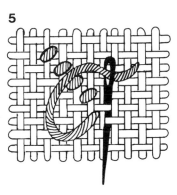

5

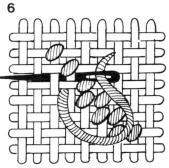

When working from bottom to top the needle is horizontal. This gives a basket weave effect on the back which is firm and hardwearing. The stitch is clear cut because the needle always goes *down* into the *previous* stitches, never *up* (as diagrams 2 and 4). The canvas does not have to be reversed at the end of each row (as do 1 and 3). These three reasons make it very practical for backgrounds. To learn the stitch, practice it as shown in diagrams 5 and 6 on an odd piece of canvas. Once it is understood that it is identical with horizontal and vertical tent stitch (1,2,3&4), only worked diagonally, it will be easy to work a corner. This is shown in diagram 8, which shows the order of working.

6

Begin in the top right hand corner, and always work the rows alternately—first from top to bottom, and then from bottom to top, starting with one stitch, and increasing each row as shown. Always leave a thread hanging in the middle of the row if you have to leave the canvas, then when you pick it up again you can tell whether you were working up or down. When two rows are worked in the same direction the Basket Weave on the back is interrupted; this makes an undesirable break which shows on the front.

8

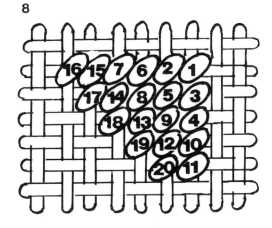

Sometimes it is necessary to work diagonal lines of tent stitch slanting from left to right as in the diagram. In this case the stitch becomes like a back stitch. The needle comes up one thread to the left and one thread below the last stitch, and goes down into the exact same hole as this previous stitch, as shown. To work a whole background of lines in this direction would not be smooth, as the stitches do not interlock as they do in diagrams 5, 6 and 8.

7

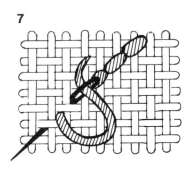

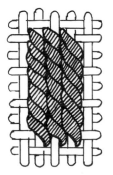

Reverse side
(vertical)

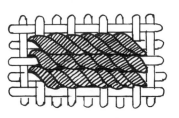

Reverse side
(horizontal)

Reverse side
(Basket weave)

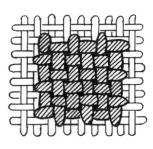

DOUBLE CROSS STITCH

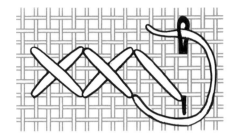

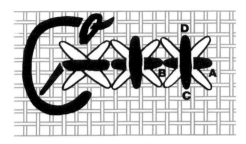

First make a line of cross stitch as shown.

Then, using a contrasting thread, make a series of crosses on top of the first stitches from A to B and C to D.

LONG-ARMED CROSS STITCH/or Twist Stitch

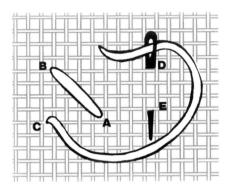

Working from left to right come up at A. Count 4 threads straight up and 4 threads over to the left, going down at B. Come up at C 4 threads directly below B; then go in at D 8 threads away and on a line with B. Come up at E 4 threads directly below D.

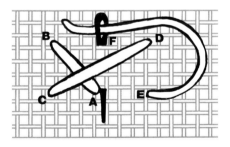

Go in at F 4 threads to the left and level with D (exactly midway between D and B). Come up in the same hole as the first stitch, at A directly below F.

Now go in at G 4 threads to the right and level with D, come up at H 4 threads directly below G.

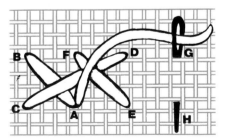

Now repeat numbers 2 and 3 to make a continuous line of stitching as shown. Note: after the first few stitches, the needle always fits back into the same holes as the previous stitches. If necessary, an extra stitch, shown at arrow, may be slipped under the bar to complete the line.

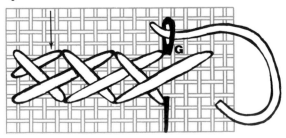

RICE STITCH

First make a cross stitch from A to B and C to D over 6 threads of the canvas. Then proceed to cross each of the four arms of the cross stitch with slanting stitches. Begin by coming up at E, midway between B and D, and go in at F, midway between D and A. Note: E and F are therefore each 3 threads away from D.

Next come up at G, halfway between B and C, and go back to E. Come up at H half way between C and A.

Continue the pattern by going in at F and up at G.

Complete the pattern by going in at H. The needle is shown coming up at J to begin another pattern.

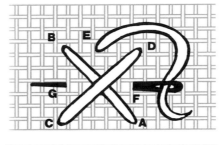
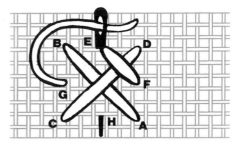
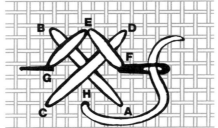
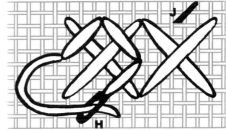

ALGERIAN EYELET

To make eyelet holes, work Satin stitches over four threads of the canvas into *one central hole* as shown in diagrams. The effectiveness of the stitch relies on the clear open hole in the center and the evenness of the stitches.

Insert scissors into hole that will be the center of the eyelet and twist so as to enlarge it taking care not to break any of the threads.

Always go *down* in the center, rotating the needle in the hole as you take each stitch, to force it open.

Draw thread tight.

Take care to place stitches side by side, do not allow them to overlap, or the hole will close up and the stitches will not be smooth.

Shows an eyelet worked to form a diamond (left)

Shows a square eyelet (right)

MONTENEGRIN CROSS STITCH

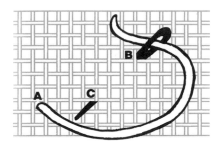

Come up at A, count 4 threads up and 8 threads over to the right, and go in at B. Come up at C 4 threads to the right of A and level with it.

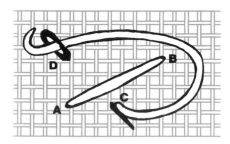

Now go in at D 4 threads directly above A and come up at C again in exactly the same hole made by the previous stitch.

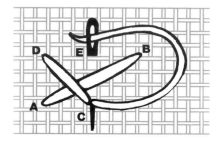

Now go in at E, 4 threads immediately above C, and come up once again at C in the same hole.

Repeat steps 1, 2 and 3 to make a line of stitching as shown.

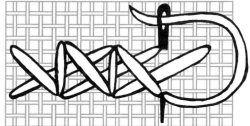

STRAIGHT GOBELIN STITCH

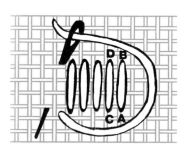

Come up at A, and go down at B 4 threads above. Repeat, from C to D, one thread to the left, and continue making a row of vertical stitches the same size, side by side.

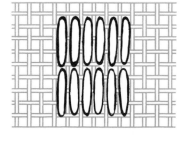

Make another row of vertical stitches underneath the first, fitting the stitches back into exactly the same holes as those formed by the stitches of the previous row. When working these upright stitches, use more threads of yarn than when you work slanting ones, in order to cover the canvas. Do not pull too tightly or spaces will form between the rows, showing bare threads of canvas. If this happens, cover the spaces by working a line of back stitch (see page 84) between each row after the whole area is filled.

ENCROACHING GOBELIN

Come up at A. Count 4 threads straight up, and 2 threads to the right, and go in at B. Come up at C, one thread to the left and level with A, and repeat the first stitch, going in one thread to the left of B. Continue to make a horizontal row of slanting stitches.

Come up at D, 3 threads immediately below C. As before, count 4 threads straight up and 2 to the right going in at E. Note: E is one thread above and one to the right of A.

Repeat DE, making a stitch from F to G. Note: This second row of stitches encroaches into the previous row by one thread of canvas, so slide your needle carefully between the stitches at G, to locate the mesh. Come up at H, and repeat to the end of the row.

Shows the finished effect with smaller stitches at the lower right and upper left to fill out the shape as needed.

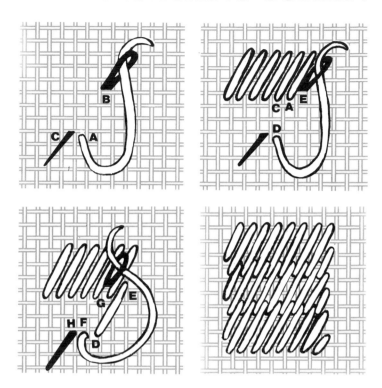

CHEVRON

Come up at A, and go down 4 threads above at B. Come up at C, one thread above and one thread to the left of A. Go in at D, 4 threads above C and one thread to the left and above B. Continue, from E to F, and G to H, going one thread higher with each stitch, always going over 4 threads, as shown.

Then work downwards (from J to K, L to M, N to O) with each new stitch one thread below the previous one as shown. Continue, making this chevron pattern across the canvas.

Repeat below, making a row of stitches identical with the previous ones, but over 2 threads, fitting into the holes of the previous row.

Finished effect is of chevron bandings of long and short stitches worked alternately.

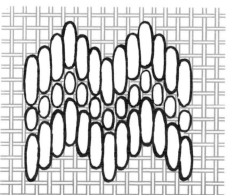

WEB STITCH

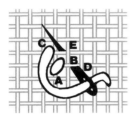

Come up at A and go down at B, making a tent stitch over one thread of the canvas. Come up at C one thread above and one thread to the left of B. Go in at D, one thread below and one thread to the right of B, making a long slanting stitch. Come up at E one thread immediately above B.

Go in at F, making a small stitch across the long slanting one, and come up at G on the other side of the stitch, one thread below and one to the right of E.

Go in at H, over the stitch, one thread to the left and one below G. Come up at J.

Now make another long slanting stitch, close to the previous one.

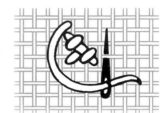

Work all the way back, placing slanting stitches across the line alternately with those of the previous row, as shown.

The finished effect has the appearance of diagonal weaving.

BRICK STITCH

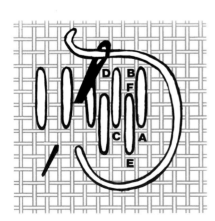

Come up at A, go down at B, 4 threads above. Come up at C, level with A but 2 threads to the left, then down at D 4 threads directly above C. Repeat across the canvas. Work the next row beneath the first coming up at E 2 threads below and between A and C, then go down 4 threads above at F.

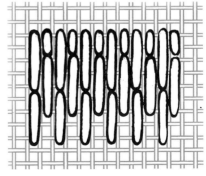

Finished effect showing small stitches used to fill in the top line making an even edge.

PARISIAN STITCH

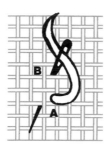

Come up at A, go down at B, 2 threads above.

Now come up at C, one thread below and one thread over to the left of A. Go in at D 4 threads above C.

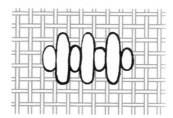

Continue, making alternate short and long stitches, over 2 and 4 threads respectively.

Each successive row fits into the previous one with the long stitches fitting below the short ones, and vice versa.

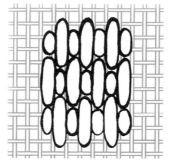

FLORENTINE STITCH

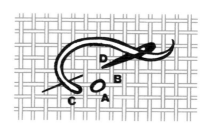

Make a slanting stitch (tent stitch) by counting one thread up and one thread to the right, from A to B. Make another slanting stitch coming up at C, level with A and one thread to the left, and go in at D one thread directly above B.

Continue working up diagonally, alternately making slanting stitches over one and two threads of the canvas.

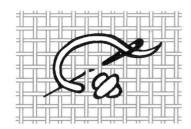

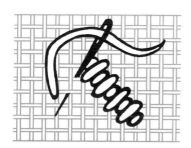

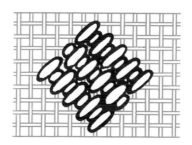

Then work down repeating steps 1 and 2 in the opposite direction, fitting the longer stitch back into the holes of the shorter stitch made by the previous row, and vice versa.

Shows finished effect.

BARGELLO

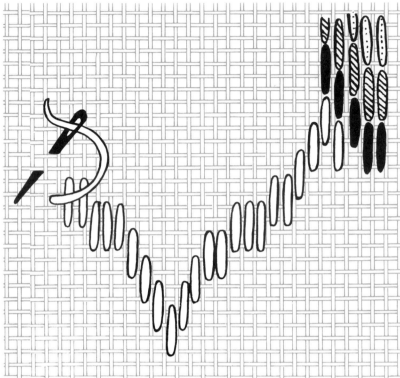

Shows the main lines of a pattern being outlined across the center of the canvas with a few stitches of each shade of the final design being put in at one side.

The color scheme can then be chosen and changed if necessary without having to unpick more than two or three stitches.

Shows a variation of the "flame stitch" pattern. Short stitches are worked in the center of the medallion.

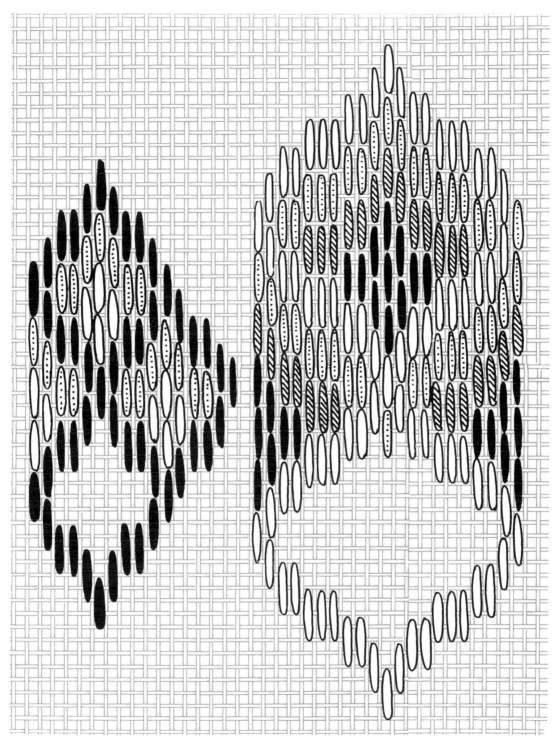

The pattern on the left forms a diamond. If you count the dark outline stitches at the upper left of this small pattern you will see that they are identical with the light outline stitches at the upper left of the large pattern on the right, except that in the larger one three stitches have been added in the center of the line. This slight difference alters the characteristics from a diamond to a flowing ribbon effect. With different shadings and outlines unlimited variations may be made with Bargello patterns.

MILANESE STITCH

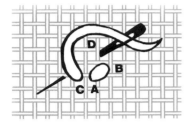

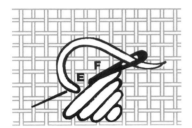

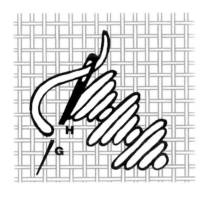

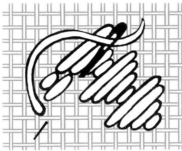

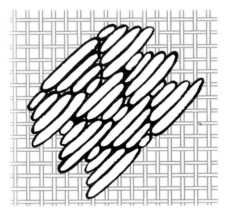

Come up at A, count one thread straight up and one thread over to the right, and go in at B making a small slanting stitch, just like a tent stitch. Then make another slanting stitch beside it, from C to D, counting two threads straight up and two to the right.

Then make two more slanting stitches, over 3 threads and then over 4 threads, and start again over one from E to F, as shown.

Continue, making these blocks of four slanting stitches, which will automatically form a diagonal line across the canvas.

Now work back in the other direction, making another set of blocks of slanting stitches.

Work first over one thread from G to H, then over 2, then 3 and finally 4, fitting the stitches exactly into the holes of the previous row.

Finished effect, showing the interlocking blocks of stitches.

FLAT STITCH

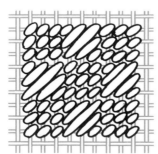

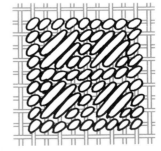

Make slanting stitches diagonally over one, two, three, four, three, two and finally one thread. This forms a perfect square as shown. Repeat, fitting the squares close together so that they all go into the same holes, as shown.

A variation of this stitch is to alternate the squares with blocks of tent stitch (see page 154). Alternatively, the squares of flat stitch can be worked with each block slanting in the opposite direction.

Another variation is called Scottish stitch because it looks like a plaid. This is done by outlining each block of flat stitch with lines of tent stitch. Mosaic stitch is just like flat stitch, but forms squares worked over one, two and one thread of the canvas.

BLOCKING

Finished needlepoint should be smooth and flat, so blocking it right side downwards helps to make the final effect beautifully even—below.

Crewel and crewel point should always be blocked face *upwards*, so that the raised stitches will not be crushed—as in the mouse at right.

Detailed instructions for blocking are shown on the next page.

"Hunca Munca Housewife" was adapted for needlework by the author, from Beatrix Potter's "Two Bad Mice."

Needlepoint needs special attention in blocking because sometimes the stitches are apt to pull the design very much out of shape. If you are sure your pattern is permanent and your work does not need cleaning, block it before you wet it; it will be easier to handle. Lay it out, right side down, on a board or an old table which has first been covered with a sheet. Use a chip or particle board, not plywood, otherwise the tacks will be hard to hammer in. Then with carpet tacks (not thumbtacks, which are not strong enough) nail down the four corners first, measuring the opposite sides to see that they are even and making sure the corners are true right angles. You can use the two sides of the board or table to guide you by placing the first two sides of the design close to them to begin with. (See page 108.)

Don't worry if the tacks stain the canvas with rust marks; this will be cut away with the "turnings" (the extra canvas which disappears in the seams). You may have to pull the design out firmly with pliers to make sure it is really taut. Then nail down four more tacks, one in the center of each side, and then eight more in the spaces between. Continue round and round, adding in this way more tacks until they are about $\frac{1}{4}$ inch apart. Take a cloth and a bowl of water and thoroughly soak the needlepoint, rubbing hard on the wrong side to keep the work flat and smooth.

Allow the needlepoint to dry. When it is thoroughly dry, take it up, and if it is not being mounted immediately, roll it around a cardboard tube with the right side of embroidery outward, so that the stitches are not crushed against one another.

If the needlepoint needs cleaning, or if you think the paint will run, soak it in cold water in the bathtub before blocking and scrub the back of the work with a cake of Ivory soap. Take care not to rub soap on the front or you will "felt" the stitches. If the paint from transferring a design has run into the wool, it may look horrifying but it will come out quite successfully if you soak the whole thing (in cold water) overnight and, rather than squeezing and rubbing, beat it hard on the side of the bathtub like a French washerwoman! Cold or almost cold water will not affect the wool and once it is blocked and pulled out firmly no one will ever know what it has been through!

SILK AND GOLD THREADS

. . . Allso the Vice-chancellour presented a paire of gloves, perfumed and garnished with embroiderie and goldsmiths worke, price 60s. . . . In taking the book and the gloves, it fortuned that the paper in which the gloves were folded to open; and her Majestie behoulding the beautie of the said gloves, as in great admiration, and in token of hir thankful acceptation of the same, held up one of her hands; and then, smelling unto them, put them halfwaie upon hir hands. And when the oracion was ended, she rendyred and gave most heartie thanks, promising to be mindful of the Universitie.

—QUEEN ELIZABETH'S RECEPTION OF A DELEGATION FROM
THE UNIVERSITY OF CAMBRIDGE, AT AUDLEY END, ESSEX, 1578

Japanese No robe, 17th century. Silk on gilded satin. *The Metropolitan Museum of Art, Pulitzer Fund, 1932*

SILK was said to have been cultivated in China by the Empress Si-Ling as early as 2640 B.C. This may be mythical but a remnant of silk still exists which dates from the fifth century B.C. Though the silkworm was held in great veneration in China (a ceremony in its honor being performed every year), silk was such a commonplace material that it was used by all classes and for almost every purpose for which fabrics might be used.

The early history of silk reads like a novel of international intrigue, for the secret of its culture was jealously guarded by the Chinese, and attempts of other countries to start their own production were constantly frustrated. However, in the fifth century A.D. the King of Kustana (Khotan) sought a marriage union with a princess of the Eastern Kingdom (China), as a token of his allegiance and submission. The Chinese Emperor agreed; whereupon the king immediately sent off messengers to the princess, saying, "Our country has neither silk nor silken stuffs. You had better bring mulberry seeds and silkworms, so that you can make robes for yourself after your arrival." So the princess smuggled both across the border, hidden in her turban, for the guards never dared to ask if they could search her there.

It is said that in the sixth century two monks traveling from Khotan brought silkworm eggs in a hollow cane to Byzantium. After the Emperor Justinian established silkworm culture at Constantinople, it was jealously guarded for nearly five hundred years. In the twelfth century Italy became a center for the manufacture of silk, and there no member of the Florentine silk guilds was allowed to leave the city without a permit, and pawnbrokers were not allowed to receive silk or any tool for its weaving.

Metallic threads, too, go back into the history of ancient lands. When you consider the importance of sun worship in early cultures, it is easy to see how gold would, in the primitive mind, seem to impart the magical properties of the sun to any article. Remains of gold and silver wire thread for embroidery have been found in a tomb in Thebes, and gold threads are often referred to in the Bible.

/ 169

Embroidered glove and mitten, English 16th century. *Victoria and Albert Museum*

Part of an apparel of an alb, 14th century. Colored silks, silver and silver-gilt thread on red velvet. Background in couché rentré. *Victoria and Albert Museum*

As Moses said, "They did beat the gold into thin plates, and cut it into wires, to work in the blue and the purple, and in the scarlet and in the very fine linen." We are told that Aaron's robe, the ephod, was all blue, of one circular piece of linen with an opening for the head in the center, edged with a woven binding, and "a golden bell and a pomegranate, upon the hem of the robe round about," were wrought with "cunning work" in blue, purple, and scarlet.

Imagine the ships bearing down from Tarshish, laden with cargoes of gold, silver, ivory, apes, and peacocks, arriving at Solomon's kingdom. Since the soldiers' shields, all the drinking vessels, the ivory throne, and even the stairs of the temple, were all either made of or covered with beaten gold, we can get a glimpse of the luxury and magnificence of the costumes when we hear that the Queen of Sheba "had no more spirit in her" when she had seen, among all the other finery, the "attendance of Solomon's ministers, and their apparel, and his cupbearers and their apparel." When Solomon was building the temple, the son of a man from Tyre was brought in because he was "skillfull to work in gold, in silver and in brass, in iron, in stone and in timber, in purple, in blue and in fine linen and in crimson, also to grave any manner of graving, and to find out every device which shall be put to him, with his cunning men." He would be surely cunning indeed to be accomplished in such a wide variety of skills! But it does give us an interesting sidelight on how close the arts were to one another, for though individual craftsmen may have worked in a highly specialized manner (as later medieval craftsmen worked only within their guilds), one "overseer" would supervise a whole operation. Thus one can see how each of the arts would influence the others in design, since those who coordinated a project would have an interest and knowledge that overlapped into all media.

As the gold, beaten flat into strips, was stiff and difficult to handle, it was later found that it could be wrapped around silver bullion, which was melted down and drawn through narrower and narrower holes until, still coated with the gold, it formed a thin wire. The resulting stronger, more flexible thread was then beaten flat and twisted around a core of orange or yellow silk. This method was first developed in the Orient but a similar one is still used to this day. Gold leaf on paper is twisted around and lightly gummed to the silk, and the thread is known as "Japanese gold." Flexible, untarnishing, and of a beautiful glowing color, it can only be "couched" on the surface of the fabric, as it would naturally be spoiled by pulling it back and forth through the cloth.

The sophistication and beauty of both silk and gold thread made embroidery with these materials particularly suitable for ecclesiastical use. Only the best that the hand of man could form would be suitable for use in the house of God. One of the greatest periods in history for embroidery of this kind was in England during the thirteenth century. Church vestments made were of such excellent design and workmanship that they were exported all over the then known world. Called "Opus Anglicanum", or English work, the embroidery was done in a stitch called "couché rentré," or "pulled couching." (See page 198.) One of the most beautiful examples of Opus Anglicanum is the Syon Cope, now in the Victoria and Albert Museum. Worked in the twelfth century, probably for Coventry, it was ultimately given to the convent at Syon near London. The gray stone of Syon House rises above the rush-grown banks of the Thames at Isleworth, so often swathed in river mists. Against this background one can visualize the Syon Cope gleaming like an antique jewel, its muted colors intertwined with glints of silver and gold, the medieval panoply of its design telling the uninitiated its story without words. The central panel shows the Crucifixion of Christ. Radiating from it are scenes from his life. Between each scene are the seraphim with peacock feather wings: "with twain they did cover their face, with twain they did cover their feet, with twain they did fly."

But apart from its ecclesiastical use in the Middle Ages, embroidery with silk and gold thread was imparting a luxury to secular life. Chaucer wrote:

> I woll gyve him a fetherbed
> Rayed with golde and ryght well cled
> In fyne black sattin doutrmere
> And many a pylow and everybere
> Of cloth of raynes to sleppe on softe
> Hym there not nede to turn ofte.

Details from the Syon Cope: Doubting Thomas and
St. Michael (below). *Victoria and Albert Museum*

Jupon of the Black Prince. *Canterbury Cathedral*

LEFT

Tomb cover of John, the son of Basil Lupu (the wolf) from Jassy, capital of Moldavia. Worked in 1650, with faces in applied silk and features in stitchery; the flowers and border designs showing Persian influence

Herald's tabard of the Lord Lyon King of Arms. *Victoria and Albert Museum*

We can visualize the richness of these textiles when we know how equally magnificent the background fabrics were: damask from Damascus; velvet, an ancient material originally called fustian (see page 15); Baudekin, an Eastern fabric shot with gold, much used behind royal thrones—these were just a few of the many beautiful ones. Thomas of Woodstock, Duke of Gloucester, had listed in his inventory, "A large bed of blue baudekyn embroidered with silver owls and gold fleurs de lys" and another bed of "black baudekyn powdered with white roses."

The noble ladies were striking figures at this time, too, we are told. The clergy upbraided them and called them "foxes, whose only care is the ornament of their long tails," and condemned all these "crimple-crispings and christy-crosties and gold thread." But Byzantium was really the center of everything. As Diehl says, "The entire world, under the cold fogs of the north, by the long Russian rivers, in the counting houses of Venice and the castles of the West, dreamed of Byzantium as an incomparable city, unique in the world: all shining in a glittering radiance of gold." Sumptuous fabrics, tents of cloth of gold—Arabian and Jewish writers have said they were unable to describe the grandeur of the city—"The motley splendor of the streets filled with people so beautifully arrayed they all resemble the children of the king!"

Through the ancient trade routes, whose very names summon up visions—from the Euphrates and the Oxus rivers to the Caspian Sea, Antioch, Aden, and Palmyra—Byzantium influenced the whole of Western art. The most important part of its commerce with Germany, Bulgaria and Hungary, Venice and the Levant were textiles and embroidery. A description of the Egyptian caliphs' court at this time sounds just like the *Arabian Nights.* "The carpets of this noble saloon consisted of one piece of cloth-of-gold embroidered with bunches of roses in red and white silk; and the dome, painted in the same manner, after the Arabian fashion, presented to the mind one of the most charming objects. In every space between the columns was a little sofa adorned in the same manner . . . and looking out on the most delicious garden, the walks of which were of little pebbles of different colors, of the same pattern as the carpet of the saloon; so that looking upon the carpet within and without, it seemed as if the dome and the garden with all its ornaments had been upon the same carpet."

The splendor of needlework combined with sumptuous velvets,

cloth of gold, and gleaming silks was never more brilliantly shown than when it was used for heraldry. Created in the twelfth century, although its ancestry can be traced from Egypt, Greece, and Rome, heraldry was a language invented to give instant recognition of their knights and leaders to the fighting men in battle.

The crest, like the feathered headdresses of the North American Indians, was the most conspicuous and obvious insignia. Worn above the completely closed and visored helm, it was indeed necessary for identification. But the gleaming suits of armor had the serious disadvantage of rusting in the rain, or worse, on crusades under a fierce Eastern sun, of broiling the warrior within. Therefore, the surcoat or jupon was designed. Worn over the armor, this textile covering not only acted as insulation, it could be embroidered with the owner's crest—hence the expression coat-of-arms. To this day the jupon of Edward the Black Prince hangs over his tomb in Canterbury Cathedral, where it has hung for five hundred years. It was embroidered in gold threads on red and blue velvet, or fustian (see page 15). The velvet was backed on wool and linen and the whole coat was quilted together.

It is interesting to compare it with the herald's tabard (shown on the same page), made in the seventeenth century for the Lord Lyon King of Arms, since so many of the techniques are similar.

One of the finest examples of this elegant gold and silk work is a horse's lavish trappings with a fascinating and well-traveled history.

Part of the horse-trappings of John of Eltham, 14th century. *Musée de Cluny*

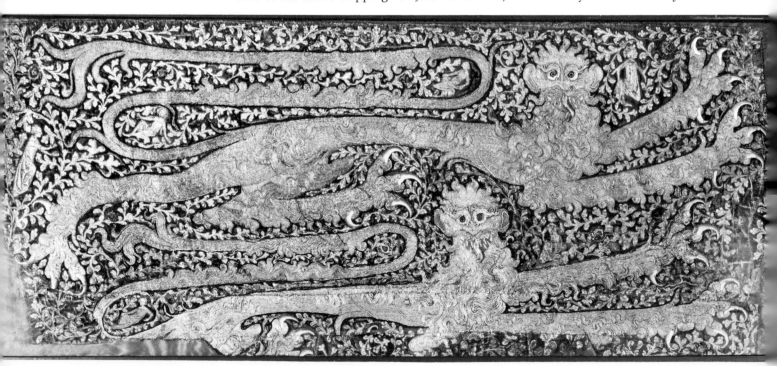

Imagine John of Eltham, second son of Edward II, galloping across the English countryside to his sister Eleanor's wedding in 1332, a glorious, awesome sight, straight from the pages of Sir Walter Scott. Even John's charger was caparisoned in fine Eastern velvet, very plush and blood-red. The three lions passant of England were embroidered with such detail on the stuff, every tawny hair was laid down with a fine gold thread. Even the full curling eyebrows were sewn in relief and the scarlet-rimmed black eyes flashed with crystal disks. Their sharp claws were raised and worked over in azur silk. The ground was so gorgeously grown with gold and silk vines that at first glance embroidered figures of men and women cannot be distinguished from the swirling foliage. (See opposite page.)

John either lost this greatly admired work in a tournament or extravagantly gave it away, but somehow the trappings reached foreign hands. They next appeared as a set of church vestments, the chasuble formed from the major part of the surcoat minus one of the lions. Finally they passed into private hands and are now in the collection of the Musée de Cluny in Paris.

Heraldic insignia and religious design served the same purpose—to communicate at a glance and without words, and all through the ages it is fascinating to observe the exchange of ecclesiastical vestments for secular use, and vice versa. Sometimes the church seemed to be in the ascendancy and magnificently embroidered hangings would be made into copes, chasubles, or altar frontals. At other times, generally in days of lesser prosperity, religious embroideries would be cut up for other purposes. During the eighteenth century, embroideries in metal were even assiduously pulled apart by ladies taking afternoon tea. "Drizzling," as it was called, became a fashionable pastime and many beautiful pieces of needlework were destroyed so that the gold and silver threads could be sold and melted down.

Compared with the splendor and lavish use of silk and gold thread in China, India, and Europe, the rather primitive rural life of the American countryside seemed more suited to the rougher texture of homespun and wool. At the beginning of the eighteenth century the "Gentleman's Progress" or the "itinerarium" of Dr. Alexander Hamilton shows how travel in the New World was indeed an adventure.

Man's vest. *Cooper Hewitt Museum of Design, Smithsonian Institution*

Dress elaborately embroidered with silver gilt and silk, early 18th century. *Victoria and Albert Museum*

Detail of man's vest. *Colonial Williamsburg*

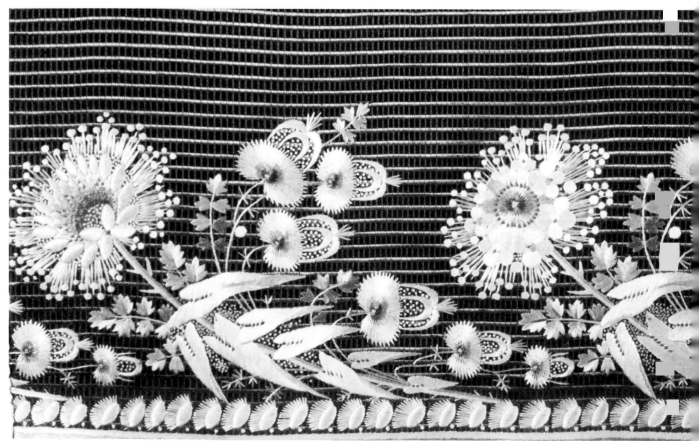

We took horse again (from Setauket) att half an hour after 5 o'clock and had scarce got a mile when we lost our way—after riding ten miles thro woods and marshes in which we were pestered by muscettos, we arrived at 8 o'clock att night att one Brewsters where we put up for all night and in this house we could get nothing either to eat or drink and so were obliged to go to bed fasting or supperless.

The people in this house seemed to be quite savage and rude.

When I waked this morning I found two beds in the room besides that in which I lay, in one of which lay two great hulking fellows with long black beards, having their own hair and not as much as half a night cap betwixt them both.

I took them for Weavers, not only from their greasy appearance, but because I observed a weaver's loom at each side of the room.

We set out from this desolate place att 6 o'clock and rid 16 miles thro very barren and waste land.

The Colonial housewife naturally used those materials closest at hand—worsteds and crewels—to interpret in needlework those things which were a fascinating part of her new world: deer, wild turkey, beaver, raccoons and gray squirrels, peach orchards, wild grapes and fields of watermelons or pumpkins. Meanwhile the Atlantic was well traveled by ships of the East India Company, laden with rare fabrics from Teheran and Samarkand, costly perfumes, spices, ointments, and precious woods. It was inevitable that privateers and freebooters should be tempted by this booty and, plying their trade through Madagascar, the pirates ultimately conveyed it to New York. Thus New York in turn became a city of almost oriental magnificence, peopled by such colorful characters as Thomas Tew, who arrived in 1694 with great wealth from the Indian seas. He was a "slight dark man of about forty, who dressed richly and scattered gold profusely. His uniform was a blue cap with a band of cloth of silver. His blue jacket was bordered with gold lace, and further garnished with large pearl buttons. Loose trunks of white linen covered his lower limbs as far as the knee, where they gave place to curiously worked stockings. A rich chain of Arabian gold hung from his neck, and through the meshes of a curiously knit belt gleamed a dagger, its hilt set with the rarest of gems. This person, dispensing draughts of sopus ale to whoever would drink, and throwing golden louis d'or about as carelessly as though they were stuyvers, soon became a familiar object in the streets and taverns of New York."

The city, like a miniature London, but more cosmopolitan, became a center of fashion for silk and embroidered clothing, infinite in its variety and exquisite in its coloring and fine stitchery. "Broadway on a Sabbath morning, as the bells were ringing for church, must then have presented an animated and ever brilliant spectacle, for both ladies and gentlemen shone rich as emperor moths."

Imagine Nicholas Bayard, secretary of the province and colonel of the militia, wearing a cinnamon-colored cloth coat—embroidered four or five inches deep with silver and lined with sky blue silk, with breeches to match, dove-colored silk stockings, and shoes with silver buckles. He takes snuff, and afterward applies to his nose a silk handkerchief embroidered with the arms of Britain. His wife, rivaling this magnificence, wears purple and gold silk over black velvet edged with silver, with green silk stockings and shoes of fine morocco leather embroidered with red clocks.

Queen Charlotte's bedspread, colored silk flowers on white satin quilted with gold thread. *Victoria and Albert Museum*

Panel from a dress shown at the Paris Exhibition, 1851 (see sketch). Padded satin in brilliant reds, blues, greens and cream silk, on caramel taffeta. *Author's Collection*

An increased elegance in furnishings as well as dress was inspired by London fashions, though William Smith, a resident historian, observed, "by the time we adopt them they become disused in England."

Toward the end of the eighteenth century in England silk almost completely superseded wool for embroidery on bed furnishings and household articles as well as clothing, though in America some silk thread was sold from door to door by pedlars, crewel was continuously popular until the end of the century.

During the Victorian era the designs for embroidery in both countries became rather heavy and serious. Everything was overspread with needlework, antimacassars, bureau scarves, wall pockets; even meat safes and beaded milk-jug covers were considered suitable subjects for silken stitchery. The mantelpiece was covered, and even the piano was not allowed to show its legs: over it would be thrown a deeply fringed shawl,

Detail from William Morris hand blocked linen. *Victoria and Albert Museum*

or a closely stitched "table carpet" often worked in the favorite predominating colors of black, deep maroon, or filthy green!

A man who had profound influence on Victorian design, however, was William Morris, who established a factory that produced hand-blocked linens, wallpapers, and embroideries. His designs, stemming from the influence of oriental stylization of natural forms, really transcended the more mundane ones then in vogue and led the way to the graceful flowing lines of art nouveau. His gentle admonition to the Victorian embroideress is good to remember in any age and at any time.

"Now indeed it is a delightful idea to cover a piece of linen cloth with roses, and jonquils, and tulips, all done quite natural with the needle, and we can't go too far in that direction if we only remember the nature of our craft in general; and since we are using specially beautiful materials, that we shall make the most of them, and not forget that we are gardening with silk and gold thread."

Plate 9. Back of an early American bargello chair, worked on the back entirely in Roumanian stitch on linen (c.1725). *The Metropolitan Museum of Art, gift of Mrs. J. Insley Blair, 1950*

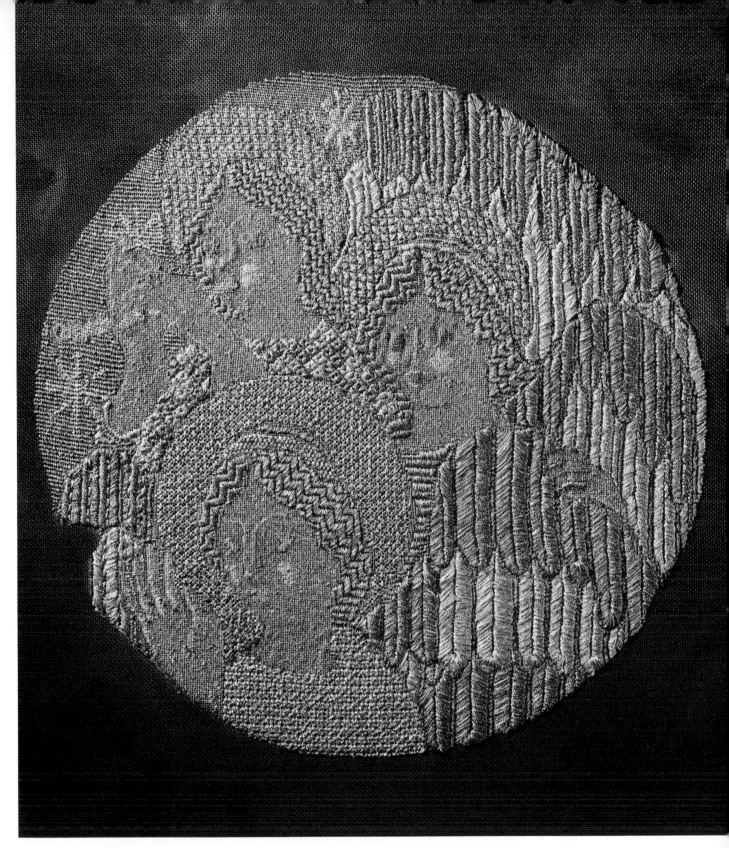

Plate 11. Needlepoint stitches in lurex on canvas; embroidery and open canvas
around it were painted with brown oil paint. *Designed and worked by
Robert Heitmann*

OPPOSITE

Plate 10. Details from a set of twelve kneelers which surround a church altar.
Designs represent the Creation, the background is symbolic of earth and
water. Christ Church, Warren, Ohio. *Designed by the author and worked
by a committee under the direction of Mrs. James Roemer. Photo by
Herbert Smit*

Plate 13. Bargello combined with cross and tent stitches on canvas—detail from a panel. *Designed by the author and worked by Natasha Josefowitz*

OPPOSITE

Plate 12. ABOVE. Tent stitch pillows, the top in shag rug wool on #7 canvas, adapted from a fabric by Jack Lenor Larsen; CENTER. Tent stitch accented with French knots; BOTTOM. Design in tent stitch, background in brick stitch

BELOW. Sofa worked in bargello, using wool and cotton; pillows in kaleidescope bargello and crewel. *Designed and worked by the author*

Plate 14. Bold colors are effectively displayed in simple tent stitch. *Designed and worked by the author*

Plate 15. Bargello stitches. *Worked by Mrs. David Epner*

Plate 16
Wild arum lily sampler. *Designed and worked by the author*

Milkweed pod in gold couching with silk thread. *Designed and worked by Dorothy Hickey*

TO BEGIN

With sophisticated gold threads and silken stitches you can create almost anything from a wall panel to a family coat of arms, an altar frontal to a mirror frame, an evening dress, a handbag, or even a devastating vest or cummerbund for a peacock husband.

Don't think that you must be restricted to rigid rules and concepts, or that because gold and silk are together in this chapter you must use them that way forever. If you turn to page 351 you will perhaps find some inspiration on how to combine various styles.

One thing leads to another, and once you have experimented with the stitches and begun to be familiar with the exciting techniques, ideas will crop up like daisies and you will develop your own individual approach to the medium. The easiest way to explore some of the fascinating possibilities is to make a sampler using the traditional threads as well as some of the many new ones. Design the sampler with simple shapes so that you can fill in areas with different methods and stitches, but make it attractive enough to hang as a wall panel; it seems a pity to spend valuable time on something that is to be hidden in a bottom drawer.

RIGHT
Blanket cover for a child's crib, all white silk, with blue collar, on white wool background. Shading effect is achieved by simply following the outlines with rows of split stitch. Designed and worked by Mrs. Joseph Berger

BELOW
Pillow from Gracie Mansion, designed by the author for Mrs. John Lindsay, worked by Mrs. Hampton Lynch, silk and wool on gold Scalamandré silk

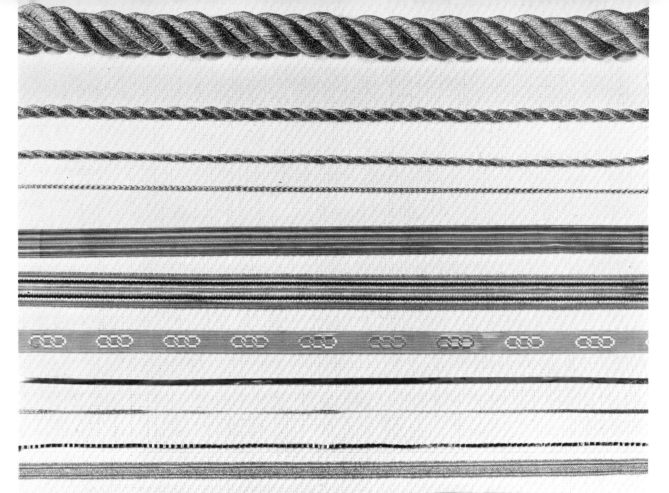

Twisted cords and flat braids; bottom right,
bullion threads of different sizes being cut

Blazer pocket, showing Nantucket yacht club
badge in gold bullion

COLLECTING THE THREADS

SILK AND COTTON THREADS

Silk and cotton threads can be used in exactly the same way as crewel wool (page 28) but, of course, with more delicate results. Real silk threads may be hard to find, although they are available in various forms, both as floss or twisted like a fine cord (Pearsall's Filo Floss and Filoselle Silk). However, cotton makes a good substitute, and the mercerized embroidery floss and various types of crochet cotton available in all the stores, though not as soft as real silk, wear better, come in a good range of colors and may sometimes be scarcely distinguishable from silk itself. Besides this, embroidery floss has the advantage of being washable, is ideal for clothing and is versatile enough to be as thoroughly at home on a blue denim work shirt as on a black satin cummerbund or evening vest. The stitches can also add a variety of effects, lacy when worked openly; or when worked closely—using stitches such as padded satin—becoming vibrant and shiny as enamel. Silk, cotton, and wool are really completely interchangeable. The only thing that sets cotton or silk apart is its finer scale and smoother texture. Therefore, any of the stitches described in crewel embroidery may be worked in silk or cotton.

LUREX THREADS

The soft pliable gold or silver Lurex threads can also be handled like silk or wool with crewel stitches. When they are fine enough, they may be stitched right through the fabric, using a large crewel or chenille needle to protect them from tearing. St. George and the Dragon (page 187) was done with a variety of flat and open-patterned crewel stitches combined with solid filling stitches on a silk background. All kinds of Lurex can be used effectively on needlepoint canvas, too, as in the Singing Angels on plate 11.

METAL THREADS

Real gold and metal threads, and occasionally some types of Lurex, need special treatment. They are either too wiry or too delicate to sew right through the fabric, and so have to be sewn down on the surface. These special techniques come into play when you embroider with such threads as Japanese gold, and use romantic-sounding materials such as gold bullion, pearl purl, and plate. The beauty of Japanese gold is that it will never tarnish; it maintains its original gleaming depth of mellow color year after year. This is because it is made of pure gold leaf on narrow strips of paper lightly coiled around a core of orange or yellow silk.

Bullion is a wire thread coiled like a tight spring and is therefore hollow in the center. Unlike a spring, however, it will not snap back into place after being stretched out, so you have to handle it very carefully. Because of its fragility it is generally cut into short lengths, and each one is sewn down like a bead onto the fabric, using a waxed thread for strength.

Bullion thread comes in three varieties. The first, "rough" or "matte" (to give both the English and French names), has a dull satin sheen. The second, "smooth" or "glissant," is a shinier gleaming bullion, and the third, "check" or "frisé," is a crinkled variety with a sparkling effect.

If these threads seem very foreign and remote to you, just look closely again at a club or army badge on a hat, blazer, or uniform. You will realize that you have often seen them before—the raised insignia which go back to the beginning of heraldry (see page 184) and are still used today. These are the threads which constitute the "scrambled eggs" on the naval officer's hat, or are used to embroider the identifying burgee of a yacht club on a blazer jacket. They would be equally effective used on a box top, for a mirror frame, for a very special evening bag, or for your own family coat of arms.

Most of the stores carry the metal threads put out by knitting wool manufacturers, so that notions departments and variety stores are the places to start looking for gold and silver threads. But all through the year and especially at Christmastime you may find different tinsel threads in the gift stores, and all kinds of cords and braids in the gift wrapping departments. Since these are nearly always Lurex they will not tarnish and can be used most effectively. However, if you want to use real gold threads, and experiment with the bullion threads mentioned here, you will have to write to some of the addresses listed at the back of this book. As the demand grows, so will the number of places where these threads are available. The best thing to do is to amass a collection of metal threads to choose from, buying them wherever and whenever you see them, so that you can select the most suitable for a particular design as you work.

St. George and the Dragon, all gold threads stitched on red damask. *Designed and worked by Mrs. Hugh M. Parrish*

CHOOSING FABRICS

There is almost no limit to the types of material you can work on, but fine linen is probably the easiest to begin with. However, if you want to work with fairly heavy gold thread on delicate white taffeta, for instance, or with fine silk on a rather stretchy open weave linen, you will find that you must back them first with another material such as lightweight linen or muslin, otherwise they will pucker. First baste the two pieces of material smoothly, together, so that they become as one. Then embroider the design by working through both layers of fabric, and when the embroidery is finished, cut away the backing material around the stitches on the wrong side.

Velvet is the most difficult material to work on, because when you transfer the design, the pile often shifts, causing the design to be placed inaccurately. Then, when you take the stitches, the pile sometimes flattens itself in some places and not in others, giving an untidy look. This limits

TOP LEFT TO RIGHT. Antique velvet, slubbed silk, rayon damask, stried upholstery satin
2ND ROW. Silk damask, wool-backed upholstery satin (mat finish), linen
3RD ROW. Cotton velvet, ribbed cotton, brushed nylon, blue denim

the stitches that can easily be done to couching, padded satin, and laid work, because these seem to lie most smoothly in the pile. One way to avoid all this is to do what was done in the fourteenth century: to overlay the whole velvet on top with fine linen or muslin with the design traced on it, embroider through both layers, and then cut away the linen from the front—very closely around the design.

Thus you can see that almost any fabric can be converted so that it is suitable for use with silk and gold threads. Not only this, but the traditional idea that rich and sumptuous threads should always be worked on equally magnificent background fabrics which harmonize with them has given way to a different approach of surprise contrasts. Today it is possible to choose rough wool or even homespun linen or cotton as a background for fine silk and gold embroidery, or to combine silk, gold, *and* wool when working on damask or brocade.

White silk on dove-colored velvet

TOP. Various bullion threads

2ND ROW. Imitation Japanese gold thread, heavy and medium; real Japanese gold; Lurex knitting thread; fine Lurex sewing threads; spool of "plate," a flat metal for couching

3RD ROW. Gold cords, heavy and fine; Maltese sewing silk or "horsetail"; Filo floss; DMC cotton

BOTTOM. String for padding; nail file (for pushing gold into place when couching), scissors, stiletto, razor blade and beeswax; felt for padding

THE TOOLS OF THE TRADE

Now that you have found your silk and metal threads, you will need to collect a few other things before you can launch into your stitching.

First, *needles.* You will need a varied assortment, because you will be working with threads of such different thicknesses (see page 16). Become like a squirrel and hoard in your workbox packets of needles which you buy whenever you come across them. Sometimes needles of the right size are very hard to find. Should they become rusty, rub them with fine sandpaper, or run them in and out of one of those little strawberry pincushions filled with emery powder.

Next, you must find silk or *mercerized cotton* for couching down the metal threads. The best for the purpose is a Maltese sewing silk, known as Horsetail, which is very strong and fine, and comes in two shades of yellow and silver gray. Any thread you use must be fine enough not to detract from the metal, and therefore must be waxed for strength.

Most notion stores have *beeswax.* This is necessary for protecting the fine silk or cotton so that it will not be cut by the metal threads when it is used to sew them down. Thread the needle and draw the silk two or three times through the beeswax before sewing with it. The wax stiffens the thread, too, making it easier to handle. Candlewax will do, but is not quite so "clingy."

A *stiletto* should be possible to find at a sewing or notion store, too, but a large chenille or pointed rug needle will do if a stiletto is not available. The stiletto is used for opening a hole in the background material, so that the extra thick ends of couched metal threads may be easily taken through to the reverse side.

You will need *felt* (of medium thickness) for padding. If you are going to cover it with gold thread, buy yellow or orange, because although it won't actually show, minute areas which are not covered influence the color of the metal thread. For silver threads, use pale blue felt. *String* is also used for padding. The best kind is not a twisted cord, but a waxed string which is smooth and firm. An average size string is #30. Anything finer than this will not raise the threads sufficiently to make an effect.

BEGINNING THE DESIGN

If you are starting with a sampler, you may get some inspiration from the one on the opposite page used to illustrate the basic stitches, or the one used to show the techniques of flat and raised couching on page 202. Alternatively, you may want to start out with a belt or handbag or, perhaps, undaunted, launch right into making a large hanging. In any case, if you have the design, the threads, the background fabric, and the tools at hand, your next step will be to stretch the material in a frame. If your background fabric is stretched out taut, it will be much easier to take accurate, smooth stitches when handling the wiry gold threads. Since many silk materials, particularly satin, show a ring if you use an embroidery hoop, and since the gold threads would obviously be damaged if a hoop were forced over them, a square frame is the best to use (page 25). You *can* work on any oval rug hoop, if the design will fit within it, but be sure the fabric which is to show will not be marked by the outer hoop.

APPLYING THE PATTERN

To be successful, traditional gold and silk embroidery must be precise and accurate. Therefore, design placement is better done on fabric that is stretched taut in a square frame rather than by the normal method of holding it flat on a table with masking tape.

To establish the center of your working area, and to give you straight guide lines for placing your design, baste contrasting colored threads through the middle of the fabric in your frame, vertically and horizontally. If you are working on linen, do this by using a blunt needle and work between the threads of the fabric, following them to keep your stitches straight. If you are working on finer fabric, use a ruler. Mark the line with pins first, and follow this with a basting line sewn with a sharp needle. Place your frame over some books, records, or any firm working surface, so that the material in the frame does not sag as you lean on it, and transfer the design to the fabric by the most suitable method on pages 18–22.

All this preparation may seem like a great deal of trouble at first, but it will be worth it in the long run. Following the correct method really saves a good deal of time and effort later on.

Wild arum lily, illustrating the stitches shown on the following pages (see key below)

A. Random Couching
B. Brick Pattern Couching
B.* Couching with diagonal, straight and radiating line patterns
C. Mille Fleur Pattern Couching
D. Couching in a Circle
E. Italian Shading, following the contours of the shape
F. Burden Stitch, gold horizontal lines with silk stitching on top (see page 56)
G. Couché Rentré
H. Couched "plate" and braids (see page 190)

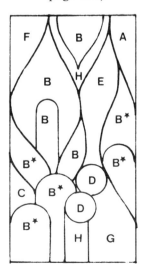

THE STITCHES

Since almost any stitches under the sun may be worked in silk or cotton, the important methods to describe here are those which are best suited for working with metal threads. The first and most versatile of these is couching. This can be done with so many variations and with such different effects it is scarcely recognizable as the same stitch. Therefore, the best way to become familiar with its different aspects is to experiment on a sampler. The wild arum on page 193 shows eight different methods which are described below.

✳COUCHING   (Letters refer to sampler, page 193.)

Random Couching (A)

Begin with the simplest form, random couching. Thread some waxed Maltese sewing silk (or any fine gold-colored buttonhole twist or mercerized sewing thread) into a #9 or #10 crewel needle. With this, sew down two threads of Japanese gold, following the directions for simple couching on page 85, making a random meandering line as shown. Couching with *any* gold thread should always be done by sewing down a pair of threads rather than a single one. To sew individual threads would require too many couching stitches, diminishing the effect of the gold. Conversely, couching three threads at a time is apt to bunch them together, and it would be difficult to maintain a smooth flat line. Leave the ends of the couched gold threads lying on the surface until the whole area of stitching is complete. Then, using a large-eyed needle, take them through to the wrong side and cut them off. Leave the ends about ¼ inch long and let them hang loose on the back. The ends are too stiff and bulky to be secured on the reverse side, and they are so firmly stitched on the front that they will not work loose. If you take them through to the back *before* the area of needlework is completed, however, your stitches are apt to tangle with the ends on the back, making smooth stitching difficult.

Couched gold butterfly, designed by the author, worked by Mary Haddon, showing mille fleur pattern in upper wings

Come up at A, and go down at B over the threads, sewing down the gold in a meandering line, with stitches at right angles and at regular intervals. When the line is complete, take the ends of gold through to the reverse side, as shown on the right.

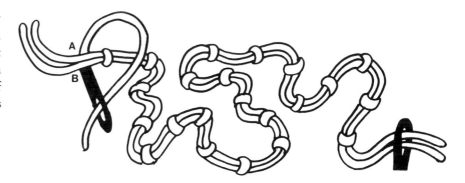

Brick Pattern Couching (B and B*)

Fill the area with horizontal rows, turning the threads sharply at the end of each row by stitching each individual thread of the pair into its place separately, as shown. "Brick" the couching stitches to make a regular pattern by spacing them alternately as in the drawing. This method of couching is used to fill bandings, borders, and larger shapes solidly. If the brick pattern is done with matching gold-colored thread, the couching stitches become almost invisible, giving the effect of a solid gold fabric laid down on the surface.

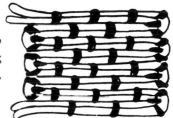

Place the lines of gold close side by side, but not so tightly packed that they overlap one another. As you turn at the end of each line, hold the corners out square by placing two stitches on the outer gold thread, one on the inner. Then continue along the line, alternating the couching stitches to form a brick pattern.

Mille Fleur Pattern Couching (C)

Next, try making patterns other than the brick, such as the "mille-fleur," using a contrasting color thread. You may find it helpful to mark out the material with lines at regular intervals to guide you as you work down, row by row.

Repeat B, but arrange the stitches to form the grouping shown here. Other patterns can easily be made, as you hold down each row with couching stitches, such as diagonal or wavy lines, or chevron patterns.

Couching in a Circle (D)

Then try couching to fill a circle. With a pencil, lightly draw regularly spaced lines radiating out from the center of the circle, and use these as a guide for your couching stitches. Fold in half one length of gold thread to be used for the couching and start by sewing down the loop end of this doubled thread in the center of the circle. Work round and round in widening rings, sewing down the two gold strands together, and placing a couching stitch on each pencil line. Make sure no material shows between the rows of couching, yet do not crowd the rows so closely that they overlap one another. To end off with a smooth outline at the edge of the circle, plunge one gold thread through the fabric slightly ahead of the other.

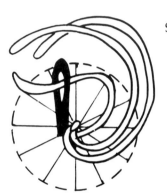

Showing the beginning, and the finished effect

Couching to Fill a Shape (B*)

Contrary to a circle, a shape like this is best started at the edge, working round and round to the center, "bricking" the stitches as shown. The dotted lines are pencilled on the fabric as a guide for the couching stitches. At each corner sew over each gold thread separately on the angle of the dotted line (as shown below).

Couching a Sharp Pointed Corner

Showing each gold thread sewn down separately at the point

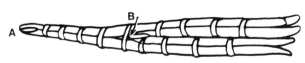

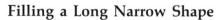

Filling a Long Narrow Shape

When the shape to be filled is very thin and tapering, take only *one* of the pair of gold threads to the outer limit of the narrow shape (at A) and sew it down with a double stitch for firmness at this point. Then double it on itself working it back to meet the second thread (at B). Turn *this* thread back sharply, stitching it with a double stitch, and continue them both together, as the shape widens, making a smooth flowing line as shown.

Couching a Square Corner

*ITALIAN SHADING (E)

Finally, you are ready to try the most sophisticated form of couching, which is known as Italian shading. This can be done in two ways. The first is to lay your gold thread in the contours of the shape, using the couching stitches for shading. You can shade by varying both the colors and density of the tiny stitches as you take them over your gold thread (as shown in the wild arum at E).

The second technique is to lay your gold threads in row upon row of straight lines touching one another, creating a design or pattern with the couching stitches as you go along. (E on your sampler.) In this technique the gold becomes merely a solid background surface, and the design is created by the variation of tiny couching stitches that are used to hold the gold thread flat. The spacing or closeness of these stitches allows the gold to shimmer through occasionally, giving a mosaic effect. The best way to work is to have several needles threaded, each with its own color, so that you can use them as you reach each area to be worked in that shade, as shown below. (Note: It is not necessary to wax your couching thread for Italian shading, see page 200.)

Shading, following the contours of a shape. The gold threads have been completely covered with close couching stitches inside the lily to give a dark shadow effect. The couching stitches are then spaced gradually wider apart and the colors lightened towards the outer edge of the shape. This couching is done line by line, just like B.

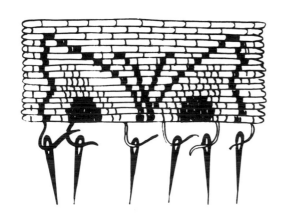

Italian shading, building up the pattern as you go along, line by line, each needle threaded with the color required for that area

*BURDEN STITCH (F)

A variation of Italian shading is burden stitch. This stitch consists of regularly spaced threads laid horizontally across the shape, held flat with a brick work of vertical stitches on top. Though the stitch is frequently worked with wool in crewel embroidery (page 56), it can be most effective with the horizontal stitches underneath in gold and vertical ones on top in silk. When worked in this way it really resembles Italian shading worked openly instead of solidly. First couch down the horizontal rows of gold thread, using a matching waxed silk thread, so that the stitches are invisible. The spacing between each row depends on the background fabric, and how fine or bold you want the finished result to be. Then work the vertical stitches in silk to form a brick pattern on top. This top stitching may be so close that the gold just gleams through, or could be of such gossamer fineness that the silk or cotton only forms a light network over the surface of the bold metal threads.

*COUCHÉ RENTRÉ (G)

When discussing intriguing variations of couching, one cannot ignore the medieval method of couching called couché rentré. This magnificently effective stitchery is a means of completely covering the background linen with gold threads, and has the effect of flame stitch or bargello stitchery in solid gold (page 162). It can be done on canvas or linen and you may ask why not sew with regular brick stitch to get the same effect? The answer is that even the most pliable Lurex is sometimes a difficult thread to use for large background areas when you have to stitch right

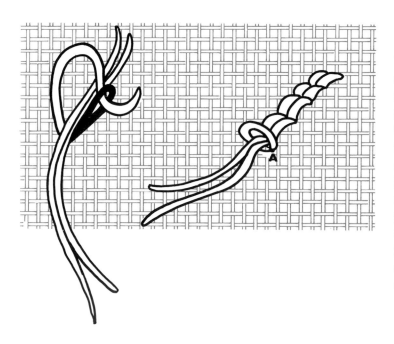

The stitching is shown on a mesh background to suggest the open weave linen necessary for couché rentré. The fabric must be stretched firmly in a frame and a strong waxed double silk or cotton thread should be used to couch the pairs of gold threads. Come up at A, go over the gold threads and return to A again, going down in the exact same hole. Pull sharply, so that the gold thread jumps right through the fabric, and continue to repeat the procedure for the next stitch. Work in straight lines, cutting the threads and "plunging" them (see page 200) at the end of each line. This makes an easier and neater edge than turning them at the end of each line, on the open weave linen.

By varying the relative positions of the couching stitches, all kinds of patterns can be made, as shown here.

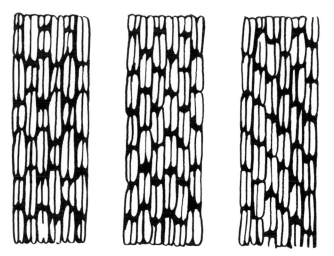

through the fabric. Small lengths of thread would have to be used or they would tear as they pass through it, and of course Japanese gold would be out of the question, as it would be much too fragile. Therefore, couché rentré with its surface couching, which only *appears* to be stitched right through, is an excellent solution.

*COUCHING CORDS

Couching gold, silk, or wool cords can be done invisibly so that the cord appears to be lying on the surface without stitches to attach it. Braids are a little more difficult, and usually have to be sewn with minute stitches first on one side, then on the other to hold them invisibly.

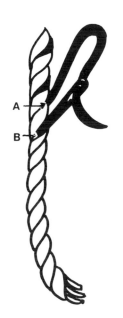

Come up at A, on the outside of the cord but close to it. Go down at B right in the center of the cord, between the twists. This makes a small slanting stitch, which, when pulled firmly, lies parallel with the twists and disappears completely. Place the stitches about two or three twists apart. It is not necessary to stitch every one.

Shows a wide braid, sewn with small, almost invisible stitches on either side

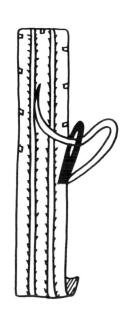

RAISED GOLD OVER STRING/Raised Outlines

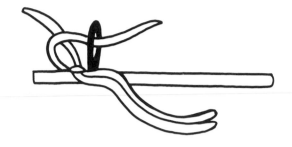

1. Sew two threads of gold (or one of silk, and one of gold) over a line of string which has been stitched to the fabric. Take a double stitch over the gold, close to and parallel with the string.

2. Then fold the gold over the string and repeat this double stitch on the other side. "Plunge" the ends of gold through the material when the line is complete.

PLUNGING

To "plunge" heavy cords or braids you may need to pierce a hole in the material with a stiletto (see page 190) or a large needle. Then you can easily take the ends of the thread through this hole to the wrong side. Ease them through, one by one, to avoid damaging them, and cut them off, leaving the ends to hang loose, about ¼ inch long.

Shows a heavy cord being plunged by taking the needle into the fabric, and then threading it. Push the ends of cord only a little way through the eye, so that the thread will not be too heavy to pull through. If necessary, open a hole in the fabric with the closed ends of sharp pointed scissors, or a stiletto, so that the cord will slip through more easily.

Things to remember about couching:

1. Always wax your silk or cotton couching thread to protect it and prevent the metal from cutting it. One exception is Italian shading, where the close stitches provide such strong protection that waxing is unnecessary.

Further, the waxing tends to darken the thread, which would spoil the vibrant color necessary for Italian shading.

2. Keep couching stitches at right angles to the gold threads, and space them so that the gold is held firm; yet not so closely covered with stitching that it cannot gleam through.

3. Gauge the width and tension of each couching stitch. If the stitches are too narrow they tend to pucker the two threads on top of each other, forming a wasp waist at each stitch. Alternatively, if the stitches are too wide the gold threads will move about.

4. Make all corners and points sharp and slightly exaggerated to give a crisp, clear-cut effect.

5. Handle the Japanese gold as little as possible. Should it separate, twist it back and hold it in place so that the silk core is covered as you sew it down.

6. "Plunge" the gold with a very large needle to avoid tearing the threads as you take them through to the wrong side. Use a stiletto to open a hole in the background fabric before plunging heavy cords or braids.

Cope designed and worked by Beryl Dean. Appliquéd cloth of gold fabric outlined with couched gold cords (see page 336).

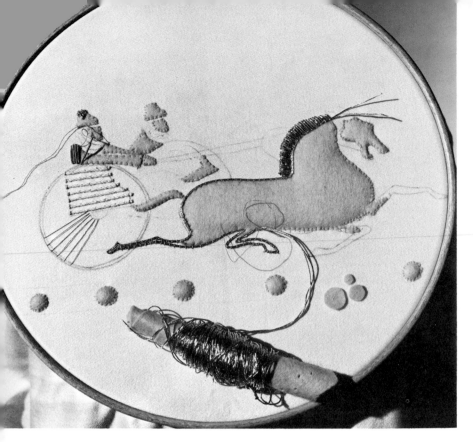

The Chariot Riders. Adapted from a Chinese clay tablet 102 B.C. *Worked by the author*

ABOVE

Chariot shows parallel lines of string stitched down horizontally. Horse and riders have been padded with three layers of felt. On lower border right hand circle shows three sizes of felt ready to be stitched down, one on top of the other.

BELOW

The completed design. Chariot: Japanese gold couched vertically over string; riders and mane: rough and smooth bullion; hats: check bullion in small chips; horse: couched Japanese gold. Lower border; couched Japanese gold, raised only at intervals over felt circles

PADDING

Couching on a padded surface achieves completely different effects. The chariot riders on page 202 shows this both in the process of work and as a finished design. First try padding with string. Fill the area to be raised with horizontal rows of string sewn down approximately ¼ inch apart. Using a fine thread, waxed for strength, sew down each length of string with small stitches taken first on one side and then on the other. To make clear edges, carefully cut the string at the end of each line with a razor blade as soon as it has been stitched in place. Take great care not to slit through the background material, cut *only* the string! Now take a pair of gold threads and couch them over the string at right angles to it.

By alternating the positions of the couching stitches you can make patterns as shown in the diagram, catching down the gold after it has passed over one line of string, then over two, then over one again to form regular repeat patterns.

PADDING WITH STRING

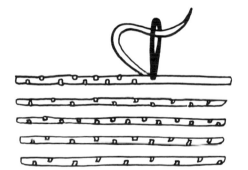

Sewing down evenly spaced rows of string.

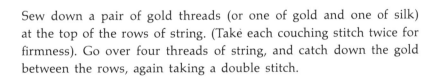

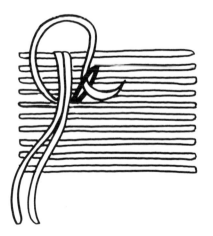

Sew down a pair of gold threads (or one of gold and one of silk) at the top of the rows of string. (Take each couching stitch twice for firmness). Go over four threads of string, and catch down the gold between the rows, again taking a double stitch.

Next, go over two threads, then over four, then over two again as shown. Work two identical lines in this pattern, side by side. Then work two more lines alternating the pattern (going over four threads next to the two taken on the previous row, and two next to the four, etc.). This will form a brick pattern as shown. Any number of patterns can be worked out by simply couching the threads over different numbers of rows of string

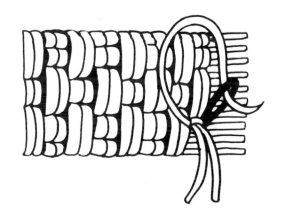

PADDING WITH FELT

To pad with felt, draw an oval or circle on your sampler and cut a piece of yellow felt to fit it exactly. Then cut four more pieces, each one smaller than the previous one, so that you have a stack of five layers of felt each decreasing in size. Starting with the smallest first, sew this in the center of your shape, securing it all around with tiny stitches at right angles to the edge. Keep these stitches close together to prevent the edges from puckering. Repeat, sewing down successively larger layers, to build up a smooth raised surface which is higher in the center. Next draw your couching lines on the padded oval or circle (i.e., a radiating sunburst or spiraling effect). However, for a simple brick pattern there is no need to draw guide lines as the stitches themselves will control your spacing. Now couch the gold thread closely over the felt following the instructions on page 196 for couching in a circle.

Sewing down three layers of felt

Start by sewing the smallest circle of felt in the center of the shape. Come up outside the shape, and go down into the felt, making small stitches at right angles to the edge.

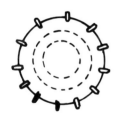

Sew the next layer on top. Finally, sew the largest top layer down.

Starting in the center, couch the gold threads round and round, stitching right through the felt.

Padded Italian Shading

Felt padding may also be used in combination with Italian shading, either following the contours or by covering the area with close horizontal lines. Here the padded felt circles were sewn down at intervals. Then couched lines of gold were taken right across from side to side. At the edges of each circle take the couching stitches close together to outline the shape. Cover the whole area by couching one line after the other right across the shape, going over both raised and flat areas with continuous lines. (See base of chariot riders p. 202.)

Silk on fine wool background, sails padded with felt. *Designed by the author, worked by Mrs. Hampton Lynch*

Pomegranate tree showing different methods of padding with felt and string; to obtain crisp edges, small leaves are sewn over cardboard of postcard thickness. *Worked by Mary Haddon, designed by the author*

BULLION

The bullion threads described on page 186 may also be worked over a padding of string or felt.

Prepare a handy board for cutting the bullion by gluing a piece of felt to a square of cardboard. The board is necessary because if cut on any smooth or shiny surface the little chips of bullion fly in a thousand directions and are lost. The felt has a kind of magnetic quality for them. To determine the length of the first piece, hold the bullion across the area to be covered and kink it gently with your scissors. Bring it back to the board and cut it right through, using this as your guide for the length of the next pieces. Do not cut bullion pieces more than ½ inch long or they will crack as you sew them down. However, if they are cut too short they will not cover the padding. Getting them just the right length is the whole skill in this technique.

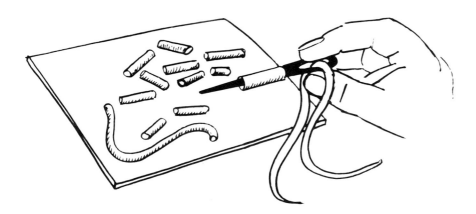

Cutting bullion thread on a board, and preparing to sew it down like a bead

Sewing down small chips of bullion to cover the padded felt, with stitches taken in different directions like seeding

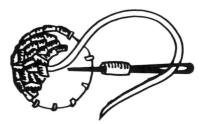

Large areas should be filled with patterns (such as brick or chevron) formed from short pieces of bullion, completely covering the padded felt area. The check or frisé bullion generally looks best when it is cut into tiny chips and sewn down in all different directions to cover the felt completely. This is more time-consuming but a great deal easier than making the smooth rows with the other types of bullion.

All the foregoing has purposely been limited to strictly traditional techniques. They are important to know since, just as in classical ballet where the disciplines of traditional steps are the foundations of modern dance, the knowledge will improve your ability when you take off on free contemporary experiments. Once you have tried the traditional methods there is no reason why you could not take the bullion or pearl purl and couch them down with other threads as in the milkweed pod on plate 16. Or incorporate long strips of bullion sewn down flat with gold clock wheels, or semi-precious stones—or fake ones! Or you could combine

Various bullion threads worked flat and over string. *Designed and worked by Barbara Dawson*

the silk and gold threads with appliqué, with crewel wool stitchery, or with stump work, experimenting with the stitches in any way you please.

BLOCKING AND CLEANING

Plain silk embroidery can be blocked just like crewel (page 108), but face downward, as a flat smooth finish is generally desired. Before blocking, test the color of the embroidery thread and the background fabric to make sure they are colorfast. Most silk and cotton threads are boilfast, but it's certainly better to be safe than sorry!

Since most gold and silver embroidery has to be done on a frame it will probably need little blocking. If it should have been rolled, or the background material folded, press it face down into thick layers of white Turkish toweling, covered with a smooth hand towel, or even a soft pillow slip. Use a warm iron and press firmly, allowing the plunged ends of couching, which are often bunched together on the wrong side, to remain free. Do not press them down flat; they may leave an unwanted impression on the front of the material.

Cleaning could be a problem when water tarnishes the gold. It is fortunate that Lurex threads are completely washable. In the sixteenth century, metal threads were burnished by being rubbed with red velvet to restore their luster, but all through the ages the best cleaning agent has been white bread, crumbled up and rubbed over the surface. French chalk, that fine powdered talc-like substance, has also been a mainstay. Let it lie thickly on top of the embroidery for as long as possible (overnight or longer), then bang and shake the needlework to remove all traces of powder and, hopefully, the dirt!

BLACK WORK

ITEM: *One paire of shetys of fyne Hollande clothe, wroughte with Spanysshe worke of blacke silke upon the edgies.*

—FROM AN INVENTORY OF THE WARDROBE OF CATHERINE OF ARAGON

By the Lady Jebson, one smock all over wrought with black silk, the sleeves wrought with gold.

—QUEEN ELIZABETH'S NEW YEAR GIFT, 1561

BLACK work, a form of embroidery which uses black silk and gold thread on cream linen, originated in Spain, and rose to the zenith of its popularity in sixteenth-century England.

Compared with the magnificent exuberance of other Elizabethan embroideries, black work has a delicacy and restraint which, above all other work of that time, shows a tremendous strength and style. Beautifully formalized flowers, enclosed by sweeping stems and strong outlines, were worked with lacy filling stitches by counting the threads of the fine white linen background. The whole design was often enriched by the sparkle of gold thread and a powdering of "owes" (better known today as sequins) to make it glisten.

So many influences and types of embroidery probably contributed to its origin that it is very difficult to say exactly where and when black work began. By the 1400's Spain had been under the domination of the Moors for eight centuries, and the interlaced strapwork patterns and geometric designs which were characteristic of Spain at this time were the ones which appeared first in England, being used generally for borders, done with great lightness and delicacy in a stitch called double running.

Looking at the geometric, bold contrasts of Arab designs, sometimes woven and re-embroidered, which have changed so little through the centuries, it is easy to see where the roots of black work began. Then, through its growth in Spain, and its final blossoming in England as a style all its own, we can see how other influences, such as the beginnings of printing and the popularity of wrought-iron work and even the ubiquitous Celtic strapwork coming down through the centuries, all played their part in forming its final beauty.

Black work—or Spanish work as it was often called—had undoubtedly been done in England before the 1500's. Chaucer refers to it in his *Canterbury Tales.*

> Whit was hir smok, and broyden al bifoore,
> And eke bihynde, on hir coler aboute,
> Of colblak silk withinne and eke withoute,
> The tapes of hir white voluper
> Were of the same suyte of hir coler.

/ *211*

opposite. Panel for a man's vest—black silk, cotton, and gold thread on white linen. *Designed and worked by author*

And in 1493 John Wylgryse of Coventry left among his effects a *"Pintheamen consutum cum serico nigro."*

Around the time of the arrival of Catherine of Aragon in England in 1501, black work began to be more popular than ever before. Fortunately, we have whole galleries of oil paintings to show us in exact detail what the black embroidery on ruff and cuff, on partelett and bodice, on sleeve and jacket, was like; the portrait painters paid as much attention to the magnificent costume as to the sitters themselves. Perhaps with reason, for the artist who painted the portrait might well have been also attached to the household to design embroideries for costume and furnishings.

At first, the embroidery was mainly done on fine linen for the neck ruffs and frilled cuffs of shirts. When outer sleeves were slashed to allow the shirt to show through, then the sleeve underneath had to be decorated, and eventually the top sleeve was in two pieces, just caught together in several places at the edges. As time progressed, patterns became more elaborate and black silk embroidery was used all over the sleeves, stom-

Black work sampler, English, 16th century. *Victoria and Albert Museum*

Portrait, dated 1587. A high necked shirt with double running and black work sleeves is worn under a jewelled black velvet dress. *Royal Academy of Arts, London*

Hood, with a typically Elizabethan
design, shaded with seeding and
speckling stitches
Victoria and Albert Museum

A "pillow-beere"
Victoria and Albert Museum

achers, bodices and caps, on gloves, on handkerchiefs, and on hoods. The stomacher, or partelett, mentioned above, was a long inverted triangle which filled in the bodice. Very often it had sleeves—which were detachable—embroidered to match it. One of Queen Elizabeth's New Year gifts in 1601 was "A partelett and a peire of sleeves of sypress wrought with silver and black silke."

But black work was not restricted only to costume. The Elizabethans loved to make themselves comfortable. Beds were hung with silk and embroideries, and sometimes had as many as three different coverlets made to match the hangings. The reason for this is explained when one reads the Hardwick Hall inventory for My Lady's Bed Chamber: "A coverlett to hang before a dore . . . three coverlets to hang before a windowe . . . a counterpoynt (coverlet) of tapestrie before an other dore. . . ."

All this finery would be on view, for the bedroom was not then the private place it is today. Carved oak benches and chairs would have soft cushions specially made to fit them; but the "pillow-beres" which were so popular for black-and-gold embroidery would probably have been used on the bed itself, designed to be framed by being surrounded with plain white "Holland" linen, or a simple quilted coverlet. Being more flexible and softer than needlework on canvas or embroidery in silk and metal threads, black work was particularly suitable for use in the bedroom, even for night shirts, which were just beginning to be worn. Up until this time, people either went to bed naked, or slept in the shirts or smocks they had worn underneath during the day. The whole idea of special bedclothes was new. Nightcaps, sometimes enriched with that most difficult stitch, the plaited braid stitch, in gold thread, would be worked in fine designs of tiny black stitches.

> and the beau would feign sickness to
> show his nightcap fine

. . . . and before retiring he would rub his teeth with a linen cloth edged with silver lace instead of a toothbrush! "From Mistress Twist, the Court laundress; Four tooth cloths of holland, wrought with black work and edged with bone lace of silver and black silk. . . ."

Later, the nightcap became so beautiful it was not worn in bed for sleeping but in the house during the day. Sir Walter Raleigh even wore one to the scaffold, under his hat, and gave it to a bystander who was cold. The latter may not have been a customary fashion, though, for it was a bitter cold day when Sir Walter Raleigh was executed and he was afraid that he might shiver and that this would be mistakenly interpreted as fear.

The nightcap was really the man's equivalent of the woman's coif, which was so often edged with lace made of silver or gold thread, and like the coif was decorated closely with beautiful patterns in fine stitchery. The overall lines of stem tracery enclosed the motifs inside them. Peas, whose golden pods could be lifted up to disclose the seed pearl peas within; strawberries, the most decorative and popular of all fruits, costing one penny a bushel at the time; grapes; flowers of every kind; beasts and butterflies—all were stitched with black and gold threads on the fine white linen. Some designs were obviously inspired by engravings and woodcuts, and were worked entirely with a speckling stitch which imitated this, called seeding (right, below), instead of the counted diaper patterns which gave the effect of beautiful appliquéd lace.

A nightcap. *Montreal Museum of Fine Arts*

A cap with speckling. *Cooper Hewitt Museum of Design, Smithsonian Institution*

Portrait of Mary Cornwallis by George Gower, showing sleeves with black work embroidery under fine lawn. *City Art Gallery, Manchester*

Sometimes black work would be covered or veiled with a soft transparent lawn, perhaps to protect it, perhaps to soften the sharp black-and-white contrasts to better suit the less brilliant climate of England than its country of origin, Spain, or simply perhaps because new linens enabled a very fine thread to be spun, and the novelty of a transparent cloth would be too fascinating to be ignored. We read of "his wrought pillow overspread with lawn," and, from Ben Jonson, "Shadow their glorie as the Milliner's wife doth her wrought stomacher with a smoakie lawne or a blacke ci-press."

Linen cambric became so fine it was called cobweb lawn, and Henry VIII, while playing tennis, was much admired for a shirt of such transparent linen gauze that his "blond skin shone through."

Old inventories always list "Spanysh work" separately from "Black work," but without being able to see the actual embroidery they describe it is impossible to tell whether the names were really interchangeable. It seems probable, however, that Spanish work was used to describe the

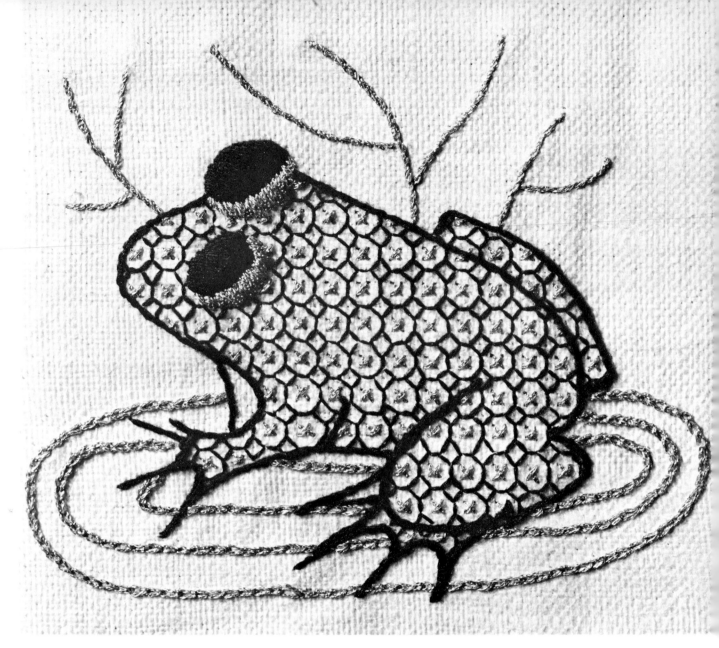

Large stitches used for bold effect. *Designed and worked by the author*

earlier double running and darning patterns that were more familiar in Spain, and that black work came to be synonymous with the later black-and-gold embroidery done with filling stitches or seeding. Often the double running was known as Holbein stitch, because Holbein's portraits so often showed designs of this kind. Sometimes, though more rarely, they were worked in red instead of black, and were seen throughout the Continent as well as in England.

OPPOSITE. Modern use of Holbein stitch or reversible double running on table linen. *Author's collection*

Four hundred years later we still have a remarkable number of exquisite black work embroideries in our museums. Unfortunately, the silk has badly worn in some of them, but when you consider a typical recipe for the black dye you wonder how they have lasted at all!

15 lb Elderbark
12 lb of soot (oak shavings or sawdust)
10 lb vitriol
2 lb wild marjoram
6 lb brown wood
1½ lb Calcined Allom and Vitriol mixed
4 lb Filings
as much lye as necessary
10 lb Walnut shells.

Black work was popular throughout the sixteenth century, perhaps because Mary Tudor's consort Philip II still maintained England's link with its country of origin, but since then little black work has been done.

To collect a sampler nowadays of the many beautiful black work fillings is an idea which could lead to all sorts of combinations. The size and scale of present-day black work can be varied according to temperament, but enlargement in stitches in itself gives the embroidery a fascinatingly contemporary appearance. The following pages may inspire some idea of what is possible, not forgetting that "black and gold" may also be effectively combined with other types of embroidery.

TO BEGIN

Black work must be done on an evenly woven material, because part of its effect is working geometric stitches to fill the different areas of design, using a monochromatic color scheme. It really looks beautiful when worked with fine black silk on a crisp white linen with gold thread, but it can also be embroidered with blue and silver, or red and white, or green and gold. On page 240 is a design worked with white thread on black linen to give a reversed effect.

Black work lends itself, among other things, to evening bags, picture panels, mirror frames, boxes, table linen, vests, and cushions. Traditionally its nature is fine, delicate, and sophisticated, but it would be interesting to experiment with bolder effects—perhaps even working a carpet on needlepoint canvas with coarse rug wool, making the lacy repeat patterns very large in black wool, and filling the background in with white tent stitch. (See Chapter 2, Needlepoint.)

It is a good idea to begin by collecting some of the black work stitches on linen so that you can see their effect. They look so entirely different when they are worked, compared with their effect in a photograph or drawing. Only when it is embroidered can you see how the same pattern done in bold crewel wools can look utterly changed from one done in fine black silk. Then you can use this sampler to refer to when you are embroidering your main design.

Companion picture to the frog, page 218
Designed and worked by the author

CHOOSING FABRICS

Fine, evenly woven white linen is the traditional fabric, but monk's cloth or coarse white linen, even nylon or coarse wool material, would be excellent for black work as long as the weave is regular enough. There is an oriental wallpaper which is manufactured with widely spaced canvas—a white linen weave thread laminated to a white paper background. These threads are spaced out evenly and held in place by the paper backing, making this firm fabric most suitable for pictures and panels in bold black work. Alternatively, you could use a regular needlepoint canvas with single weave (mono), leaving the canvas open as a background and backing it afterward with white fabric.

The most important thing is to find a material with a clear even weave, as all the stitch patterns have to be counted out on the background following the mesh.

Match the thickness of your working thread to your background material. Your working threads should be approximately the same thickness as those in the fabric.

TOP, LEFT TO RIGHT. Black linen; even weave canvas wall covering; the same in natural
BOTTOM, LEFT TO RIGHT. White coarse-weave linen; medium-weave linen; monkscloth, similar to "Binca" evenweave cotton

THREADS AND NEEDLES

Fine fingering knitting wool or acrylic fiber, or fine tapestry wool are all good for black work, as they are rounded threads, smooth and not hairy—the better to work clear-cut, crisp, geometric patterns. Six-stranded mercerized cotton embroidery floss, buttonhole twist, or sewing silk are all good for finer effects. The best way is to collect various threads and try them out on your linen. As to the gold thread, various sewing companies put out a gold you can sew with—a fine Lurex variety which is nontarnishing. (See page 190.) These may be sewn or couched onto the fabric and, together with sequins, are often the final touch—the frosting on the cake—which just finishes the design.

Use blunt (tapestry) needles in a size to correspond with the thickness of your wool and background fabric, so that you can pass between the threads of the linen without splitting them. For outlining, for gold threads, and for any patterns which are not worked by the thread of the linen, use sharp needles, either crewel or chenille, again large enough so that the threads pass easily through the linen. A specially large-eyed needle is necessary to protect the fragile gold thread as it passes back and forth through the fabric. When very fine, it is a good idea to knot the gold thread around the eye of the needle to prevent it from constantly slipping out.

BEGINNING THE DESIGN

Patterns for black work must necessarily be stylized, since the design is to be worked with geometric repeat fillings. This does not mean that your design must be limited to abstract shapes, or that the pattern must be made up of squares, circles, or triangles. It can consist of simple silhouette shapes, like those on the beautiful Elizabethan caps and bodices. These shapes may be filled with different lacy patterns worked both closely and lightly for contrast of texture—or blocks of the repeat patterns may make a design themselves, worked on a large scale.

Pictures in black work can be as strong and dynamic as a woodcut, or as delicate as the copies of early prints embroidered in speckling or seeding stitches (see page 107). A contemporary inspiration might be to work out a version of the much enlarged photos from newspapers or printed black-and-white photos, which, when blown up, appear as a series of large dots. The scissor-cut designs, or Scherenschnitte of Switzerland, with their beautiful silhouette shapes, are also excellent for black work (see page 225).

Before you begin to embroider, make a "cartoon" or drawing of your final design on paper, and fill in the areas to be stitched with three shades of any color: light, medium, and dark. You can do this with pencil, paint, or felt pens. This will show you which areas should be worked with close solid stitching (painted dark) which should be medium, and

A contemporary example of decorative black work, with gold thread accents. *Designed and worked by Mrs. Grover O'Neill*

Pillow with tree inspired by Scherenschnitte, backed with brilliant green velvet

Snail, showing stitches in large scale on coarse white linen. Grass in chain stitch using gold lurex. *Both designed and worked by author*

BELOW. The design inspired by silhouette work

Swiss Scherenschnitte or silhouette work

which light and airy (painted light). The effectiveness of the whole thing relies on your good balance between solid and open stitching. Therefore, it is best to see this finished effect on your cartoon first, since any unpicking is apt to leave the material looking tired and gray!

Once you have applied your pattern by the methods on pages 18–23 (deciding which one seems most suitable for your background fabric), you will be ready to begin the stitching. You will find it much easier to count the threads of the linen if it is stretched tight in an embroidery frame or hoop (see page 24). If you are using gold thread, work with a square or stretcher frame since round hoops might squash and split the metallic threads.

Stylized designs to use for black work

THE STITCHES

Whether you have begun by making a sampler, or whether you have launched right into your final design, practice the stitches you are going to use on the edge of your work, or on another piece of the same linen. Then you can see how they will work out on your particular cloth, and how they will look when you use different thicknesses of thread. Try out both close and open stitches to see which are best in conjunction with one another.

The patterns are all counted onto the linen, but they are not complicated, for they are based on three simple stitches: cross, running, and back stitch. Always begin stitching in the center of each area to be filled, as it is much easier to count out one complete section of the pattern first than to start in an awkward corner where you will be interrupted by converging outlines. You can then fit the pattern into the corners, once you have established one or two unbroken repeats in the center. Combine the counted stitches with blocks of solid satin stitch for contrast, seeding, and all the squared fillings (see pages 103–104), using both black and gold threads for good variety. You can combine gold thread with the black silk or wool in other stitches, too; whipped stem and whipped chain

Panel, Black work stitches combined with fine black net. *Designed and worked by Mrs. Daryl Parshall*

Trotting

are good for stems and outlines, using black thread and whipping in with gold, or vice versa (see pages 39, 61). Raised stem and raised buttonhole, braid stitch and raised spiders' webs are excellent stitched with plain gold threads. Sequins sewn down with matching yellow silk or a black French knot give richness to the design.

Below is a listing of the main and most important stitches used in black work.

BASIC BLACKWORK STITCHES	STITCHES FOR SOLID CONTRASTS AND OUTLINES	
Geometric counted stitches	Padded satin stitch	French knots
Darning stitches	Stem (plain and whipped)	Spiders' webs
Squared filling stitches	Chain (plain and whipped)	Braid stitch
Seeding	Raised stem, chain, and buttonhole	Bullion knots
		Buttonhole
		Laid work

Detail from an Elizabethan lady's coif. *Victoria and Albert Museum*

*GEOMETRIC BLACK WORK STITCHES

Geometric Black Work stitches are counted out on to a regular weave background fabric and should always be worked with a blunt (tapestry) needle. Most black work patterns are based on two simple stitches, cross and back stitch. Try out the stitches as shown opposite and below. Then use the pages that follow as guides for other patterns. You will find that eventually you can make up your own.

*CROSS STITCH

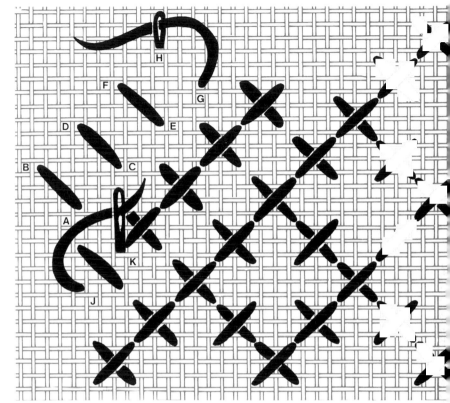

Start with the easiest stitch which is Cross.

Using a blunt needle come up at A, count 3 threads up and 3 threads to the left, go down at B. Now count 6 threads to the right of B and come up at C.

Stitch CD repeats AB. Continue from E to F and G to H making a diagonal line of identical slanting stitches.

Now complete the cross by making stitches in the other direction from J to K so that you have a diagonal line of completed cross stitches. Each top stitch of the cross should always lie in the same direction for evenness. Once you have completed one diagonal line, make a pattern of diagonal lines which intersect on every other stitch as shown on the right of the diagram.

*BACK STITCH

Next try a pattern based on back stitch. Using a blunt needle, first practice back stitch as shown at right—up at A, down at B, up at C and down at A again. Then make the honeycomb pattern as shown on the left.

First make a series of slanting back stitches over 2 threads of the linen from A to B as shown.

Then work vertical stitches over 2 threads from C to D.

Complete the honeycomb with another line of stitches as in #1 and continue repeating steps 1, 2 and 3.

Finally, work a single vertical stitch over 2 threads in the center of each honeycomb.

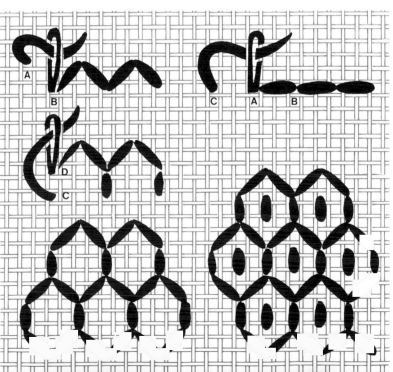

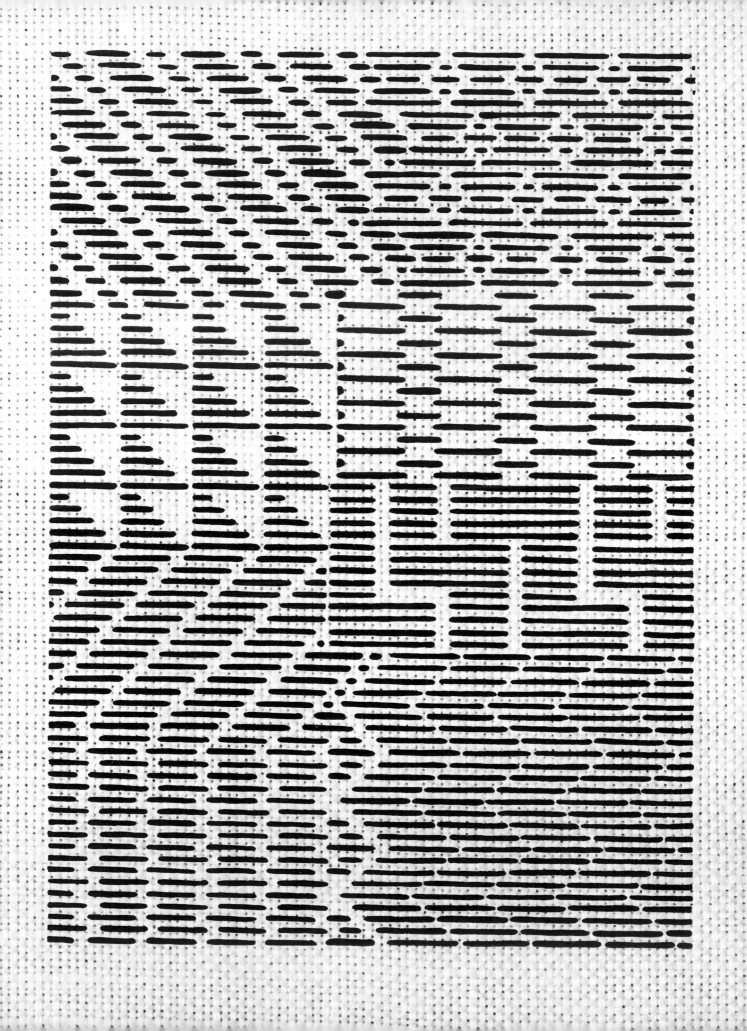

*DARNING STITCH

Using a blunt needle and a thread approximating the size of your linen, weave horizontal lines across the fabric to make the pattern shown below.

Come up at A, go over 7 threads, go down at B and under 3 threads.

Come up at C and go over 7 threads—again go down at D and continue, repeating these stitches along the line.

On the next line immediately below, come up 1 thread in from A and go over 5, under 2, over 1, under 2, and over 5 again. Repeat along the line.

On the next line come up 1 thread in from the line above and go over 3, under 2, over 3, and under 2.

Now repeat steps 4, 3, 2 and 1 in that order to form the diamond pattern as shown in the diagram. All kinds of patterns can be built up in this way as shown on the opposite page.

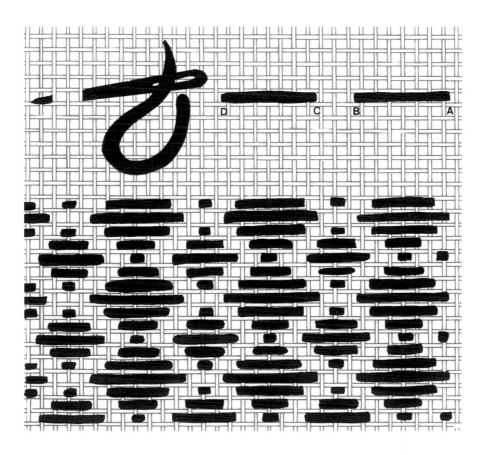

DOUBLE RUNNING

Using a blunt needle, come up at A, go over 3 threads and go down at B. Come up at C, 3 threads away and go down at D, over 3 more threads. Continue, making even stitches in a straight line.

Turn the work completely around and fill the spaces between with running stitches, going into the same holes as the previous ones to make a continuous line of stitching, alike on both sides.

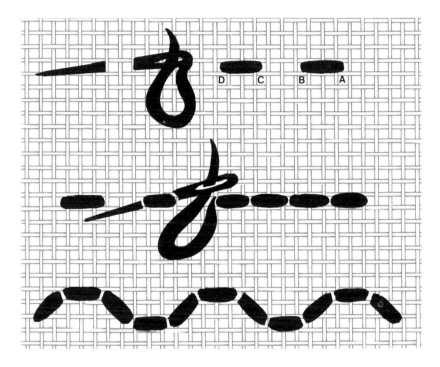

Double running or Holbein stitch. *Victoria and Albert Museum*

When the design is finished, it can be blocked by the method described on page 108. But if you have used gold threads which may tarnish, wetting the fabric may injure them. Therefore, press the design face downward into several layers of thick white Turkish toweling, using a damp cloth under the iron.

Black work techniques for a design adapted from a brass rubbing, worked in white on a black ground. *Designed and worked by the author*

WHITE WORK

*Arachne first invented working with the needle, which this mayd of Lydia learned from the spiders, taking her first samplers and patterns from them in imitation.**

—EDWARD TOPSEL, *History of Fourfooted Beasts and Serpents,* 1608

*Beautiful, young, and talented was Arachne—but boastful! She claimed she could spin and weave better than anyone in the world—even the goddess Athene. When Athene visited her, disguised as an old woman, Arachne unknowingly challenged her to a duel at tapestry weaving, which, of course, the goddess won. Arachne, in horror, hanged herself, and Athene, as a warning to all conceited mortals, quickly changed her into a spider so that she could spend eternity perfecting her stitches!

Fine white work apron showing darning and openwork stitches. Medallion on left reads "Anne Bullock Her Apron 1715." *Metropolitan Museum of Art*

WHEN Arachne first learned to imitate the spider, it must surely have been white work that became her first sampler! For nothing could be better compared with white work's textured patterns and airy openwork stitching than the lacy delicacy of a spider's web.

Because it is worked with white stitching on a white background fabric (hence the name!) white work needs a contrast of texture to give it its full effect. In fact, it is a sort of baccalaureate for the embroideress, an ultimate test of ability—for in its purity and restraint all depends on the excellence of delicate stitchery. Like a painter of still life, where the artist's true ability is shown without distraction of subject matter, the white-work embroideress has to channel her enthusiasm into the confines and limits of a monochromatic color scheme. A casual observer, accustomed to rainbow-hued crewel wools or exotic gold and silken threads, might be forgiven for not immediately appreciating its beauty.

Perhaps it needs an acquired taste, like that for caviar (to fit our idiom, the white Iranian kind, served only to the Czars!) to take delight in this form of stitchery which is not interchangeable with any other medium. Crewelwork may imitate oil painting, and silk embroidery, water color. Stump work may resemble sculpture, and needlepoint, tapestry. Even black work may be compared to etching. But white embroidery stands uniquely alone, its sparkling whiteness as refreshing as crisp air on a snowy winter's day. No wonder John Taylor, the seventeenth-century's "Water Poet," referred to it in his book *The Needle's Excellency* as "frost work." "For Tent-Worke, Raised-Worke, Laid-Worke, Frost-Worke, Net-Worke—All these are good and this we must allow, that these are everywhere in practise now."

White work seems to have been done all through the ages in almost every country in the world. Sometimes it was in the ascendancy of fashion, sometimes overshadowed when other types of embroidery gained more attention. But it was always there—the delicate Indian muslins, the crisp white cuff that contrasted so beautifully with the Elizabethans' sparkling

/ *243*

Fine white panel with chinoiserie figures, showing geometric filling stitches. *Cooper Hewitt Museum of Design, Smithsonian Institution*

Christening robe trimmed with tambour work
Metropolitan Museum of Art (see page 255)

English baby bonnet in fine drawn work
Author's Collection

gold and silken sleeve; the Scandinavian openwork or the finely wrought Scottish baby bonnet—serving its purpose as a washable lightweight decorative cloth for shirts, underwear, bed pillows, coverlets, baby clothes, shawls, dresses, and altar linen.

The Egyptians were probably the first to use it, and it does seem logical that white embroidery would originate in countries where the finely woven background material was best suited to the tropical climate. Very primitive white work has been found in Coptic tombs; Cleopatra was known to have worn gossamer-drawn thread work; and when the Queen of Sheba visited King Solomon all his trumpet players were arrayed in white linen, which was more than likely to have been embroidered.

In China, it may have been closely related to the "forbidden stitch" (the French knot which was so fine and closely worked that the embroideress ultimately went blind!), for the finest work seems to have been done there since before recorded time.

Perhaps from China, Persia, Turkey, and Arabia, along the ancient trade routes, the tradition of the craft found its way to India where, on the banks of the Ganges and the Malabar Coast, a special caste of washer-*men* starched and pleated fine lightweight muslins for the Indian nobility. Princesses changed their clothes several times a day, a subject of amazement to later European visitors who seldom changed theirs at all!

The muslins were blanched with lemon water and given poetic Indian names such as "dew of light," "running water," "woven wind," and "scorched tears" and were so fine as to be almost transparent; in fact, a Dutch visitor to India in the seventeenth century wondered if the wearers weren't nude! These muslins were woven from the earliest days of India's history, for a historian describing the period from A.D. 320 to 420 wrote: "She wore a gown of white, bleached 'netra' cloth [a net with gold thread interwoven], lighter than a snake's slough, flowing down to her toes. Underneath gleamed a petticoat of saffron tint . . . a divine woman wearing a dazzling muslin robe embroidered with hundreds of diverse flowers and birds gently rippled by the motion of the breeze."

When the Portuguese navigators began to open India to the West at the turn of the sixteenth century, Vasco da Gama brought back, among the riches from the fabled East, a gift for the Queen of Portugal. It was

Close stem stitching on fine linen silhouettes the hunting figures. *Metropolitan Museum of Art*

a "white embroidered canopy for a bed, the most delicate piece of needle-work, like none other that has ever been seen; this has been made in Bengal, a country where they make wonderful things with the needle."

The tradition of needlework in India was certainly ancient, originally having been done to join and strengthen fabrics and eventually developing into a beautiful decoration.

One of the oldest literary documents in existence, the Rig-Veda, refers to it in a hymn in an invocation to Raka, the goddess of the full moon. "With never-breaking needle may she sew her work, and may she bestow on us a son who is worthy and will possess immense wealth." (The Hindu, by gifts and praise, always hoped to coax those invincible elements, such as the sun, the storm, and the lightning into friendly acquiescence, and to provide him with the material things he needed.) This illuminates for us not only what an important part needlework played even in early Indian history, but also how valuable and fragile was a needle of hand-beaten gold, copper, or bronze.

The white embroidery that came from Madras, Delhi, Calcutta, and the area around the Ganges was called "Chikan." It was worked on filmy muslin which was woven from cotton, hemp, or the fiber of the pineapple

Detail from panel

tree, and stiffened with rice starch. The embroidery was done with a double row of back stitches on the reverse side, which gave a shadowy effect. This was contrasted with an openwork stitch made by pulling a fine thread tightly to form regular holes in the gauzy fabric.

According to the Roman poet Lucan,* Cleopatra had robes which were made by a similar technique. In describing the fabric he said, "which wrought in close texture by the skill of the Chinese, the needle of the workman of the Nile has separated, and loosened the warp by stretching the web." Or, as he put it more romantically in verse,

> Her snowy breast shines through Sidonian threads,
> First by the comb of distant Seres struck
> Divided then by Egypt's skillful toil
> And with embroidery transparent made.

European embroideresses, accustomed to heavier linens, must have found the fine muslins fascinating, but the convolutions of the openwork stitch must have been almost impossible to unravel. For when the fine thread is pulled so tightly that only the open holes show, the method of working is completely concealed. Who knows, therefore, if a French or English lawyer might not have been inspired by that Indian name for muslin embroidery to add the word "chicanery" to the language to describe some particularly involved and intentionally deceiving piece of legal verbiage!

In Europe, where beautiful altar frontals were made in the thirteenth and fourteenth centuries in Switzerland, Saxony, and Germany, the white-on-white embroidery was worked with geometric patterns. Moorish tradition, which may have spread through Portugal, then at the height of its European influence, was perhaps the inspiration for filling the stylized designs with textural repeat patterns. These altar frontals were often done in convents. "Nuns with their needles wrote histories also," closely stitching and counting the threads of the fine linen to illustrate stories from the Scriptures for the unlettered. Many a wellborn lady who, jilted by her lover, had repaired to a nunnery, might have soothed her sorrows by sewing a design of the Annunciation of the Virgin, the Adoration of the Magi, or the Crucifixion of Christ. Similar embroideries were done in color, and

*Lucan was a young and romantic poet, who at the age of twenty-three was forced to take his own life, after an unsuccessful plot to overthrow Nero.

Medallions on an altarcloth from the cloister Feldbach, Thurgau, Switzerland. *Historisches Museum, Basel.* BELOW. Detail

Shirt with Chikan work. *Author's Collection*
(see pages 248 and 274)

Embroidered shirt worn by Charles I at his execution.
By gracious permission of Her Majesty the Queen

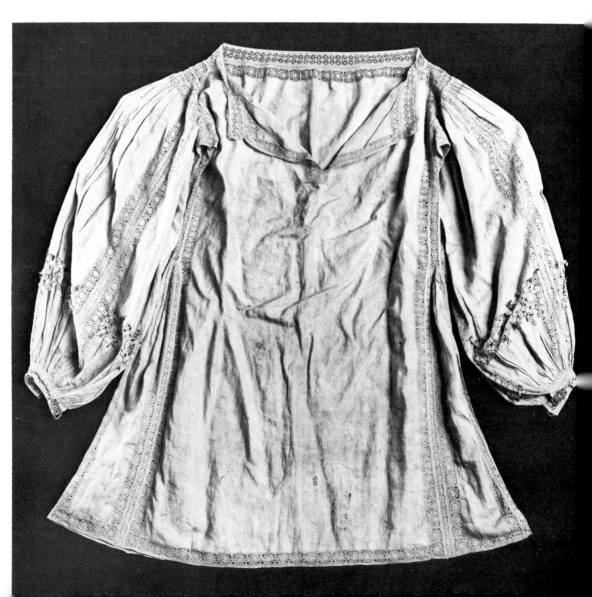

indeed these seem to be the forerunners of the later embroidery on canvas (see page 249), but white to symbolize the purity of the Virgin was used for altar cloths and, for Lent, large hangings were worked as veils, hung to separate the altar and the choir from the congregation. Seen with the soft light glimmering through them, silhouetting the shadowy figures with their rich variety of textured patterns, the designs must have appeared restrained and beautiful.

The linen was often woven in France and Germany, but the soil of Flanders and the Netherlands seemed particularly suitable for growing the flax. So excellent was the Dutch fabric that up until the eighteenth century, the word for the strongest linen was simply "Holland" or "Holland cloth."

Though fine, the linen was not transparent like the Eastern muslins, and sometimes the nuns would draw out the threads of the background to give a lighter effect. This led to a more openwork form of stitchery which they used for borders of sacramental and burial robes, keeping their methods a secret, and using the finest flax thread grown at Brabant and steeped in the waters near Haarlem. Besides, this openwork and drawn-thread embroidery was an ancient technique of knotting threads derived from fishnets. The *lacis* (network), as it was known in France, was then woven with solid patterns darned in and out with the needle. St. Paul's Cathedral in England had a cushion of this work in 1295 and Exeter Cathedral three pieces for "use at the altar."

Similar to *lacis* was hollie point, a needle lace made entirely of buttonhole stitch. The background of the pattern was solid, made by working the stitches close together, and the design itself was outlined by open holes formed by working the stitches wider apart. Was it called hollie point because of these holes, or because this early form of lace may have been of Arab origin and was brought from the Holy Land? No one is really sure.

Still another type of openwork, where buttonholed bars were connected across a linen surface which was afterward cut away, came from the Ionian Isles and Corfu, and was later known in Venice as Reticella. This "cut work," so called because the background was later removed, caused the astonishing and exciting discovery of the century—that a background linen was not really needed at all and that the stitches could be built up by themselves—and *"punto in aria,"* literally, *"a stitch in the air,"* was born. This light and delicate stitchery became the first real needlemade lace, and Vinciolo, the Venetian who published a book of patterns for it in 1587 and who took it to France to the court of Catherine de Medici, became world famous. Venice, that glittering port, receiving the spoils of the fabled East brought back by Marco Polo, must have also received the finer, stronger, and more plentiful flax thread spun by the Saxon wheel invented in Nuremberg in 1530.

Not only was the sixteenth-century *punto in aria* new and different, it was available for the first time outside the church. For centuries thereafter all varieties of lace continued to be high fashion for costume and household articles, as well as church furnishings. Noblemen sold acres of land to be

Three examples of *punto in aria*. Cooper Hewitt Museum of Design, Smithsonian Institution

able to afford the expensive luxury. A French courtier of 1630 boasted that he wore "thirty-two acres of the best vineyard . . . around his neck." The plain sleeve edge disappeared for three hundred years, to be replaced by frothy layers of lace, and the collar, heavily starched, rose up to become a ruff, subsided to being a wide cape, and finally became a cravat, always made either entirely of lace or of fine linen bordered with deep bands and flounces of it. Knee breeches for men had wide frills of lace, and extravagant dress for both men and women was ornamented with gimps, braids, laces, and ribbons. The diarist Evelyn describes a fop at this time: "It was a fine silken thing I espied walking th' other day through Westminster Hall, that had as much ribbon about him as would have plundered six shops and set up twenty country peddlers. All his body was drest like a May-Pole, or a Tom o' Bedlam's cap. A fregat newly rigg'd kept not half such a clatter in a storme as this puppet's streamers did when the wind was in his shrouds; the motion was truly wonderful to behold."

Side by side with the needlemade lace or *punto in aria* in the sixteenth century, came the knotting of threads known as *macramé*, the forerunner, perhaps, of bobbin lace. Neither of these is really needlework, for true embroidery always must be worked on a background fabric, but both are so closely allied to it that they can really be considered as one. Thread knotting must have been at least as early a craft as embroidery itself; the necessity for knotting two threads together very soon developed into decorative bands and fringes. The trappings for horses, camels, and elephants shown in early paintings from the East clearly illustrate this. From earliest times, too, it must have been used by sailors, who on long sea voyages found it both amusing and practical. In fact, it was French sailors in the eighteenth century who gave it the name of *macramé*, and it was in that century that it really became the rage all over the Continent. Even Queen Mary of England, wife of William of Orange, was known as the Royal Knotter, "Who, when she rides in coach abroad,/Is always knotting threads."

It was said that "the Queen was oftener seen with a skein of thread about her neck than attending to affairs of state" and, "so fashionable was [this] labour of a sudden grown that not only assembly rooms and visiting rooms, but the streets, roads, nay the very playhouses were witnesses of this pretty industry."

Officier du Roi, French, 17th century. *Metropolitan Museum of Art, Elisha Whittelsey fund, 1957*

Early 19th century sampler showing ladies in white work dresses. *Cooper Hewitt Museum of Design, Smithsonian Institution*

In Queen Anne's time in England, the fashion for finely embroidered aprons worn by ladies as a purely decorative garment rose to a new height. Though many were done in silk and gold thread, white ones were popular, too. This fashion was decried by Beau Nash who, at a gathering in the assembly rooms at Bath, tore off the white apron worn by the Duchess of Queensbury and flung it into a corner, saying white aprons were worn only by serving women. With the advent of the neoclassic period and the interest in Greece and Rome came a fashion for white-work dresses in muslin and gauze in devastatingly simple designs compared with what had gone before. Perhaps the fashion was a close reproduction of ancient marble statuary, for ladies clad all in white-on-white embroidery would go to balls in dresses dampened to accentuate their clinging filmy transparency.

With the development of Arkwright's and Crompton's looms, which meant that fine muslins and cottons no longer had to be imported from India, Britain began an industry of white embroidery which was highly successful until the late nineteenth century. Worked on a ring hoop or tambour frame (which gave the embroidery its name), it was done in chain stitch, sometimes with a fine crochet hook, like the Indian embroideries, and sometimes with a needle. Another type of white work, known as Broderie Anglaise, was done by cutting eyelet holes into the linen, which were then closely stitched around the edges. This, combined with tambour embroidery, was developed into a very competitive cottage industry in Ayrshire and Belfast. Cottagers would gather for the companionship of working together, pay a child a penny to keep the needles threaded, and contribute to the family earnings, though the highest pay was ten shillings a week for their labors.

In the eighteenth century a religious group from Germany settled in Bethlehem, Pennsylvania. They were the Moravian sisters, and they opened a school where they taught "fine needlework as an extra" for seventeen shillings and sixpence, Pennsylvania currency. Among the types of work they taught were tambour work, together with ribbon work, crepe work, flower embroidery, and pictures on satin. It is said that they embroidered Count Casimir Pulaski's banner, which his legion carried all through the Revolutionary War until his death at the siege of Savannah in 1779.

Perhaps the sisters fostered, or at any rate encouraged, the vogue for the "French embroidery" which became so popular between 1750 and 1840. Being similar to the Ayrshire work of this period in England, this embroidery was stitched by American ladies who made christening robes, baby bonnets, ruffled men's shirts, and gowns with long trains. At first the designs were done simply with padded satin stitch, but eventually all kinds of cut and pierced work gave way to real laces.

In the sixteenth century an English parson named Lee invented a knitting machine, but he died, disappointed and brokenhearted, without finding recognition for his work. Even Joseph Jacquard, who had just produced a net-making machine, when brought before Napoleon I, was asked, "Are you the man who pretends to do that which the Almighty

Man's commemorative handkerchief embroidered in fine lawn: "Lafayette and Washington, 1777 and 1824." *Litchfield, Conn., Historical Museum*

Unfinished piece showing use of padded satin stitch. *Metropolitan Museum of Art*

cannot do, to tie a knot in a stretched string?" But the first patent for a machine which exactly duplicated hand embroidery on a multiple scale was taken out in 1829, remarkably enough, fifteen years before the machine for plain sewing was invented in America. The Jacquard loom, which was originally designed to reproduce knitting, was found to adapt magnificently to laces, and so in the nineteenth century modern science overtook the vast hand industry for white embroidery and lacemaking which had developed throughout the world.

Now that versatile and prolific machines can turn out as many thousand yards of white work as the trade demands, white embroidery by hand is done only in limited quantities by skilled professionals in places such as Hong Kong, Madeira, and Venice. This beautiful traditional work often passes unnoticed, most people imagining that such delicate stitchery could not possibly be done by hand.

Today, with the great revival of interest in handwork, the techniques of other centuries may be adapted to contemporary styles; if so, the results will be exciting and fascinating.

TO BEGIN

The most beautiful white-on-white embroidery can be worked with fine threads and delicate stitchery, to make such things as a monogrammed man's shirt, a throw pillow for a bed, a lampshade, table mats, a child's first dress, or an heirloom christening robe. The stitches can be as fairy-like and lacy as time and eyesight will allow, and the designs contemporary, even though you are using traditional techniques. But you can also take those techniques and expand them with dramatic results. Imagine a gauzy Dacron or organdy window curtain, shadow-stitched with snow-white angora on the reverse side. The bold wool stitchery (instead of the usual fine cotton) gives a clear opaque silhouette which contrasts beautifully with the sheer background fabric. Or visualize a Roman shade window curtain in coarse off-white linen with bands of needle weaving in natural rug wool. A wall hanging done with this large-scale openwork stitching could be illuminated from the back to show its airiness, or hung as a room divider to be seen from both sides.

One of the fascinations of white work is that instead of doing surface stitchery you really take a plain piece of fabric and transform it, either by drawing threads or cutting holes, or combining these with geometric patterns in self color to give a surface texture as well. There are literally hundreds of traditional variations on this theme, which go all the way from close solid stitching to needlemade lace. So many different styles and names may be confusing. Wherever do you start when confronted with names such as Hardanger and Hedebo, Richelieu and Reticella, Battenberg and Broderie Anglaise? But it is simpler than it seems, for basically there are only two main types of white work—coarse and fine. Coarse white, in spite of its name, may be worked on any *opaque* fabric which shows clear individual threads, from coarse burlap weaves to the finest linen. Then you count the mesh to make geometric surface textures, draw out threads to form lacy patterns and borders, or cut the material to make openwork holes.

Fine white is the type of stitching which is done when the linen is too sheer to draw threads, so the effect is made either by letting in net, working shadow stitch on the reverse side, or by drawing the fine threads

Example of Norwegian Hardanger embroidery. Geometric satin stitch patterns are worked on even-weave, double thread linen. Open work fillings are then cut as on page 266, and this drawn threadwork mesh is strengthened with needleweaving, page 269. Because the special double thread Hardanger linen is so firm, it can be cut close against the satin stitch without fraying. *Norwegian-American Museum*

tightly together to give an effect of open holes. This pulled stitching, as it is called, may also be done on coarse linen with a loose sleazy weave, so that large holes can easily be made in it. In other words, an open lacy effect is formed by pulling the threads together instead of drawing them out or cutting them.

So you can see that, opaque or transparent, it is the background fabric which really controls what type of stitching you do. If you start by making two samplers, one of coarse white and one of fine, you will be able to learn the basic techniques, recognize them when you see them in traditional white embroidery, and experiment with them and combine them in all sorts of different ways on future pieces of needlework.

COARSE WHITE WORK

MATERIALS, THREADS, AND NEEDLES

Use opaque linen of coarse, medium, or fine weave. Naturally, the fibers must be distinct enough to see the mesh clearly, and tightly twisted enough so that the threads can be drawn out without disintegrating. Monk's cloth, homespun, nylon or Dacron, and coarse wool or cotton as well as linen fabric may all be suitable. The best and sometimes the only way to tell whether a fabric is suitable is to take home a small swatch of it and experiment.

The traditional thread for coarse white embroidery is either tightly twisted linen thread or cotton embroidery floss—the six-stranded variety available in all notion stores. But, as suggested earlier, you could use any thickness of wool on heavy linen or any kind of white crochet cotton in various thicknesses.

Your needles must necessarily fit the thickness of thread you are using. They should be heavy enough to make a clear opening in the fabric

TOP, LEFT TO RIGHT. Monk's cloth; coarse open-weave linen; open-weave jute
BOTTOM, LEFT TO RIGHT. Natural coarse-weave wool; natural medium-weave linen; white medium-weave linen

so that the thread can follow smoothly, but if they are too coarse it will be hard to keep the stitching even. A package of assorted sizes embroidery, crewel, or chenille needles will be best, so that you can find exactly the right size for a particular stitch (page 16). For needle weaving you will need blunt tapestry needles since you are weaving between the threads of the background fabric, being careful to avoid splitting them.

TRANSFERRING THE DESIGN

Transfer your design by making a perforation, using carbon paper or tracing paper as shown on page 21. For the perforating method (page 18), use a very fine paintbrush and blue watercolor, since white work must be washable, and the blue paint will eventually wash out and will act like an old fashioned "blue bag" which will make the work appear whiter.

To position a design that may come in the four corners of a cloth or a table mat, fold the cloth in half diagonally and then in half again, creasing a diagonal line through all four corners (be certain not to stretch the fabric). Baste these diagonal lines across the cloth in both directions, using a contrasting thread. Place the design in the correct position in one corner, transfer it, and repeat in the other three corners.

THE STITCHES

TEXTURED SURFACE STITCHES

Flat geometric stitches
Padded satin
Seeding
Mountmellick stitch
Trailing

OPENWORK STITCHES

Drawn thread work borders
　with Hemstitching
Needleweaving
Open fillings
Cut work

Coarse white work consists of two contrasting types of stitches, those that are raised, giving textured interest to the surface of the material, and those that are open. In the first group are the geometric border and filling stitches, padded satin stitch, trailing, seeding, and Mountmellick stitch, to list some of the most basic ones. In the openwork group are drawn-thread-work borders, openwork fillings, and cut work.

*FLAT GEOMETRIC STITCHES

Using a blunt tapestry needle and an even weave linen so that the threads may be counted, you can work out geometric borders or fillings for silhouette shapes. These may be done in white on a colored linen, or in an entirely monochromatic color scheme such as white on white, or in a deeper shade such as natural on an off-white background.

You should use embroidery floss or heavy cotton to give you a crisp regular silhouette. Wool, with its hairy texture, is only suitable if a rough homespun look is desired.

White geometric stitches on a dark blue ground. *Author's Collection*

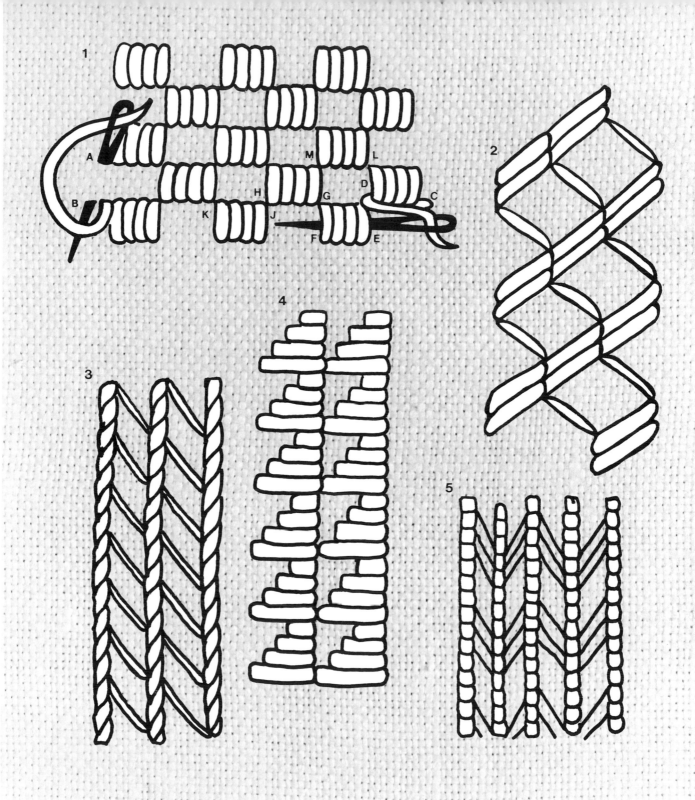

1. Make a chequer board pattern of blocks of stitches four threads deep, and four stitches wide, coming up at A, and going down at B. Then, using a blunt needle, weave through these blocks of stitches. Slide under the first block from C to D. Then go under the lower block from E to F. Slide through the next upper block from G to H, then go down and slide through from J to K and so on. The needle only slips under the stitches, not through the material. Repeat this on the next row above, starting through the upper part of block CD, then going through the next block above from L to M and so on. The weaving draws the blocks of stitches together making an even, slightly raised pattern. 2. Slanting stitches making a three-dimensional pattern. 3. Lines of stem stitch, connected by diagonal lines. 4. Blocks of satin stitch, counted out on the linen. 5. Back stitch combined with fishbone stitch in blocks of three

PADDED SATIN AND SEEDING

Padded satin stitch worked with fine cotton has a raised, shiny, very white effect which contrasts beautifully with openwork stitches in both coarse and fine white embroidery (see page 49).

Seeding produces a shadowy light effect which blends into the background and gives the material a textured appearance (see page 107).

Besides seeding and padded satin stitches, there are other surface stitches such as bullion knots, coral, chain, and whipped stem—in fact, almost the entire vocabulary of crewel embroidery, which can be very effective if used in white-on-white stitchery (see page 241).

Bedspread showing raised white stitches. *Cooper Hewitt Museum of Design, Smithsonian Institution*

MOUNTMELLICK STITCH

Mountmellick is a surface stitch which has been used traditionally in white work only. It gets its name from the town in Ireland where it originated in the 1830's. It is a bold stitch with a raised effect, achieved by working heavy white cotton on a background such as satin or linen.

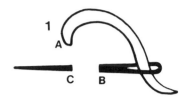

This stitch is worked vertically, and each individual stitch has three movements. Come up at A. Go down at B slightly to the right and below A, and come up at C directly underneath A. Pull through to form a slanting stitch.

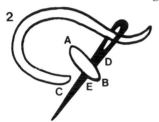

Slide under this stitch from D to E (do not go through the material).

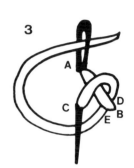

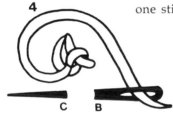

Take a vertical stitch, going into the same holes from A to C, and looping the thread under the needle, draw through. This completes one stitch.

Repeat #1 again, taking another stitch under the first which is exactly like B to C at #1. Then repeat #2, sliding the needle under the slanting stitch as before.

Now repeat #3, but go down at the arrow right *inside* the previous stitch, just like a chain. Loop the thread under the needle as before, and repeat, to make a continuous line of stitches.

The finished effect. This stitch is best worked in heavy thread.

Corner of a cloth with Mountmellick stitch predominating. *Atlanta Historical Society*

*TRAILING STITCH with OPEN FILLINGS

Trailing is the most basic and useful stitch for white-on-white embroidery and is used in both coarse and fine white work. It is done by taking fine whipping stitches closely over a bundle of three or more loose threads, to form the effect of a smooth raised cord. Trailing may be used independently for linear designs; it may be used as an edging around other stitches, and when worked in double lines it makes a firm framework for openwork filling stitches.

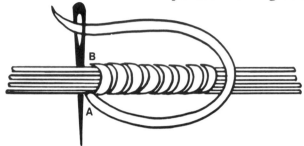

Trailing

Come up at A, go over the bundle of threads and down at B, almost in the same hole as A. Repeat, placing each stitch very close side by side.

Trailing is done most easily with the fabric stretched tightly in a frame. As you take each stitch, pull the bundle of couching threads firmly in the direction you are working. This helps to make the line smooth and firm, like a cord (right above).

Open fillings (see opposite)

Working on clearly woven even-weave linen, outline the shape with two lines of trailing, side by side, worked one after the other. Then cut and draw out the threads of the linen inside the shape. Cut two threads and leave two threads in both directions, just inside the trailing, to give an over-all lattice effect as in the enlargement at left.

With fine thread in a blunt needle, whip these fabric threads together as shown in both directions. Then following the directions for Squared Filling #3 (page 103) work over this mesh in both directions, to give the effect shown here.

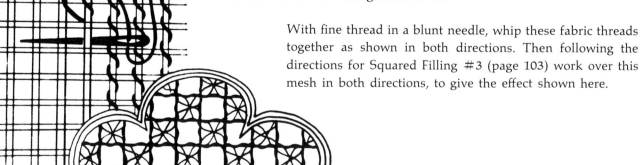

Openwork fillings are done by first completely outlining the shapes with two lines of trailing worked side by side. Then the linen is cut away close against the trailing, inside the shape, leaving alternate groups of threads uncut to form a trellis pattern. See sleeves and skirt, page 241. These threads are then whipped together to form a mesh into which other patterns can be woven, if desired.

Ornamental initial illustrating trailing, used as a pole screen, showing Mrs. Cabot's house in Murray Bay, Canada. *Worked by Mrs. F. Higginson Cabot and designed by the author*

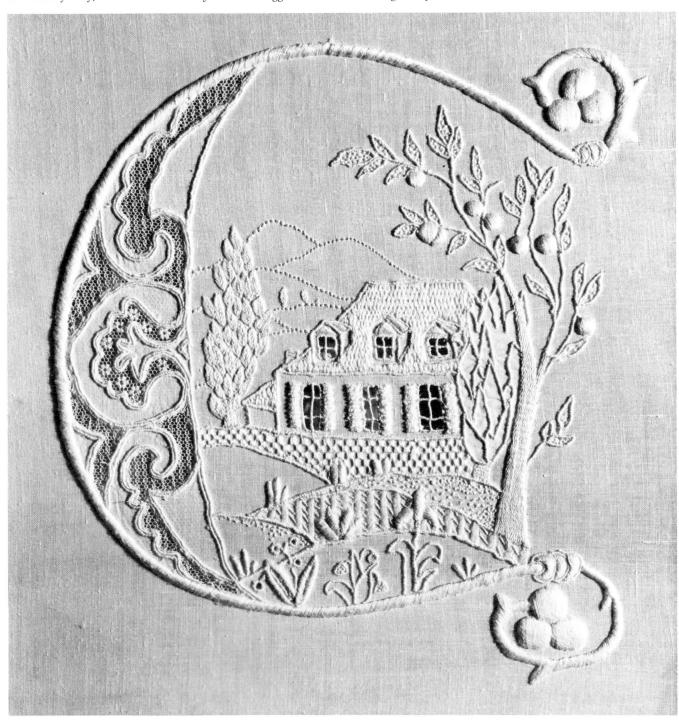

DRAWN THREAD BORDERS

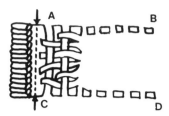

Determine the width and the length of the border you want to make, and draw one thread out of the linen on either side of it (at AB & CD). Then work a band of buttonhole (see page 70) between A and C, with loops facing inwards towards the border. Then work a second band at the other end. Next cut a vertical line between A & B (at arrows), carefully cutting each *horizontal* thread (*not* the upright, vertical ones). Repeat this at the other end, cutting close against the buttonhole stitching. Draw out the threads, one by one, until the border is composed only of vertical threads as at #2.

HEMSTITCHING

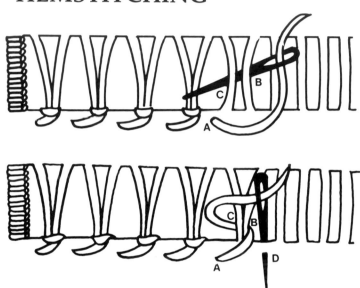

Secure the vertical threads of the border by hemstitching. Using a blunt, tapestry needle, come up at A, just underneath the border. Slide the needle under a bundle of two or more threads (from B to C).

Wrap round these threads and slide the needle into the fabric again at D as shown. Continue, repeating 2 and 3. Pull tight, and then hemstitch the opposite side of the border. Either hemstitch the same groups of threads to form a ladder effect, or split the groups, taking one bundle from one group and one from another, hemstitching them together on the opposite side.

NEEDLEWEAVING

Hemstitching the edges of the border is optional for needleweaving, it may just be left plain.

Prepare the border as in #1. Then, working on the reverse side, and using a blunt tapestry needle, weave over a bundle of approximately eight threads, then *under* a bundle of eight. The needle always goes down in the center of the two groups, first pointing from right to left, as shown, and then from left to right. Push the stitches together with the needle as you go, so that they are even and firmly packed. To end off, run the thread back under the stitching. Needleweaving may be done over three or even four groups of threads, or woven with many variations, some of which are shown on the opposite page. Each block of needleweaving shown here has been alternated by a single bundle of threads closely wrapped round and round.

Sampler of drawn thread borders. *Designed and worked by the author*

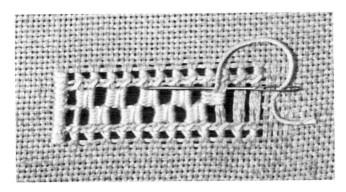

Needleweaving; in crochet cotton, above, and in coarse wool, right

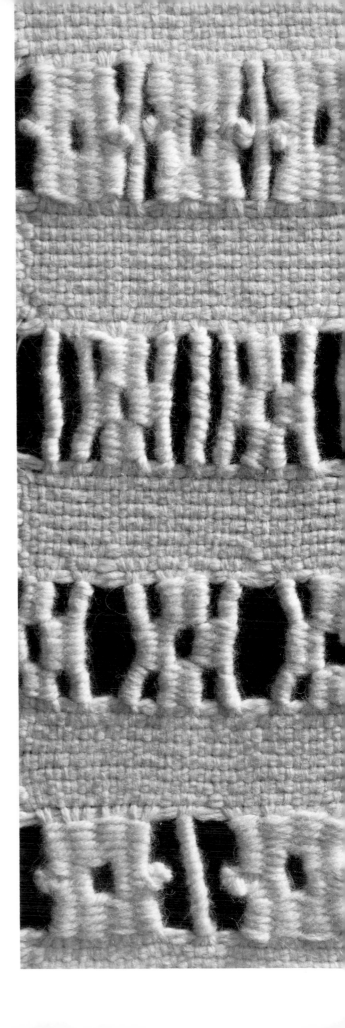

ABOVE. Dress with hand-worked panel of Broderie Anglaise. *Designed and worked by the author*
BELOW. Detail of a petticoat from a Roumanian peasant costume

BRODERIE ANGLAISE

The shapes to be cut are first strengthened by outlining them with running stitch around the edges. The fabric is then cut inside these shapes, leaving hems which are turned back and closely oversewn right over the running stitches. If the holes are so open that they might gape, they are held firm by working bars across the wider parts. Instead of simple oversewing (traditionally used in Broderie Anglaise and Danish Hedebo), sometimes buttonhole stitch is used instead. Richelieu is the name usually given to this type of work. The buttonhole bars of Richelieu may be further ornamented with small "picots," or decorative loops, which give the plain edges a frosty appearance (see page 285).

Round eyelets:

With a long enough thread to complete the working of a circle, make a line of running stitches all around the outline.

Leaving the thread hanging, cut four slits in the material from the center, out to the running stitch, as in the diagram.

Fold back these four flaps, one at a time, and closely sew over and over all around the edge, working right over the running stitches.

In the finished effect the oversewing stitches should make a smooth, narrow banding round the edge. Cut off the frayed turn backs on the wrong side. Small holes should not be cut, but pierced with the closed ends of a pointed pair of scissors or a stiletto, after outlining the eyelet with backstitch (page 84) instead of running.

FINE WHITE WORK

MATERIALS, THREADS, AND NEEDLES

Organdy, sheer Dacron, lawn, batiste, transparent loosely woven linen and wool, muslin, net—in fact any sheer fine white fabrics of varying opaqueness may be used for this embroidery.

Just as in coarse white, the most usual traditional thread for fine white is six-stranded embroidery floss, but there is no rule which says you may not use white angora, for instance, on organdy, for shadow work in bold scale. For pulled stitches, such as point Turc and point de Paris, the effect is made by holes. Therefore the thread should be fine and strong, and match the background fabric as closely as possible. Use a fine linen thread for this when you are working on an open weave linen, and a fine sewing silk or just one thread of six-stranded embroidery floss on lawn or organdy.

The needles you must use for punch stitch must be large enough to open holes in the fabric, so they should be quite heavy in comparison

TOP, LEFT TO RIGHT. Fine-weave casement cloth; medium-weave casement cloth; open mesh curtain fabric
BOTTOM, LEFT TO RIGHT. Dacron organdy; scrim; batiste

to the size of your thread and background material. As you are sewing through the same holes several times, a blunt needle is ideal to avoid splitting threads and to keep the openings clear. On organdy, a tapestry needle #18 is best for this stitch (see page 16).

The same blunt tapestry needle is good for darning stitches on net, so that you can weave easily between the mesh. If you are going to do fine trailing on batiste or lawn you will need a hair-like needle, perhaps a #10 crewel, to use with a single strand of embroidery floss.

Since your needles will depend on the kind of background material and threads you are using, a package of assorted size crewel or embroidery needles will be the best thing to keep on hand. Because crewel needles have long eyes, they are easy to thread even when they are very fine.

TRANSFERRING THE DESIGN

Transferring the design for fine white embroidery is very simple. You first outline the pattern on white paper with India ink or a fine felt marking pen. When it is completely dry, lay the fabric on top, positioning it correctly, secure it with masking tape, and lightly trace the design onto the fabric with a very hard pencil (2H). Always be sure the paper with your design is *white*. If your design is on tracing or layout paper, put several other layers of paper underneath it. The more contrast between the white paper and the black design lines you have, the more clearly will your design show through the material. Never use too sharp a pencil for transferring the design since it may cut through the cloth.

If your fabric is too opaque to use this tracing method, you could use the tissue paper technique explained on page 21.

If you are going to work on net you must transfer your design to oilcloth or similar vinyl or plastic material. (Plastic-coated shelf paper is good.) You can then baste your net to this and embroider the whole design, weaving and darning the stitches, following the outlines, which clearly show through the net. Your blunt needle will not penetrate the plastic because it glances off the shiny surface, and your work will not stretch out of shape because it is basted to this firm background. When you have completed your design, separate the plastic by removing the basting stitches. This same method is used for the openwork stitches of needlemade lace, known as point or Renaissance lace.

THE STITCHES

SURFACE STITCHES

Trailing
Seeding
Padded satin
Chain stitch
Shadow stitch
Shadow appliqué

OPEN STITCHES

Pulled stitches (point Turc
    and point de Paris)
Darning on net
    or tulle embroidery
Net inserts
Needlemade lace
    (Renaisance or point lace)

SURFACE STITCHES

Trailing (page 266), seeding (page 107), and padded satin stitch (page 49) are excellent when used in combination with one another, and really look beautiful on both opaque and sheer fabrics. Seeding on transparent fabrics forms a shadow effect as the thread passes from one stitch to another on the back. The result is white close stitching instead of the light speckling, formed when seeding is worked on an opaque ground.

One of the great advantages of working on sheer fabric is that you can obtain shadow effects. Certain stitches give you a clear silhouette which stands out beautifully against the transparent background. Shadow stitch (a row of close herringbone stitches worked on the reverse side), is one of the best of these.

Shadow stitch is done by working close herringbone (also known as double back stitch) across the area of design, on the reverse side of the fabric. The stitches, crossing on the back, give a solid or lacy white effect, depending on how closely they are worked.

DOUBLE BACKSTITCH or SHADOW STITCH

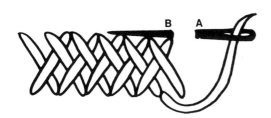

On the reverse side of the design, work a row of herringbone stitches. Take one stitch from right to left (A to B) on the lower outline of the design, and repeat it at the upper edge, going right into same hole formed by the previous stitch.

White shadow stitch combined with colored silk on organdy tablecloth. *Designed and worked by the author*

Reverse side

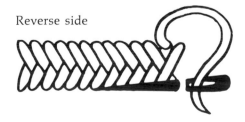

The effect is best if the stitches are taken very close together, as shown here.

When worked on sheer material, the effect on the right side is an opaque band bordered by a row of back stitches, above and below. The closer the stitches, the more opaque and distinct this band will be.

Right side

CHAIN STITCH AND SHADOW APPLIQUÉ

Chain stitch in white cotton provides a bold contrast when worked on a sheer background such as ninon, organdy, or filmy batiste. A similar effect can be obtained by stitching another layer of the same fabric either to the front or the back of the background material. This is known as shadow appliqué

Shadow appliqué is done by basting another piece of the background cloth or another white material of contrasting texture such as satin, to the *reverse* side of the transparent background. On the *right* side of the fabric, the design is then outlined with point Turc or point de Paris (pages 278, 279). Finally the extra material is cut away close to this stitching on the back.

The word shadow seems a misnomer for these techniques, for it is actually the surrounding fabric which appears to be shadowed, contrasting with the whiter effect of the design.

Detail of apron in Ayrshire work with bold chain stitch in cotton on lawn, and net inserts. *Author's Collection*

Shadow appliqué with point de Paris outlining the shapes. *Author's Collection*
(see page 278)

OPEN STITCHES

Point Turc and point de Paris (Turkish stitch and pin, or Paris, stitch) can be done either on open weave linen or on any fine materials such as lawn, muslin, organdy, or silk.

The effect of both point Turc and point de Paris is a series of openwork holes made by pulling the fabric tightly together with fine thread. These holes then become dominant and the connecting stitches almost invisible (see page 280).

POINT DE PARIS

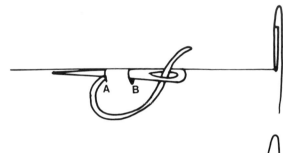

This stitch is particularly useful for holding 2 pieces of fabric together, so it is shown here used for a hem.

Using a blunt tapestry needle, come up at A under the hem, go in at B and return again at A in the same hole.

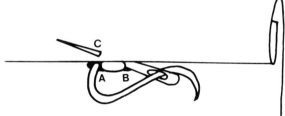

Go in again at B, and come up at C, directly above A in the hem.

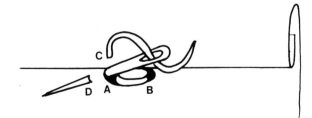

Return again to A, and come up at D.

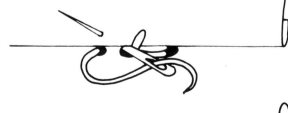

Now repeat steps 1, 2 & 3, wrapping each stitch tightly to form large holes.

Shows finished effect.

Plate 17. Persian horseman, silk and gold on damask. *Designed and worked by Mrs. Daryl Parshall*

Plate 18.   Handbag in gold bullion and silk; butterfly in silk and Japanese gold
(shown in skeins at right)

Plate 19.   Rooster in silk laid work and long and short stitches. *Designed and worked by the author*

Plate 22. English spring flowers, with lines from "Love's Labour's Lost." *Designed by the author for* The Erica Wilson Creative Needlework Society

Plate 23.   ABOVE. Pillow in wool and cotton thread. *Designed by Linda Ormesson*

BELOW. Timmy Willie in a peapod. *Both designed for* The Erica Wilson Creative Needlework Society

Plate 24. Puffy couching, Turkey work, French knots on stalks and raised stem stitch give a three-dimensional effect. *Designed and worked by the author*

PUNCH STITCH or POINT TURC

1

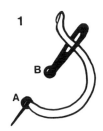
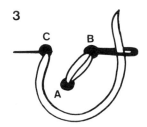

Using a blunt needle and fine thread come up at A, go in at B (above and to the right of A). Then return to A again. (The needle is slanting.)

2

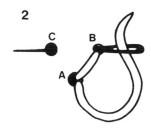

With the needle horizontal, go in at B again and come up in C, level with B (but beyond A). The distance from A, B, and C should be the same, so that they form a triangle.

3

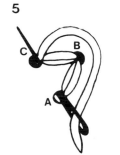

Repeat #2, going from B to C again, with the needle horizontal.

4

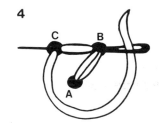

Take this BC once again, forming a double stitch. (Again the needle is horizontal.)

5

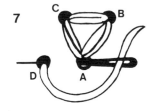

Go in at A and up at C.
(The needle is slanting.)

Go in at A and up at D, level with A, but beyond C so that AB, BC, CA, and AD are all the same size stitches. (The needle is again horizontal.)

6

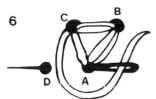

7

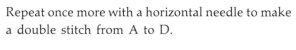

Repeat #6 going from A to D with the needle horizontal.

Repeat once more with a horizontal needle to make a double stitch from A to D.

8

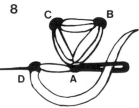

Repeat steps 1 to 8 to make a line of stitches. This diagram shows the way in which the stitch is worked.

9

#10 shows the finished effect. Once the stitch has been mastered as in #9, pull each stitch tightly to open large holes in the fabric. The stitches should be so tight they almost disappear, and the entire effect is formed by the holes between.

10

Point Turc may be worked in individual lines, or rows may be worked back and forth to fill an area. If one line is worked over a flat seam, the raw edges may be cut away so close to the stitching on either side that the seam appears only as a row of decorative openwork.

Point de Paris is most suitable for hems, and is particularly effective in shadow appliqué; it borders the applied shapes with a row of openwork holes.

In order to hold the holes firmly apart, each stitch must be wrapped twice. Therefore, it is best to first practice point Turc and point de Paris with heavier thread, working loosely, so that you can clearly see each stitch and master the repeated movements of the needle.

When you have learned how to do them, work with a single strand of embroidery floss and a large blunt needle and *pull tightly!* If you are working on lawn or organdy, use a tapestry needle #18, but once you have realized the effect you want to achieve you can find the needle which best suits the fabric you are using. Because you must pull tightly, work in your hand, wrapping the material firmly round your finger to hold it taut as you stitch. The lightness of the background fabric, the large size of the needle, the fineness of the working thread and the firm way you pull your stitches, all control the size of the holes.

Point Turc combined with chain stitch. *Designed and worked by author*

To make this shadow appliqué pillow, first cut a rectangle of white felt to fit within the finished shape. Fold the rectangle in half, in half again, and in half one more time. Then cut semicircles and triangles out of the edges of the folded felt, just as children make paper doilies. (If you prefer, practice with paper first!)

Open up the felt fretwork, and lay it between two layers of organdy. Baste all three layers together, and work Point Turc around the outlines, close against the felt, securing it firmly between the organdy. (Point de Paris was used to surround the outer edges.) Finally, embellish the pillow with whipped spider's webs (page 98) and spider's webs worked inside Broderie Anglaise eyelets (pages 271 and 285).

DARNING ON NET, TULLE EMBROIDERY

Mark out your design with a permanent felt-tipped pen on any stiff, shiny blue paper. A suggestion might be to use self-adhesive wallpaper (without removing the protective backing) or heavy duty plastic-coated shelf paper.

When the design is thoroughly dry, firmly baste your net to this paper and proceed to weave the outlines and patterns, following the lines which show clearly through the net. Use six-strand embroidery floss, varying the number of threads according to the effect you want, lacy or bold. Use a blunt needle which will slide easily over the plastic, and between the threads of the net without splitting them. Outline the shapes first with running stitch, using as many as six strands of cotton for a heavier effect. Then fill the shapes with geometric patterns, counting the threads of the mesh and using only one or two strands of cotton for a lacy effect.

Pattern #1

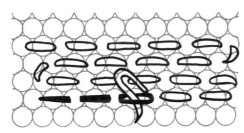

Care must be taken in starting and ending threads, as all joining will show clearly. End off if necessary by running a few threads back beside the ones you have just taken on the outlines. Preferably join by making a lace knot (page 288). This means you can join a new thread to your working one and continue stitching. The tiny knot will disappear invisibly into the embroidery.

Pattern #2

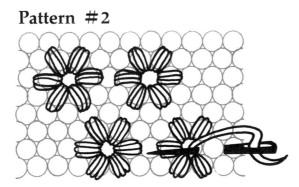

Pattern #3

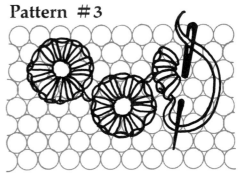

Pattern #4

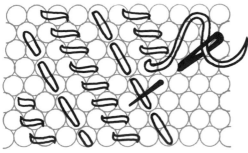

Pattern #5

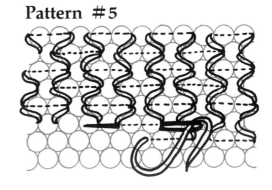

Darning on net. A frame is useful for working the filling
stitches. *Designed and worked by author*

NEEDLEMADE LACE

The variations of needlemade lace are too many to mention, but the simplest, point or Renaissance lace, is composed of braids which are knotted and looped together by buttonhole stitch.

Machine-made braids, which were available in the nineteenth century, but are now hard to get, may be replaced by making your own braids of hairpin lace or buying ribbons.

Start by outlining the design, with double lines, on blue plastic-coated paper, as on page 282. Then baste the braids or ribbons down within these lines, folding and tacking them where necessary. Then work button-hole bars and spiders' webs to connect them, using a blunt needle, and embroidery floss or crochet cotton. Connecting stark white braids or ribbons with these bold simple stitches gives a dramatic effect, but alternatively all kinds of lace stitches, based on buttonhole stitch, can be worked to give a delicate or more solid effect, depending on the thickness of the thread.

Renaissance lace mats with braids held together by looped stitches and spiders' webs in coarse cotton thread. *Author's Collection*

NEEDLEMADE LACE/Spider's Web

Baste the ribbons, braids, or bands of hairpin lace to firm paper, (such as vinyl, coated shelf paper), in any openwork pattern (see opposite).
Fold or pleat the braids if necessary to form smooth curves, (at A, B and C) and hem them together where they join each other (at arrow).
Then with a blunt needle and firm thread (such as buttonhole twist), connect the braids with bars. The circle shown here has threads crisscrossing the center (from D to E, F to G, etc.) so that a spider's web can be woven. (see page 98, diagrams 3, 4, or 5). Conceal the threads by running through the braids as invisibly as possible from one bar to the other, and join on new threads with a lace knot (page 288) to save ending off.

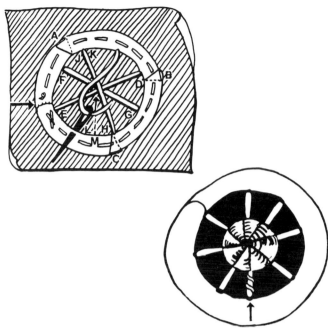

Shows the finished spider's web. To pass invisibly from one place to another in the openwork part of the design, wrap the working thread several times around one of the bars (at arrow).
When the whole design is finished, cut the basting threads to free the needlemade lace.
(Cut them on the reverse side of your paper backing, to avoid cutting your stitches!)

NEEDLEMADE LACE with Buttonhole Bars and Picots

First baste the braids in position. Using a blunt needle, connect the braids with three bars, ending the final bar on the left, so that you can work close buttonhole stitching over the bars to the center. Slide the needle downwards into the last buttonhole stitch, and twist the working thread three (or more) times around it, as shown.

Draw through, holding the twists between finger and thumb, just like a bullion knot (see page 106). Then slide the needle upwards through the same buttonhole stitch, and pull through. Finish buttonholing the bar right across.

Shows the finished picot with the completed buttonholed bar. Buttonhole bars with picots may be used in cut work, as edgings, or with any open work or surface stitching as well as needlemade lace.

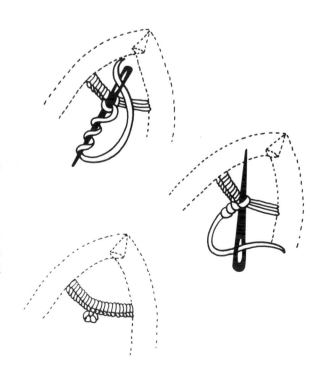

"To grow," wall hanging based on button-hole lace, using wool and linen threads. *Designed and worked by Virginia Bath, courtesy of The Art Institute of Chicago*

DETACHED BUTTONHOLE FILLING for Needlemade Lace

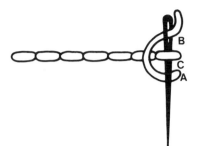

To work this stitch on fabric, first make a border of back stitch, as shown. For needlemade lace, take your stitches right into the braids themselves. This stitch is worked entirely free from the background. Using a blunt needle, come up at A on the right. Go through the first back stitch or braid from B to C. With the thread *under* the needle, just like a buttonhole stitch, draw gently through.

Repeat #1 to the left.

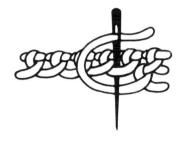

At left is the complete line, going down into the fabric or braid on the last stitch, to secure it.

At left is a second row, working again from right to left, and going into each stitch of the previous line, as shown.

For variation, a completely different effect can be formed when you work the first row from right to left, and the second from left to right, as shown here.

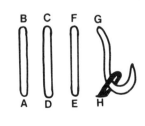

KNOTTED GROUND and DRAWN THREAD BORDER

First lay parallel threads across the area to be covered, coming up at A, down at B, up at C, etc.

Using a blunt tapestry needle, slide under the first bar from right to left. Take the working thread over, then under the needle and draw through, pulling gently upwards to form a knot.

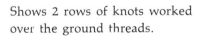

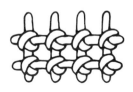

Repeat on the next bar.

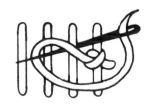

Shows 2 rows of knots worked over the ground threads.

The same knot can be used to hold a bundle of threads together on a drawn thread border. Secure the thread in the center of the buttonholing at either side of the border. (see page 268)

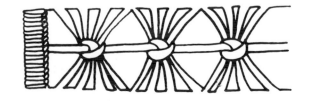

LACE KNOT

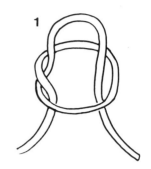

Begin as though you were making an ordinary knot in the thread, but instead of pulling the end through, pull through a loop as shown.

Push the end of the new thread to be joined through the top of this loop.

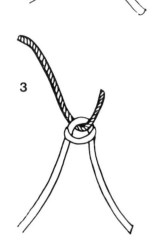

Holding the new thread firmly, pull the loop of the first thread tight.

When it is quite tight, pull sharply on *both* ends of the first thread. You will hear a little click as the new thread pops through the knot as shown here.

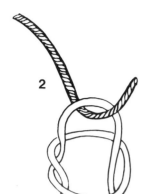

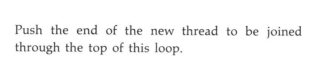

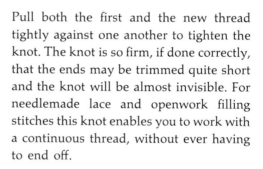

Pull both the first and the new thread tightly against one another to tighten the knot. The knot is so firm, if done correctly, that the ends may be trimmed quite short and the knot will be almost invisible. For needlemade lace and openwork filling stitches this knot enables you to work with a continuous thread, without ever having to end off.

FINISHING

Since white work is generally soft, pliable, or delicate it does not need blocking. Instead, it is best to soak it in cold water, and while it is still wet, press it face downward into a thick cloth. You can cover a Turkish towel or a blanket with a smooth hand towel or a sheet, and use this as a thick pad underneath.

STUMP WORK

Court gown at the wedding of the Prince of Orange to the daughter of
George II:

*Embroidered with chenille, the pattern a large stone vase filled with ramping flowers,
that spread over a breadth of the petticoat from the bottom to the top; between each
vase was a pattern of gold shells and foliage, embossed, and most heavily rich, the
gown was white satin, embroidered also with chenille mixed with gold ornaments,
no vases on the sleeve, but two or three on the tail!*

Side panel from a Stump work box shown on page 303, using stitches such as Ceylon and Trellis (see pages 317 and 318). *Victoria and Albert Museum*

CURIOUSER and curiouser!" said Alice, following the twisting path of the White Rabbit. This might be the perfect way to describe the "raised" or "embossed" work of the seventeenth and eighteenth centuries, which later became known, strangely enough, as "stump work."

The raised work done in England at this time, where it seemed to be particularly fashionable, consisted mostly of mirror frames, boxes with compartments for toilet and writing articles, with perhaps even a secret drawer, and pictures and small bags. These were done in the very finest of stitches, with tremendous virtuosity and finesse, often by young girls who had suddenly discovered the delight of stitching these charming little motifs in relief on white satin.

The designs were often similar, nearly always consisting of two central figures on either side of a fountain, the surrounding garden being a space-filling of flowers, fruits, plants, and animals, all happily oblivious of scale. Into these charming formalized gardens went ladies and gentlemen all looking remarkably alike with their ruffs and bodices, brocaded skirts and pantaloons, whether they were supposed to represent James I and his Queen, Susannah and the Elders, the Five Senses, or even the Four Continents.

Why this raised embroidery should suddenly have become all the rage and why it should have been called "stump work" are mysteries fascinating to explore.

Two explanations for the name are generally given. One is that, because the raised effect was sometimes obtained by covering little box-wood molds with stitching, the technique came to be called "embroidery on the stump." Or, perhaps because patterns printed on satin were available to the embroideress for the first time, "embroidery on the stamp" eventually became "stump work." Neither of these explanations seems totally satisfactory, however. For the curious, a third is worthy of some sleuth work. *Estompé* is the French word for embossed. In 1678 the phrase stump drawing—directly derived from *estompé*—was introduced into the Oxford

Dictionary for the first time. Stump drawing was a form of shaded pencil sketching which gave to the flat picture the effect of high relief. Pencil-shaped cylinders of paper, soft leather or India rubber, called stumps, were used to rub down hard pencil lines and produce soft rounded effects. It seems logical to suppose, or at any rate interesting to conjecture, that a new and fashionable word describing drawing in relief might also have been borrowed to describe embossed embroidery. It was only after this date, in the eighteenth century, that raised or embossed needlework became generally known as "stump work."

By the eighteenth century, raised embroidery with gold threads,

Scenes from the Biblical story of David in typical 17th century style. *Victoria and Albert Museum*

The Lord Chancellor's Purse, in a design dating back to the 17th century. *Crown Copyright*

pearls, and jewels had become a tradition in France, where almost every girl seemed to have been born with a needle in her hand. As early as the twelfth century, French cathedrals and churches were so numerous and their contents so rich that a popular contemporary phrase was "happy as God in France." The lavish splendor of the court of Le Roi Soleil had not subsided when Louis XV took his place, and embroidery was used to enrich everything: no longer was it restricted to ecclesiastical use. In fact, Louis XV himself claimed that he could do better embroidery than anyone else in his entire kingdom!

This description by the Marquise de Créqui of the dress of one of the ladies of Louis' court shows to what lengths (or rather, heights!) raised work was sometimes taken. "The dress was of rich red velvet. The folds of the ample skirt were held in position by brooches of Dresden china made in the semblance of butterflies. On a front panel of the dress was embroidered a design showing an orchestra complete with musical instruments. *The latter were worked in relief* and the musicians embroidered on cloth of silver were arranged in six rows. Within the skirt was a hoop of nearly six yards in circumference."

English ladies, intrigued by a technique so new to them, developed a completely original approach in design and concept, in the same way as their Colonial cousins, who were transplanting the English crewelwork into their own American idiom at almost the same time.

Although the designs and techniques of English stump work seem unique, there are several logical reasons for its development apart from its continental influence. Gardens, samplers, and pattern books, for instance, all played their part in inspiring the designs, while in stitchery the influence may have come from raised embroidered book bindings, canvas work appliquéd to velvet, and needlepoint lace, with its variety of stitches worked free from the background fabric.

First of all, the fascination of the embroideress for the garden setting is better understood if we realize that in the seventeenth century everything was relatively new to the young girl, whose preoccupation was translating this excitement into silken stitches on satin. Until then, gardens had been cultivated exclusively at monasteries or castles, and even when they became part of the surroundings of the manor house, they were reserved at first for herbs and vegetables.

Because "sallads" were so popular, "longwort, liverwort and purslane" were grown together with yarrow, sorrel, and borage, which caused Parkinson, in 1629, to suggest that the kitchen garden be removed from the front of the house, "for the many different scents which arrise from the herbes such as cabbages, onions, etc., are scarce well pleasing to perfume the lodgings of any house." However, "sallets," as they were also called, included the candied petals of roses, violets, cowslips, and strawberry leaves, and it is easy to see how these favorites would take their place alongside such sophisticated flowers as the opium poppy from the Middle East, the sunflower from Mexico, potato and tobacco plants from the New World, and the tulip, newly arrived from Istambul via Holland. The Elizabethan flower gardens, with their formal borders and hedges of musk, lavender, and rosemary, their new flowers—hyacinths, pinks, marigolds, and iris—all blending their fragrances around a central fountain and pool "whose shaking crystal was a perfect mirror for all its other beauties," could rightly inspire Sir William Cecil to say: "For if delight may provoke men's labour, what greater delight is there than to behold the earth apparelled with plants, as with a robe of imbroidered works, set with orient pearles and garnished with great diversitie of rare and costly jewels."

And so, with great "diversitie," the stump-work garden would be planned, peopled with figures whose faces were sometimes raised with sculptured wooden molds under the silken stitching, whose stomachers or bodices, padded with wool or horsehair, often surmounted skirts in brilliant petit point. These were embroidered separately, then gathered or pleated, and attached only at the waist, so that the skirt could be lifted to disclose a froth of lace petticoats and perhaps a pair of golden shoes. Butterflies, flitting among the flowers, would have two sets of wings—one embroidered flat on the satin background and the other free-standing in lacy buttonhole

A garden scene from Petrus Crescentius *Opus Ruralium Commodarum. British Museum*

Left and right side
of an 18th century
mirror frame

stitches. Peapods that could be raised to show the tiny seed pearl peas within, caterpillars in fluffy chenille threads, and of course the fountain in gold or silver bullion, were all primly surrounded by the rainbow-hued flowers.

The young lady who loved stump work must necessarily have learned the basic stitches on her sampler when she was a child—cross stitch, then possibly tent stitch, Florentine and rococo stitches, or even plaited braid or chain stitch in gold thread on the linen. She might have interspersed these with panels of cut and drawn work, or made a separate record of those in a white work sampler.

Indeed, it was the custom to teach girls their alphabet at the same time as needlework. As early as the seventeenth century, the importance of this exercise in their education, and the extreme youth of the students, are shown by this extract from a letter written by the Countess of Traquair. Practically penniless and in exile in Paris, she nonetheless struggled to provide her daughter, Lady Anne Maxwell, with the "necessarys." These were masters ". . . of whom she has 4, a dancing master, a singing master, a harpsicall master and a French master. For since perhaps she may never have wherwithall to portion her, she stands more in need of good qualitys, so that I am willing to squeeze it out, even out of necessarys to myselfe, thinking her education preferable to my wants. . . . But between all these her day is pretty well employd; for she has her English reading, and her sampler, and has done already the 24* letters twice over, both sides alike, and all her masters are satisfyd with her." All this, and Lady Anne not yet five years old!

Yet there are no samplers entirely worked in raised embroidery remaining to us today. This is probably because the stump work was almost a sampler itself: a progression from the basic stitches to a chef d'oeuvre which would incorporate the more complex techniques from many types of embroidery. It was almost as though the young lady, carefully schooled from her early years, would graduate with a beautifully worked cabinet or mirror frame which would show all her skill in one magnificent piece.

One part of this grand project with which she did not have to struggle was drawing her own design. Numerous herbals, gardening books, and bestiaries, even designs on separate sheets, were available to the

*I and J and U and V were interchangeable in early alphabets.

Elizabethan embroiderer for the first time, to arrange as she liked. Many of the plates from the few rare books which have survived are pricked for copying.

> Here followeth certaine Patternes of Cut-workes newly invented and never published before. Also sundry sorts of spots as Flowers, Birdes and Fishes, etc., and will fitly serve to be wrought some with gould some with silke, some with crewell in coullers, or otherwise at your pleasure. (London, printed in Shoe Lane at the Sign of the Faulcon, by Richard Shorleyker.)

> A catalogue of Plates, and pictures that are printed and sold by Peter Stent dwelling at the sign of the white Horfe in Gilt Spur Street betwixt Newgate and Py Corner. (1662)

Just as gardens, samplers, and pattern books played their part in forming the design for stump work, so three styles of needlework originating in the sixteenth century all contributed to the development of its stitchery.

The first was the fashion for stitched book bindings. One of the earliest known embroidered books was given as a New Year's gift to Queen Elizabeth in 1583. It was described as "a large Byble in Englysshe covered with crymson vellat alover embrodered with venys gold and seade perle."* Later book bindings embroidered in silk on satin were found to wear much longer if seed pearls and raised gold were combined with the flat stitching. In many cases, the gold used was "purl" or "bullion," a silver gilt wire coil, which the embroideress would cut into short lengths and sew down like a bead, threading the needle through the center of the coiled tube (see page 206).

This raised effect gave the book covers a tremendous richness, and several that have been left to us today are in perfect condition because they in turn were enclosed in embroidered bags to protect them. The gold bullion embroidery worked on book bindings also was used for stump work. Fortunately, like the books, a very few embroidered cabinets were preserved in specially made cases, which enables us to see even today the brilliant sparkle of the gold thread, instead of a tarnished and lusterless gray.

A second influence, which inadvertently gave the effect of slightly raised relief, and which may have made embroideresses realize the potential

*Now in the Bodleian Library, Oxford.

The Metropolitan Museum of Art, gift of Mrs. Thomas Watson

The Bible in embroidered crimson velvet presented to Queen Elizabeth I. *Bodleian Library*

A book of prayers, handwritten by Elizabeth I as a child, with a cover embroidered by her in silver and light blue. A New Year's gift to her stepmother, Queen Katherine Parr. The pansies are padded and raised. *Bodleian Library*

of three-dimensional work, was the fashion for applying needlepoint canvas to velvet. This innovation, possibly brought to England by Mary Queen of Scots, cleverly avoided the tedium of many hours spent in embroidering the canvas background. Beautifully stylized flowers and plants, just like the cuttings or "slips" which would be used to propagate shrubs and plants in the new gardens, were worked first in petit point in silk and then applied to velvet or silk material and finally edged and connected with gold threads. The novel idea of cutting out the canvas work and applying it to a soft material was particularly suitable for curtains surrounding four-poster beds because not only was it quicker, but the glow of velvet and gold contrasted beautifully with the completely worked needlepoint valances around the top of the bed. Several hangings and long cushions, done in this way by

Needlepoint slips appliquéd on velvet and outlined with gold thread. *The Metropolitan Museum of Art, Rogers Fund, 1920*

Italian lace in buttonhole stitch with free-standing details. Figures standing on Hollie point ground. *Victoria and Albert Museum*

Left front of a bodice. The flowers are in trellis stitch, very similar to hollie point. *The Metropolitan Museum of Art, Rogers Fund, 1923*

Mary Queen of Scots, with the help of the "broudistars" or embroiderers she brought from France, still remain at Hardwick Hall in England to this day.

A letter written in 1656 describes how the work was done:

> But as for the Carpet and Chayr and stoole, I should despayre of seeing an end of them if John Best had not found out a way to ease my wife. But now John takes these borders which my mother wrought and cutts out every single Flower and Leafe, and when they are so voyded, he draws some Turning Stalkes for my wife to work, upon which he will so place the Flowers and Leaves that it shall seem as if all had been wrought together and be perfectly suitable to the pattern on the Bedd.

The fashion for needlepoint lace was a third inspiration to the embroideress about to embark on her raised work masterpiece. This Italian lace, done with a needle in many forms of buttonhole stitch, was made fashionable in France by Catherine de Medici, to whom Vinciolo dedicated his book of needlelace patterns in 1587.

One closely worked version of buttonhole lace was hollie point (see White Work, page 251). Its name was probably derived from "holy" point, perhaps because it was a stitch used extensively for white ecclesiastical vestments, and was originally brought back from the Holy Land. In 1640, the Campbell inventory lists "Holland schettis [sheets] 2 pair, 1 pair schewit with hollie work," which points to the fact that hollie point was used a great deal for household items, too. It was this stitch, when closely worked in silk to resemble petit point, which became the ideal close covering for the raised parts of the stump work designs. See opposite.

Hollie point is one of the stitches used in stump work whose name we recognize today; trellis, twisted braid, bullion knots, and couching are others. But many, listed under "The School Mistris Terms of Art for all her ways of sowing," in an English encyclopedia of 1686, have vanished. What are the smarting Whip stitch, the Finny stitch, the Virgin's Device, the needlework Pearl, the Mow stitch, or the Bread stitch? The names alone inspire us to heights of fancy as to their actual appearance, just as we wonder about such mysterious hues as murray, tawnye, ladies blushe, pound cythrone, or horse flesh, colors which must have rivaled in brilliance their exotic names.

The same encyclopedia also catalogues "terms and things to work with" in the art and skill of stump work, including

Needles of several sizes	Slave silk
Cruel of all colours	Naples silk
Silk sowing of all colours	Fin white Alcomy Wyre
A Tent	Ising Glass
A samcloth, a cloth to sew on	Gum Arabic
A Canvice cloth	

Somehow, the naïveté of the English stump work with its formal treatment of stylized figures, plants, and animals gives it a certain charm and quaintness. Some of the later designs, however, became more and more flamboyant, eventually imitating sculpture to such a degree that whole gardens were made free-standing with the use of wire and other threads. Gathering dust through the ages, their sparkling gold and silver tarnished to a dull charcoal color, these products of so much effort and dedication can only fascinate us today with the delicacy and variety of their stitchery. But occasionally one beautifully preserved piece will fortify our imagination as to what the others must have been. Such a one is the small cabinet in the Metropolitan Museum of Art (see plate 20).

Another magnificent example is a sixteenth-century English bodice known as the Devereux heirloom. Worked on cloth of silver entirely in gold, silver, and silk thread, with a twining design of roses, iris, carnations, peapods, cornflowers, columbine, and forget-me-nots, all interspersed with caterpillars, birds, and butterflies, it really combines the techniques of canvas, silk and crewel embroidery, as well as raised work. The stitches used are Gobelin and tent as well as buttonhole and chain, using silver and gold wire. The bodice was said to have been sent to Queen Elizabeth by the Countess of Leicester when her son, the Earl of Essex, was awaiting execution in the Tower of London.

Incidentally, this was not the only gift of embroidery designed to soften Elizabeth's heart, for Mary Queen of Scots was always planning to this end. As the ambassador reported to the French king: "The Queen of Scots, your sister-in-law, is very well, and yesterday, I presented on her behalf a skirt of crimson satin worked with silver, very fine, and all worked with her hand, to the Queen of England, to whom the present was very

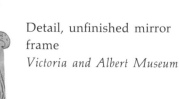

Detail, unfinished mirror frame
Victoria and Albert Museum

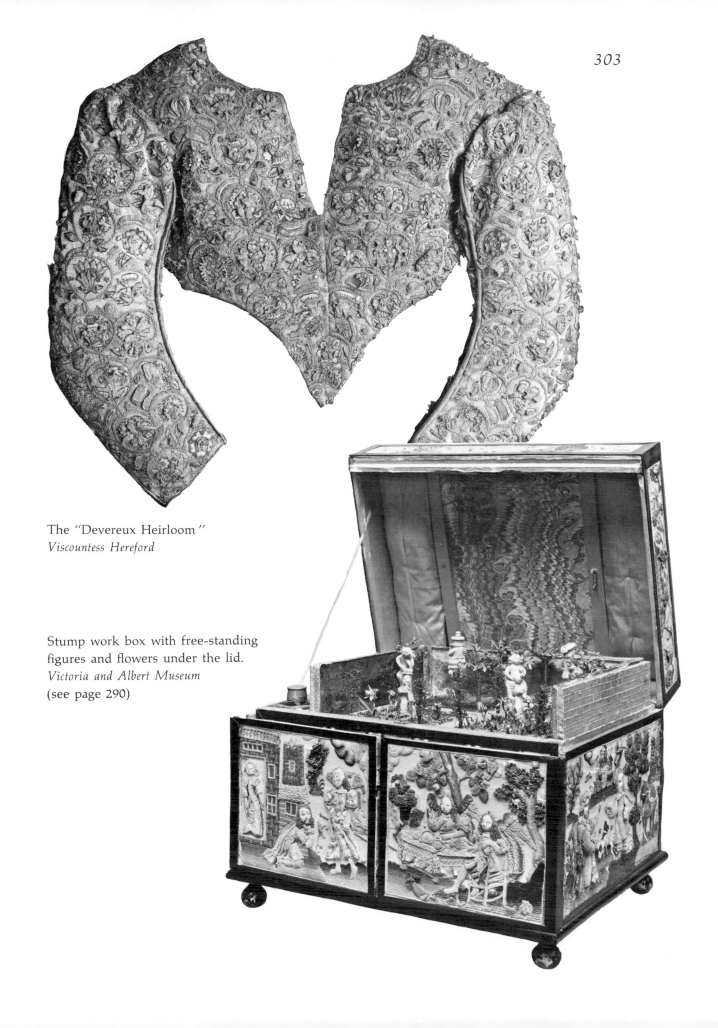

The *"Devereux Heirloom"*
Viscountess Hereford

Stump work box with free-standing
figures and flowers under the lid.
Victoria and Albert Museum
(see page 290)

agreeable for she found it very nice and has prized it much, and it seems to me I found her much softened towards her." Unfortunately for Mary, and for the Countess of Leicester, this laborious handiwork and the ambassador's high hopes were for nought, for while Elizabeth's heart may have been softened, her resolve was rarely undone.

Still another charming piece is an unfinished mirror frame in the Victoria and Albert Museum. Since the frame is in this state, it is possible to get an idea of how the shapes were gradually built up. The stitches are trellis, long and short, couching, bullion knots, and padded satin, with appliqués of embroidered satin and rice stitch on canvas (see page 302).

Tastes change. Toward the end of the 1700's, for an unknown reason, the fashion of stump work suddenly vanished, never to appear in the same form again. Its nearest counterpart, however, would be the raised wool embroidery of the Victorian era, which is fascinating in its own way and considerably bolder in its technique, since it uses only wool threads.

Raised wool embroidery became very popular in the United States as well as in Europe, which is interesting because so few examples of the earlier stump work with silk and metal threads have been found in

America (opposite). This may have been because of the difficulty in obtaining the suitable materials in the eighteenth century, for while the English lady was stitching with imported silk and gold threads, the Colonial embroideress was spinning and dyeing her own wool and weaving her own linen for crewelwork.

When in the nineteenth century Berlin wool work became so popular (see page 129), special sheep were bred in Saxony to provide the correct soft merino wool which could be dyed with jewel colors, and this same wool was also used for the raised embroidery. Pictures with sprays and baskets of flowers done in this manner were mounted in deep shadow boxes so that the glass would not crush the raised stitches. Unfortunately, the wool was beloved by moths, who often managed to penetrate the sealed containers. Unfortunately, too, the wool often has faded, but its mellowed

Victorian raised wool.
Author's Collection

softness today is perhaps more attractive than the original harsh contrasts caused by the newly invented aniline dyes.

These raised wool pictures are similar to the designs in Turkey work of the same period. The Turkey work designs were always done on canvas, and the stitching was clipped to follow the modeling of the subject. This was so finely done it often resembled velvet, and was sometimes called "plush" stitch instead of Turkey work.

When one realizes that stump work and raised embroidery were the culmination of so many styles and influences, one can see that this combination of different stitches is rather like a historical forerunner of today's mixed media (see page 351).

Today, stump work is enjoying a revival, but in a form that would be unrecognizable to the ladies who made the original beauty boxes and mirror frames of the seventeenth century. Bold hangings with raised appliqués, and crewel-embroidered panels with all kinds of raised wool stitches, are being done by embroiderers, and painters developing the technique of collage are experimenting with threads and fabrics, so that their medium sometimes overlaps into true embroidery.

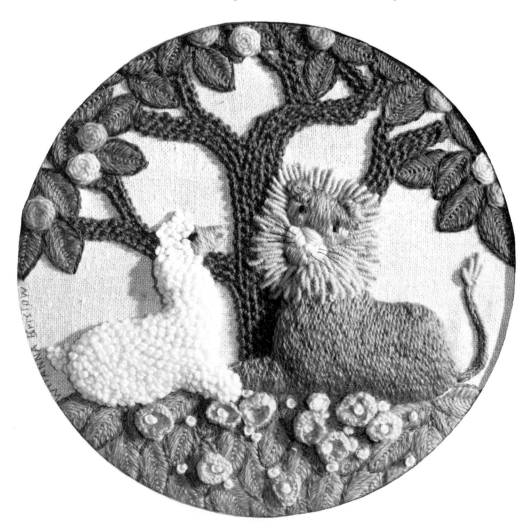

TO BEGIN

There are all kinds of possibilities for contemporary stump work; appliquéd fabrics can be raised by padding, raised wool embroidery can be done with stitches such as buttonhole, trellis, and Turkey work, and an almost unlimited variety of three-dimensional embroideries can be made from combinations of both these techniques. You could cover any sort of box, from a magnificent jewel box or sewing cabinet, to a pill box (plate 21). Jewelry itself, a very special eyeglass case, a handbag, a mirror frame, a tabletop under glass, or a picture or panel that could become a conversation piece, all can be subjects for the experimental needle.

MATERIALS, THREADS, AND TRANSFERRING THE DESIGN

Because the field is open to such a wide variety of effects, the choice of materials is almost unlimited. Silk, satin, antique satin, felt, or even leather and suede, needlepoint canvas, linen, cotton, and wool may be stitched with silk, wool, cotton, beads, or metal threads. Therefore, all the materials listed for the different techniques in this book may be incorporated in this medium.

In order to raise the fabrics and stitches you will first need muslin for lining the padded area. For the padding itself you can use regular cotton from the drugstore, or the Dacron wadding used for stuffing pillows. Even more resilient is the lamb's wool sold in some drugstores for protecting corns! You can also use felt or string to raise the stitches, as described in gold embroidery on pages 203 and 204.

Transferring the design will depend on the choice of fabrics and therefore you can select the method that seems most suitable from the listing on pages 18-23.

Because the stitches are to be raised, you should work on a square frame or on a hoop frame which is large enough to enclose the whole design (page 25). Besides being extremely difficult to push down over the embroidery, a small hoop might crush the padded stitches as you move it from one area of the design to another.

OPPOSITE. The lion and the lamb. Note raised cup stitch flowers (see page 318). *Designed and worked by Wilanna Bristow*

THE STITCHES AND TECHNIQUES

Traditional stump work was done on white satin with fine silken stitches, using gold threads, such as bullion and velvety chenille as well as silks. Faces and hands were raised with wooden molds and all kinds of lacy stitches such as hollie point and trellis, which were raised by paddings, were combined with stitches such as long and short and laid, worked flat on the background material.

Similar to stump work were the Victorian raised wool embroideries with fascinating three-dimensional realism, done with all kinds of raised crewel stitches, such as Turkey work, bullion knots, and padded satin (page 305).

If you take a liberal approach, combining traditional stump work with this raised wool needlework, you can use them both as a basis for all kinds of modern abstract creative stitchery. You can work with the

Adam and Eve have padded bodies; felt, beads, raised wool and metal thread complete the design. *Designed and worked by the author*

traditional delicate tracery of silk and gold stitchery, or explode the scale of these stitches by substituting the fine threads with bulky wools and cords, making the whole effect unrecognizable in its new textural form.

The most important technique used in stump work is, obviously, padding and stuffing. This can be done in various ways.

You can apply any material to the background fabric (see page 343, appliqué), cutting out the shape to be applied a little larger than the design, so that when it is sewn down a "bubble" is formed in the center, which will be filled with the stuffing. Leave enough of the edge unstitched so that you can push a padding of cotton between the two layers of fabric, using the points of your scissors to help you. Push the cotton in firmly, but not so hard that it loses its resilience and becomes packed into solid lumps.

Another variation of padding is sewing down a muslin lining which,

Lamb, showing Pekinese stitch and detail above. *Wilanna Bristow*

after padding, will be completely covered with stitching. These stitches should not be sewn down through the padding, but should closely cover it, lying completely on top. Sewing through the padded area is not only difficult, but might flatten the final effect; therefore detached surface stitches such as weaving, trellis, or buttonhole lace are best for this technique. Apply and pad your muslin exactly as before (applying fabric, above), and try out various detached stitches which cover your padded area, yet remain free from the ground except at the edges. Start with weaving, then try trellis stitch, then hollie point and Greek lace filling.

These are the most basic stitches, but any of the lace stitches based on buttonhole for the close weaving stitches which are detached from the background are suitable for working over a padding (see page 287).

If you want a variety of stitches on your raised fabric, or if you only want to put in details such as features or outlines, embroider them first on a separate piece of material, *then* appliqué this and pad it. You can also apply a finished piece of needlepoint canvas according to the instructions on page 316, and raise this with a padding. Or, if you want to go one step further, you can turn back the edges of these stitched materials and hem or oversew them. Then you can either sew them down to the background material, just like patches, or leave them free standing, just catching them down where necessary. This can work equally well for the petals of a flower or for an entirely abstract shape in a design.

A further development of this is to stitch your shape so that it may be seen completely in the round, like sculpture. By threading wire inside the shapes you can make them stiff enough to stand up on their own, away from the background. An excellent example of this is "before" and "after" on plate 21, showing a caterpillar and a butterfly as the free-standing decoration atop a pair of pillboxes.

Alternatively, you can raise the background fabric from behind, rather like quilting, by basting muslin over the back of your design, stitching closely round the outlines—back stitch is the best (page 84)—and then pushing the padding cotton in between the muslin and the background fabric, from behind.

You can also pad with any of the methods described for gold embroidery (page 183), using layers of felt or string and working with either gold, silk, or wool on this raised surface, as you please.

Plate 25. Detail from a panel illustrating the story of the Golden Cockerel. Design based on an illustration in a children's book and worked in silk and gold on linen twill, predominantly in split stitch, by Mrs. Theodore Roosevelt, Jr. *The Smithsonian Institution. Photos by Vladimir Kagan*

OVERLEAF *Plates 26 and 27.* Complete panel of the Golden Cockerel

Plate 28.   Screen panel adapted by the author from a Chinese lacquer screen, worked in wool, silk and gold threads. Note the use of bargello stitch on fabric. *Worked by Mrs. B. P. Bouverie*

OPPOSITE

Plate 29.   ABOVE. Wheatfield in wool stitchery combined with appliquéd net. Clouds worked in angora, held in place by net. Foreground is emphasized by the use of bullion knots. *Designed and worked by Mrs. E. J. Thomson*

BELOW. Sun and moon in a variety of gold and silver threads on silk shantung. *Designed and worked by Dorothy Hickey*

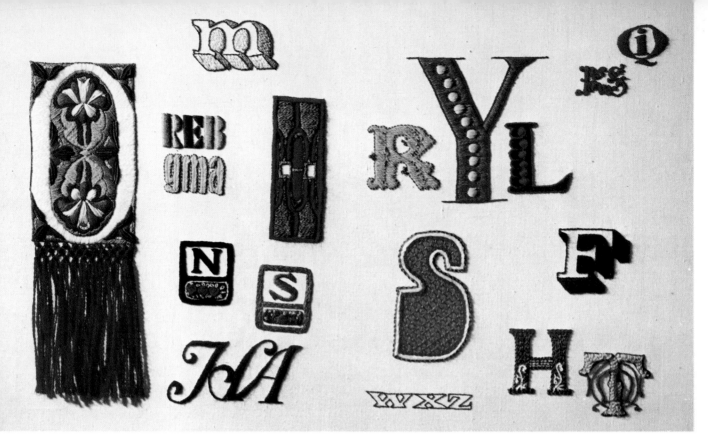

Plate 30.   Ideas for letters and monograms, using cotton and wool threads

San Blas Indian reversed appliqué

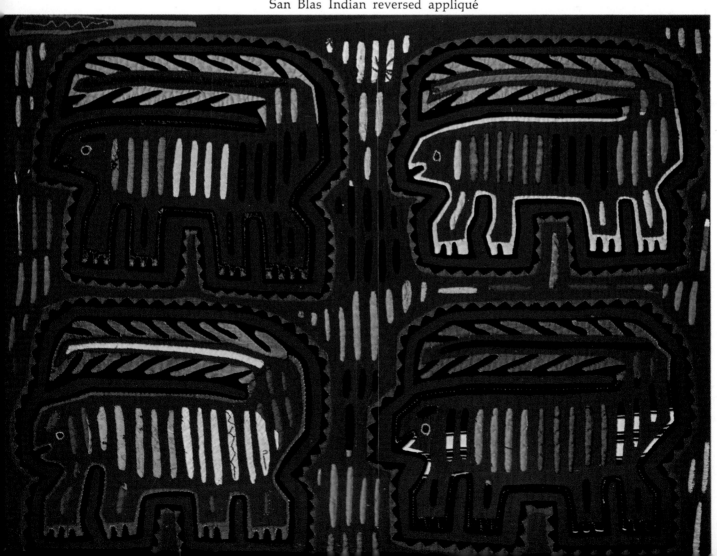

Plate 31. Lion appliqué from Dahomey; Indian temple cylindrical hanging; San Blas reversed appliqué

Plate 32.   Sketches with felt pens are useful in making simplified designs for embroidery such as the stylized birch trees. Here the whole background was worked in plate stitch, leaving the birch trunks in the bare ribbed fabric.

Ecology panel with flat and padded appliques and raised stitchery. As the panel was made for six year olds in a San Antonio school, the mouse squeaks, the frog croaks and the possum holds baby possums in a zippered pouch. *Designed and worked by Wilanna Bristow*

RIGHT. Sailor in padded needlepoint appliqued to a gobelin stitch background, worked in a bargello pattern. *Designed and worked by Mrs. Carroll O'Connor*

FAR RIGHT. Lady with a pekinese, needlepoint completely in the round. *Designed and worked by Robert Heitmann*

THE STITCHES

If you want to raise your embroidery by stitching alone, you can use the traditional raised wool work as your inspiration, and, with a lightness of touch which is contemporary, work normally flat crewel stitches in high relief. Plate 24 and page 313 show the effect of some of these stitches, which are included in this listing:

Raised seeding	Raised needleweaving
Raised rope stitch	Raised chain (on a raised band)
Looped stem	Raised buttonhole
Raised close herringbone	Raised stem
Puffy couching	Raised spiderwebs
Trellis and raised cup stitch	Ladder stitch

As you see, you can achieve exciting effects by working these stitches, alone or in combination with regular raised crewel stitches, such as padded satin, French knots on stalks, and Turkey work. Alternatively, you can combine them with the smooth texture of flat crewel stitches to give dramatic contrast.

Strawberries in trellis stitch. *Designed and worked by Mrs. William Sloan*

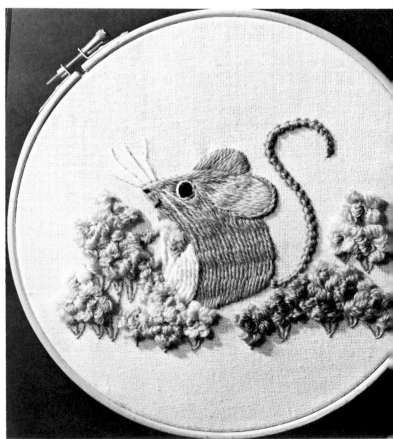

The mouse in plate stitch, tail in knotted pearl, flowers in raised seeding. *Designed and worked by the author*

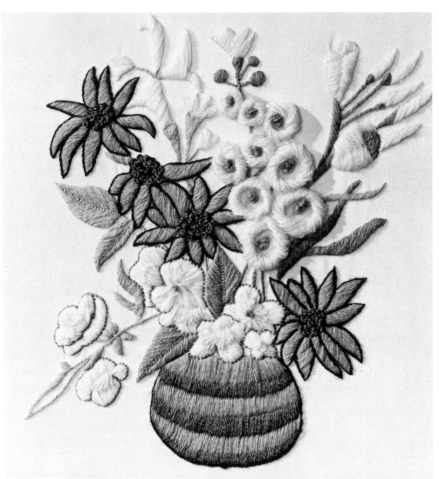

Raised rope stitch in enlarged detail
Designed and worked by the author

*✳PADDED APPLIQUÉ

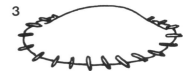

Cut out your shape (slightly larger than your finished area) and apply it to the material as described on page 342. Leave one side open as shown.

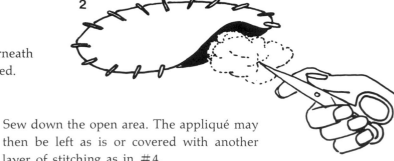

With your scissors push cotton underneath the padding until it is sufficiently raised.

Sew down the open area. The appliqué may then be left as is or covered with another layer of stitching as in #4.

Prepare to weave across the surface by laying threads diagonally across as shown. Do not pull too tightly to destroy the effect of the padding.

Using a blunt needle and starting across the center of the shape weave in the opposite direction. Carefully push threads close together as you weave so that they do not "fall off" the curved surface. Though weaving is shown here, any close stitching may be used to cover raised appliqué, such as trellis, ceylon or raised chain, stem or buttonhole.

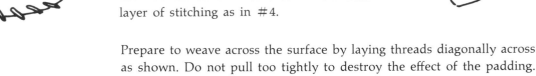

Turkey work cut and uncut. *Designed and worked by Jeri Kilgroe*

*PADDING WITH MUSLIN ON REVERSE SIDE

Baste muslin to the reverse side.

Outline your design with back stitch on the right side.

Make a slit in the muslin, push in the cotton, pushing it well into the corners until it is sufficiently padded. Next stitch together the slit in the muslin. Extra muslin may then be trimmed away around the design.

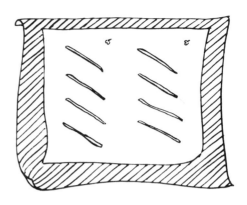

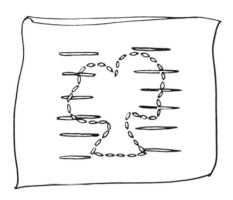

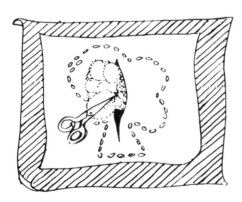

Ferdinand the Bull, under a cork tree with real corks, is embroidered in Turkey work, cut and uncut. *Designed and worked by Jeri Kilgroe*

APPLYING FINISHED NEEDLEPOINT TO FABRIC

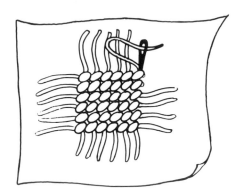

First unravel your raw edges around your finished needlepoint so that single threads appear on all four sides as in the diagram. Then pin and baste the needlepoint in position on the background material. With a large-eyed needle take each thread through to the reverse side of the fabric.

Turn to the reverse side and knot the needlepoint threads together in pairs, pulling snugly so that the canvas is held firmly in place on the front.

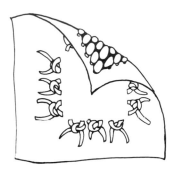

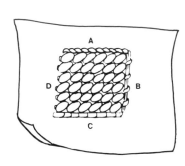

Now turn to the right side again and outline the canvas with any edging stitch you prefer. In the diagram, stem stitch is shown at A, couching at B and a couched cord at C. D shows the needlepoint canvas left plain without an edging, which is also equally effective if desired.

FREE-STANDING STUMP WORK USING WIRE

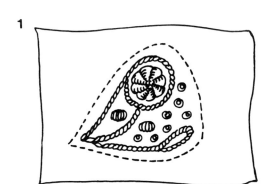

Embroider shape on fabric.

Join it to backing, with right sides facing. Leave one section open (shown by dotted line). Snip notches in the turnbacks for smooth seams and rounded finished edges.

Turn to the right side and insert a loop of wire through the open end. Leave ends of wire long enough to use for attaching to main design.

Attach by taking wire through to the wrong side. Blind stitch the last opening by stitching it together with small invisible stitches. Add final embroidery details (body, etc.).

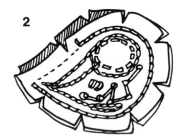

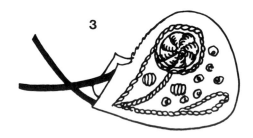

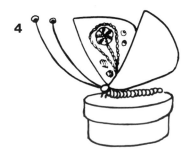

*TRELLIS STITCH

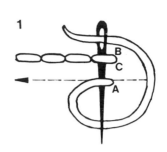

1. Begin with a row of back stitch to make a foundation on which to begin working. Using a blunt tapestry needle, come up on the right at A, immediately below the first back stitch.

2. Slide the needle vertically under this first back stitch, and then fold the working thread (which comes out of the fabric at A), first over the needle, and then under it, as shown. Draw gently through and pull up to form a knot.

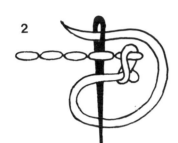

3. Continue, repeating this stitch to the end of the line. Go in to the material at D, and taking a vertical stitch, the size of one knot, come up at E.

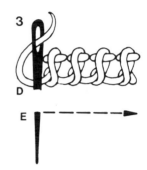

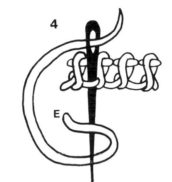

4. Now, work from left to right, repeating the first line, but in the opposite direction, slipping the needle under the bars which connect each stitch.

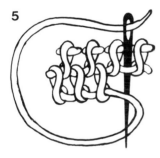

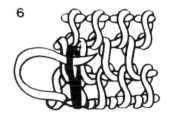

5. Work to the end of the row, drawing each stitch up gently to make an even row of knots.

6. Finally, anchor the last line by taking a small stitch over each bar of the last row.

The effect of trellis can vary tremendously according to tension. If you stretch out the finished web the final effect is as shown here.

If you work very closely, the knots make a solid covering. Trellis may be worked in horizontal rows, or in curved lines to fit any shape. Alternatively, the whole shape may be outlined with back stitch, then decreasing rows of trellis may be worked round and round inside as shown at right. To obtain a raised circle, do not start decreasing the stitches until nearing the center. The stitches will then stand out as though there was padding underneath them. (See lady's sleeves, page 289, and strawberry eyeglass case, page 312.)

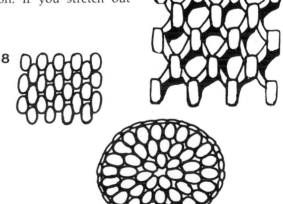

*CEYLON STITCH

Using a blunt (tapestry) needle, begin by coming up at A and going down at B to form a base line the width of the shape to be embroidered. (If the distance is wide, hold this stitch down with small stitches at regular intervals across it.)

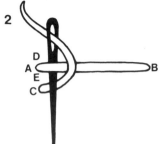

Now begin the stitch itself, which is always worked from left to right. Come up at C and slip the needle under the base stitch from D to E and over the working thread which comes out at C. Do not go through the material.

Make a second stitch to the right, exactly like #2 and continue, repeating these stitches to the end of the line.

Now come up on the left at G, immediately below C, and slip the needle behind first loop of the previous row, from H to J. Slide horizontally under two threads, where one loop overlaps another, as shown.

Continue, repeating #4 to the end of the line. Secure the final row with small stitches taken through each loop, into the material. The shape may be increased or decreased by adding or taking away stitches at the end of each row.

*RAISED CUP STITCH

Make a triangle of 3 back stitches, in the center of the area to be worked.

Using a blunt (tapestry) needle slide under one back stitch. Do not go through the material. Take the thread over the needle, then under it as shown.

Pull through gently to form a knot.

Repeat, making a second knot beside the first one on the same bar. Pull through, gently.

Continue, making two knots on each bar to make a complete ring around the back stitches. Then make a second ring of stitches by sliding the needle under the bar between each knot (at arrow).

Finished effect
(See flowers on
tree, page 289.)

Work round and round, if necessary occasionally working two knots into the bars to increase the size of the cup.

* LOOPED STEM

Work lines of regular stem stitch (see page 34) but use heavy thread and leave each stitch loose to form a loop, as shown. The thickness of the thread worked into a fairly fine linen will hold the loops firmly in place. (See page 289, grass under lady's feet.)

* RAISED ROPE

Work rope stitch (see page 66) but leave the stitches loose to form a raised ridge. This is particularly effective when worked in a circle. (See page 313, close-up of rope stitch flower in vase.)

* RAISED SEEDING

Work seeding (see page 107) but leave each stitch loose to form a raised "bump" on the fabric. As in looped stem the thickness of the thread will hold the seed stitch in place. (See page 312, mouse with flowers.)

PUFFY COUCHING

*Work a line of couching, (see page 85) but instead of laying the threads flat on the fabric, lift them with your needle as you take each couching stitch to form the raised look shown here. (See plate 24, close-up of orange zinnias.)

*RAISED CLOSE HERRING BONE

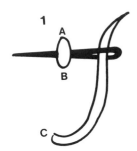

Come up at A, go down at B, making a small vertical stitch at the top of the shape. Then come up at C, slightly to the left at the base. Using a blunt needle, slide through stitch AB from right to left. Do not go through the material.

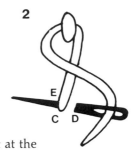

Go into the fabric at D, slightly to the right at the base, and come up at E, immediately above C on the outline of the shape.

Slide through stitch AB from right to left again, taking care that the stitches lie smoothly side by side.

Go into the material at the base again, going down on the right, and up on the left, just above the other stitches.

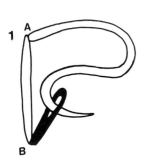

Continue, repeating 2, 3 and 4 to the top to make a raised leaf.

Shows finished effect as seen from the side.

* RAISED NEEDLEWEAVING

Using a blunt needle, come up at A, down at B and repeat, coming up at A, down at B again, so that two stitches lie side by side. Do not draw too tight.

Coming up at A once more, start to weave, (without going through the material). First pick up the left hand thread, pushing the needle through from right to left.

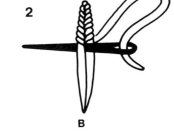

Then pick up the right hand thread, pushing the needle through from left to right. Continue till the two underlying threads are completely covered. From time to time pack the weaving threads together by pushing them up with the needle. Keep the tension even so that the line will be smooth.

*RAISED SPIDER'S WEBS

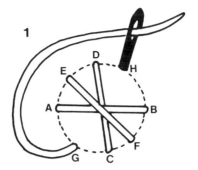

Using a blunt (tapestry) needle, come up at A, down at B, across centre of circle.

Then come up at C, and down at D, (C to D should be slightly off centre as shown). Come up at E, down at F, up at G and down at H. (H goes in quite close to D.)

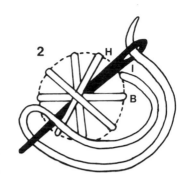

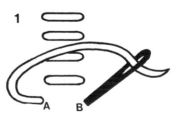

Pulling the knotting thread upwards, take another blunt needle threaded with any contrasting colour and push it under all the spokes.

This leaves a space for the needle to come up finally at I, a point midway between H and B. Then slide the needle under all the threads at their inter-section. Take the thread and loop it across the needle and then under it as shown. Draw through and pull upwards to knot threads together in centre.

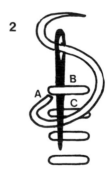

Unthread this needle and pull upwards with both strands of this contrasting thread, so that all the spokes are taut (as shown). Continue to hold it upwards whilst weaving round and round as in ordinary Woven Spider's Webs. Push in enough rows of this weaving so that the spider's web stands up in a point. Finally pull out the contrasting working thread, leaving the spider's web firmly raised.

*RAISED BUTTONHOLE

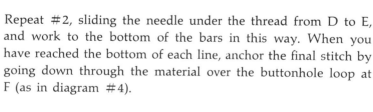

Using a blunt needle, come up at A, form a loop with the thread, and without going through the material, slide under the first bar from B to C (as shown). Draw down towards you until the thread is snug. This forms a Buttonhole Stitch on the horizontal bar.

Repeat #2, sliding the needle under the thread from D to E, and work to the bottom of the bars in this way. When you have reached the bottom of each line, anchor the final stitch by going down through the material over the buttonhole loop at F (as in diagram #4).

Work several lines close side by side, always beginning at the top, working downwards, until the bars are entirely covered. Do not pack too many rows in or the effect will be lost.

*RAISED BUTTONHOLE ON A RAISED BAND

(Raised buttonhole, is shown here, but any of the stitches worked on bars, such as raised stem or chain may be worked on raised bands.)

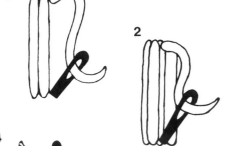

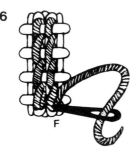

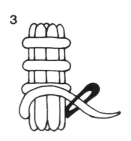

First lay a series of parallel stitches close together (as shown in diagram).

Lay a second row of stitches over the first, keeping the stitches away from the edges. Several decreasing rows may be worked in this way so that the band has a raised center.

Lay a series of parallel stitches across the band just under ¼" apart (as shown in diagram).

Using a blunt needle, come up at A, form a loop with the thread and without going through the material, slide under the first bar from B to C (as shown). Draw down towards you until the thread is snug. This forms a Buttonhole stitch on the horizontal bar.

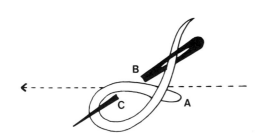

Repeat #4 sliding the needle under the thread from D to E and work to the base of the bar in this way. When you have reached the base of each line, anchor the final stitch by going down through the material over the buttonhole loop at F (as in Diagram #6).

SNAIL TRAIL

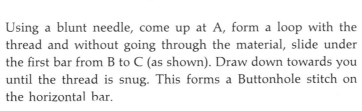

Working from right to left, come up at A. Lay the wool flat along the line you are working (you can hold it in place with your thumb) and take a large slanting stitch across this line from B to C. Before pulling through, twist the wool first over, then under the needle as shown.

Shows finished effect with fairly large stitches spaced wide apart. The effect is entirely different if you change the slant of the needle and the spacing of the stitches. Snail trail worked very close becomes Broad Rope stitch. When worked with the needle at right angles to the thread, instead of slanting, it becomes Coral.

✳ROSE LEAF STITCH

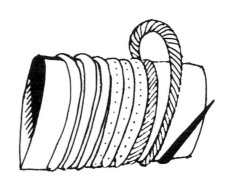

Double a piece of cardboard (postcard is good) so that it measures the size you want your loops to be (from one to two inches is a good average size, but it will depend on the thickness of the yarn and the scale of the design). Mount the work in a frame and hold the card in place along the center of the leaf shape. Using knitting worsted or a single strand of any bulky wool, come up on one side, go over the cardboard and down on the other. Go down close beside where you came up, but not in the same hole. Make three light-colored stitches side by side, three medium and three dark.

Slide the cardboard out.

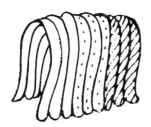

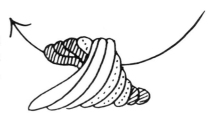

Carefully turn the loops inside out, pushing the dark ones through the light, so that when twisted the loops form a leaf or petal shape, evenly shading from light to dark.

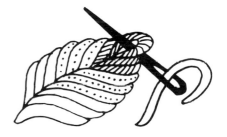

Come up at the end of the shape and sew through the last loop of dark color which has been twisted right through. Go down in the same hole as where you came up, to hold the tip of the leaf.

Work one stitch down the middle to form a vein.

Shows the stitch sewn across at the tip to form a rosebud

Shows a group of stitches forming a spray of leaves

BLOCKING AND MOUNTING

Pressing would be impossible for the raised and embossed embroidery of stump work. Blocking may be difficult if the background fabric is not colorfast, or is made of silk, which could be damaged by water. In this case, the answer is to steam the embroidery. First, mount it on a stretcher frame, described on page 25. Then place an iron upright on the ironing board, set for "linen," and cover it with a wet cloth. Hold the work so that the steam can rise through it from underneath. After five or ten minutes the stitches will stand out clearly, should they have become crushed in working.

If the work is to be framed, raised embroidery should be mounted in a shadow-box frame with plenty of space between the glass and the needlework so that the stitches will not be flattened.

CHAPTER 7

A MISCELLANY:
Monograms, Appliqué, and Shisha Work

Alphabet in needlemade lace. *Victoria and Albert Museum*

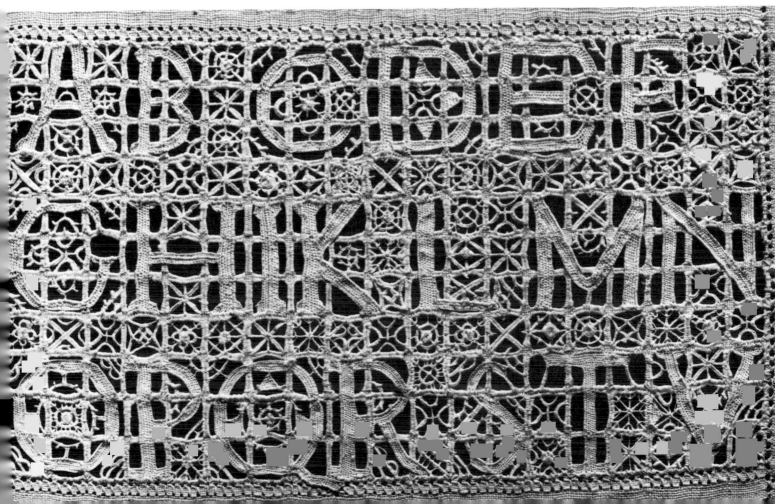

Early American sampler with alphabet in eyelet and cross stitch. *Cooper Hewitt Museum of Design, Smithsonian Institution*

MONOGRAMS

THE personal nature of hand embroidery is perhaps one of the most appealing things about it. With monograms or letters you can give special significance to a piece of needlework, whether you are making something as a gift or for yourself. The lettering can either make up the whole design, or an initial or a signature can be hidden, to become an integral part of the pattern. Inspiration can come from traditional sources such as illuminated manuscripts or from today's exciting super graphics. Just leafing through the pages of a magazine will give you wonderful ideas for different treatments in lettering.

The letters and monograms on plate 30 were designed to show the different effects of wool, cotton threads, and combinations of both. Your choice of threads will depend on what you are going to make and how the monogram is to be used; wool for an initial in the center of a pillow (plate 23), cotton for the turnback of a sheet (page 328), for instance. Embroidery floss or cotton thread is best for clothing, bed linen, or any article that has to be frequently laundered. Although you can wash wool embroidery gently by hand, like a sweater, it is best not to throw it into the washing machine!

When it comes to stitches you can choose from the whole repertoire of crewel embroidery. The possibilities are endless. Padded satin is a traditional stitch for monograms, because it is raised and clear-cut, but simply outlining the letter with chain, stem, or back stitch can be most effective, and any of the banding stitches such as Roumanian, Vandyke, or cretan are excellent either alone or when combined with other stitches.

If you want to sign a piece of crewel or silk embroidery you have done, the best way to do it is to write out your name in the correct scale on tissue or tracing paper. Then baste this to the needlework, stitch right through, and tear the paper away, following the method described on page 21. Split stitch or stem are good stitches to use for script writing, but for the smallest letters back stitch can't be beaten for it gives the finest line. Whichever you choose, reduce the size of the stitches slightly as you go around curves; it will make the letters much smoother. Sometimes it is better to overlap one stitch over the other where two lines converge. This makes a sharper point than when you bring both stitches together into the same hole. Be precise about keeping angles clear-cut, and straight lines

Monogram for sheet turnback. The letters are outlined and filled with flowers worked in embroidery cotton. *Designed and worked by the author*

Needlepoint door pillows

Cross stitch sampler, showing pattern worked on graph paper, then counted onto even-weave linen. *Designed and worked by the author*

really straight. Sometimes moving a stitch just one thread to the left or right can make all the difference to the accuracy and legibility of small size letters.

The tissue paper method of putting on the design is also excellent if you want to monogram a sweater, a man's shirt or tie, a blouse or a handkerchief. But some people prefer to see their stitches appearing right on the cloth rather than working through a layer of paper. In this case you could choose from any of the other methods of transferring designs on pages 18–23, depending on your background material.

Letters in cross stitch on linen or tent stitch on needlepoint canvas are simple to work out because they are geometric. It is best to plan them on graph paper first. Then, using a blunt needle, you can reproduce them exactly, counting the threads of the linen or canvas, following your graph (page 329).

If you want to work letters in cross stitch on a fabric where the threads are too fine to count, you can follow the method on page 23, basting a piece of needlepoint canvas over the material, working right through both thicknesses, and then drawing out the canvas threads after the work is done. The even weave of the canvas makes it possible to count out the regular geometric stitching easily.

Lettering in back stitch on linen. *Design adapted from Beatrix Potter's* Appley Dapply's Nursery Rhymes *and worked by the author*

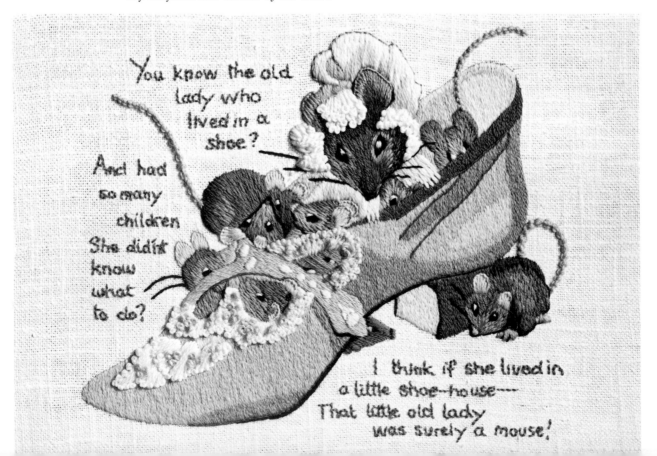

You know the old lady who lived in a shoe?

And had so many children She didn't know what to do?

I think if she lived in a little shoe-house--- That little old lady was surely a mouse!

Timmy Willie from "The Tale of Johnny Town Mouse" by Beatrix Potter. *Design adapted and worked by the author*

Our ancestors used to make alphabet samplers when they were children, and stitching a collection of letters on fabric is still a good idea. Whether you want to initial or monogram a certain something, whether you want to write out a word or a verse in embroidery, or whether you simply want to sign your name, you will have a collection of stitches and techniques right at your fingertips, waiting to be used. On the following pages are some alphabets to trace or enlarge, and stitch in any medium.

ALPHABETS

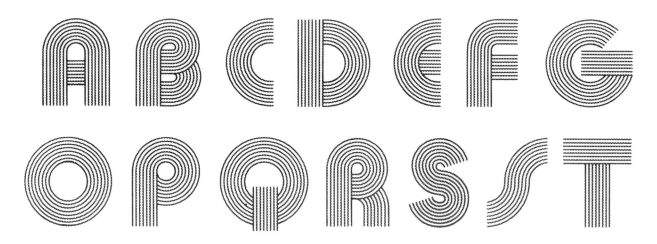

ABCDEFGHIJ
stuvwxyz

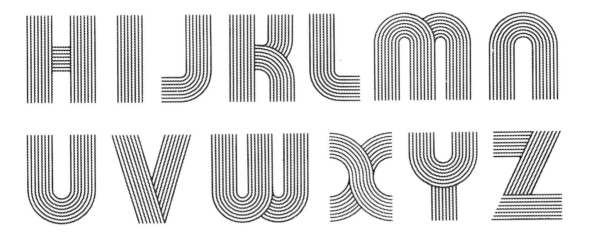

H I J K L M N

U V W X Y Z

k l m n o p q r

1 2 3 4 5 6 7 8 9 0

ALPHABETS

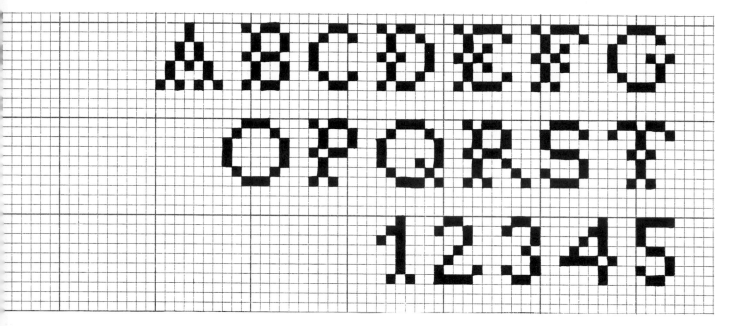

ALPHABETS

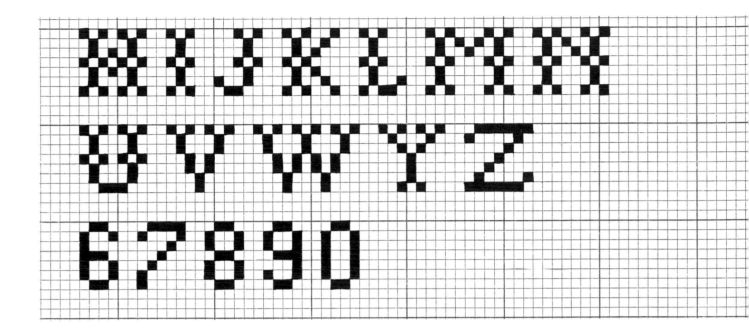

APPLIQUÉ

Appliqué comes from the French verb meaning "to put on" and is simply the cutting out and applying of one fabric on top of another. It is certainly one of the simplest, and probably one of the oldest, ways of decorating cloth, and has been part of the needlework tradition of all nations throughout the centuries. Indians in Arizona stitched dried leaves to leather thousands of years ago. The Dahomey tribe on the west coast of Africa make symbolic heraldic panels in brilliant colored cottons, and the Cuña Indians in San Blas near Panama translate everyday objects into sophisticated designs for "molas" or blouses which also have a family and historic significance.

The most primitive appliqué (like that of the Dahomey African banners, plate 31) is sewn around the edges with invisible stitches so that nothing interferes with the bold contrast of one silhouette shape on another. The effect is completely changed when the appliquéd shapes are outlined with braids or cords of contrasting color, as in the festive cylindrical banners made to hang in Indian temples (plate 31).

The result is also completely different when stitchery is added. In America, appliqué has long been combined with patchwork, quilting, and

Bedspread with velvet leaves in reverse appliqué, and rug wool flowers in lazy daisy and french knots. *Designed by Vladimir Kagan, worked by the author. Brides' Magazine*

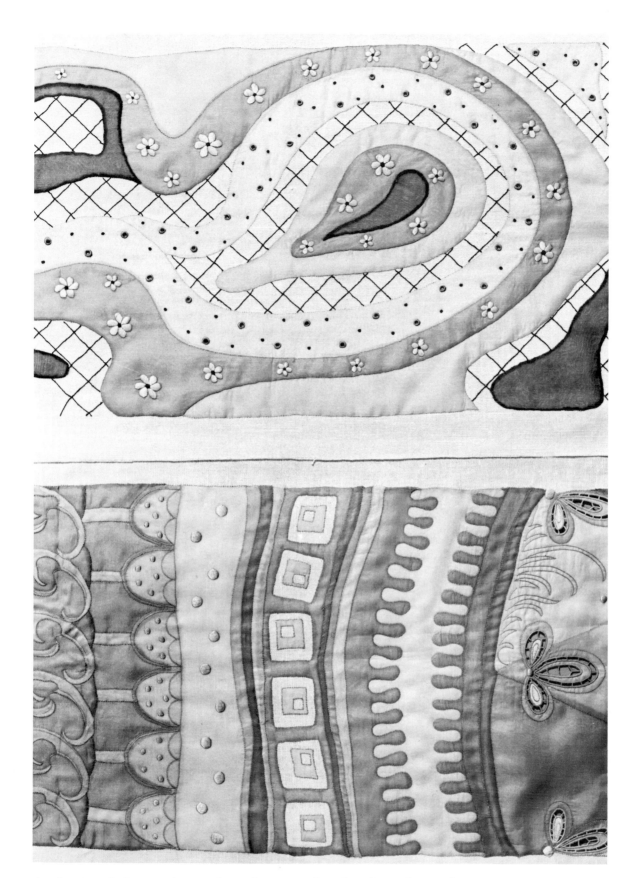

Appliqué with layers of organdy on linen, combined with stitches such as satin, stem and point de Paris. *Casa Jana, Madeira*

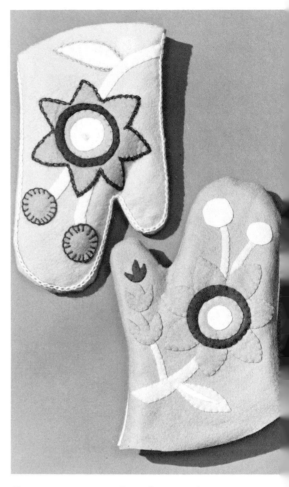

Child's bedspread, appliqué in purple, red, yellow and orange. *Mountain Artisans of Appalachia*

Oven mitts, one with outline stitching, the other without. *Designed and worked by the author*

Contemporary version of the Bayeux Tapestry done in appliqué. A set of 27 panels commemorating the 900th anniversary of the Battle of Hastings. *Worked by the Royal School of Needlework, London, courtesy Hastings Corporation*

Appliqué panel. *Designed and worked by Wibeke Beck-Friis Frisk*

embroidery, and bed coverlets were traditionally stitched with beautiful and simple geometric patterns. Materials such as velvet, silk, and damasks, as well as cottons, were combined with feather, buttonhole, chain, and herringbone stitches to great effect. But most sophisticated among the primitive appliqués is the work of the San Blas Indians, for their designs are done in *reversed* appliqué. Pieces of material, laid on top of one another, are cut away layer by layer to reveal the ones below, and the juxtaposition of complementary colors of the same value and intensity gives the whole design a vibrating glow which is exciting (plate 30).

In addition to all these variations, there is the shadow appliqué used effectively and extensively in white-on-white embroidery, (page 277) and the raised padded appliqué of stump work (page 315). The nature of appliqué lends itself to bold and stylized silhouettes. These, combined with subtle or vibrant colors, are a natural vehicle for modern abstract and strong graphic design.

TO BEGIN

Translating your ideas into a pattern for appliqué is wonderful practice for all needlework design, because the shapes must be reduced to their simplest graphic form not only to make the design effective, but to make the appliqué possible to do.

Decide on your theme and color scheme and choose the colors of your background fabric first, because this will influence your entire design.

You can make a color sketch as a guide, but you will probably never be able to match the shades with fabric exactly, so be flexible and choose those fabrics that look best together without following your sketch too precisely. Draw your shapes on brown wrapping paper, then cut them out as patterns. After a while your scissors will become as versatile as a pencil, and you will feel adept enough to cut out the paper patterns without drawing any lines; and eventually you may find you can cut out the material itself without using any patterns at all, working entirely freehand.

Pillows, tote bags, and clothing such as long evening skirts, blue jeans, or jackets can be done in appliqué, but because the areas can be so quickly and easily covered, it is ideal for large-scale designs like headboards, quilts, hangings, banners, and for anything that needs a theatrical effect and must be viewed from a distance. Appliqué can be used as a background for elaborate stitchery, or solid shapes can be contrasted with a fine line tracery of stitches, or the stitching can be invisible and all the emphasis given to the shapes themselves.

MATERIALS, THREADS, AND NEEDLES

Your choice of fabrics will depend on which style of appliqué you want to use, or perhaps in reverse. Your fabric may be the deciding factor in choosing your technique. There are really two basic variations: the type of appliqué where you simply turn under the raw edges and stitch them down invisibly (used for both applied and reversed appliqué), and the type where the raw edges are left flat, to be covered by cords or stitchery. The most suitable materials for each variation are therefore listed in two groups.

FABRICS FOR APPLIQUÉ WITH
EDGES TURNED UNDER

FABRICS FOR APPLIQUÉ WITH
RAW EDGES COVERED BY STITCHING

Fine linen

Cotton—muslin or percale
   (no-iron sheets come in a
   wonderful variety of colors)

Taffeta

Organdy

Sateen

Damask—fine light weight

Velvet	*Felt*
Heavy linen	*Suede*
Satin	*Soft leather*
Brocades	*Net*
Grosgrain	*Vinyls and other*
Burlap	*soft synthetics*
Homespun	

The fabrics in each group may be interchanged. You need not turn under
the edges of organdy or fine cotton, and you *can* if necessary turn under
those of heavy linen or brocade. You may also mix all types of fabrics
in one design. But your work will be easier if you use fabrics in the groups
as they are listed, particularly if you are trying appliqué for the first time.
Materials printed in italics, like *felt* and *suede,* are the easiest of all
because they have no fraying edges to worry about. You cut them out and
stitch them down just as they are, either with invisible stitches or with
decorative ones. But any fabrics, such as velvet, coarse linens, silks or satin,
which are to be sewn down without hems may be made as firm and easy
to handle as felt. Simply brush the back of the fabric very lightly with
Latex or paste glue, allow it to dry, and then cut out your pattern. Alternatively, you could glue some fine muslin or organdy fabric to the reverse
side, or use any thin iron-on fabric available from most notion stores. The
bonding fabric called "stitch-witchery" is excellent, as it means that you
can cut out your shapes in any fabric and sew them down flat without
turning back the edges; there will be no fraying.

Threads and needles are naturally as versatile as the fabrics and you
can use silk, wool, cotton, linen, gold, or silver thread as you wish. Crewel
or embroidery needles with their long eyes are perhaps the best for appliqué, and you will be able to find whichever size is most suitable for the
thread and fabric you are using (see page 16).

* APPLIQUÉ

First transfer the whole design to the background fabric by any of the methods on pages 18–23 which seem to suit your material best. Then transfer the designs to the various fabrics which are to be applied. On textiles with a definite weave, it is very important that the threads of the appliqué and the background should always run in the same direction. In other words, do not try to stitch a piece of cross-grain or bias-cut fabric to a background where the threads run straight up and down. Unless the threads run in the same direction the applied pieces may stretch and "bubble" and detract from the smooth flat effect you want to achieve. Therefore, once you have determined which way the grain or thread of the appliqué material is to run, cut out your shapes, leaving an allowance of about $\frac{3}{8}$ inch all around for turnbacks. With your scissors, take little snips into this hem allowance, around the curved edges, so that when creased or pressed back the contours will be smooth and even, without angles or bumps. Baste these "turnings" back with contrasting thread so that it can easily be withdrawn when the work is done.

Stretch the basic fabric loosely in an embroidery frame and pin the pieces you are applying in their positions. When one shape overlaps another, lay the underneath one down first, leaving the raw edges flat wherever an upper layer of fabric will cover them. Turnbacks are not necessary here, as they would form ridges which would show through the top layer (see #5 opposite).

Hold the appliquéd pieces flat with basting stitches taken right through the center of each shape, as shown opposite. Do not run basting stitches around the edges as this may also cause the material to bubble. Finally, stretch the fabric *tightly* in your embroidery frame and sew the appliqué down with small stitches at right angles to the edges using self-color thread (opposite). Alternatively, you may secure the appliqué by stitching it all around close to the edge with a running stitch, or with the regular stitch on a sewing machine. This shows a definite line of stitching just inside the edge, but it has a very crisp and tailored effect.

If you are working freehand without patterns, particularly in reverse appliqué, cut out your shapes, pin and baste them in position, and *then*

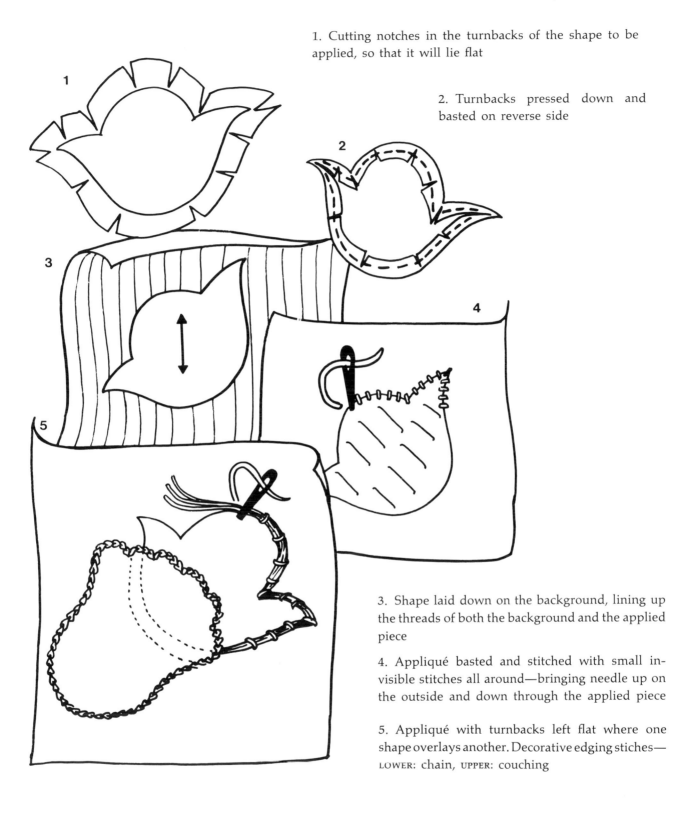

1. Cutting notches in the turnbacks of the shape to be applied, so that it will lie flat

2. Turnbacks pressed down and basted on reverse side

3. Shape laid down on the background, lining up the threads of both the background and the applied piece

4. Appliqué basted and stitched with small invisible stitches all around—bringing needle up on the outside and down through the applied piece

5. Appliqué with turnbacks left flat where one shape overlays another. Decorative edging stiches— LOWER: chain, UPPER: couching

turn back your edges with your needle as you stitch. This method sometimes works better than trying to fit precut and basted patterns into areas
of the design. Somewhere along the way these prebasted shapes often
change, and it seems impossible to fit them in without much pulling and
stretching. You should still take small snips into the fabric at right angles,
to make sure the appliqué will be flat, but you can do this as you go along.

APPLIQUÉ/RAW EDGES

This variety of appliqué is done in exactly the same way as the kind
with the edges turned back. The one difference is that since the raw edges
are to be secured or covered by decorative stitching, the shapes may be
trimmed close around the outlines, leaving no seam allowance. Therefore,
with this type of appliqué it is easy to keep the shapes clear-cut and the
outline crisp. Putting on a Latex back or using a bonding fabric for materials
which are soft or easily frayed makes them very much easier to handle.

Choose from the wide variety of "banding" stitches to sew your
appliqué down. The most basic of these are buttonhole, herringbone,
couching, trailing, French knots, coral, feather, zigzag chain and open chain.

If you would like to stitch your appliqué decoratively by machine,
cover the raw edges with zigzag stitch. The closer and more solidly you
work the zigzag the more tailored your effect will be. This machine stitch,
when worked closely, has the look of a band of satin stitch, and also resembles the trailing stitch of hand embroidery (see page 266). Since it is naturally
a great deal faster, it is excellent for large projects. First baste the appliqué
as on page 243. Then using the sewing machine, go round the edge with
an open zigzag to hold the edge flat. Finally, cover these stitches completely
with the close zigzag.

REVERSE APPLIQUÉ

In order to make this form of appliqué clear, it is described here
specifically in its simplest form.

1. Stack several layers of different colored cloths, of the same size, one
   on top of each other. (Five is a good number to start with.)

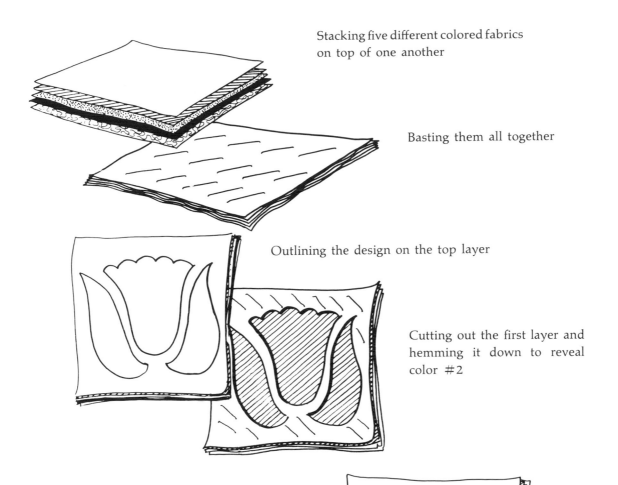

Stacking five different colored fabrics
on top of one another

Basting them all together

Outlining the design on the top layer

Cutting out the first layer and
hemming it down to reveal
color #2

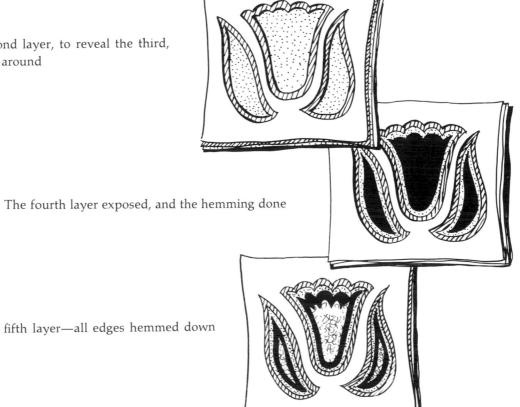

Cutting out the second layer, to reveal the third,
leaving a border all around

The fourth layer exposed, and the hemming done

The fifth layer—all edges hemmed down

2. Baste them all together with the stitch shown on page 243.
3. Outline your design on the top layer of cloth. The pattern should be made up of large shapes, covering most of the area.
4. Cut away the fabric *inside* each of the shapes of this pattern on the top layer, taking care not to accidentally snip the material underneath. Hem or stitch invisibly around the design, turning the edges under if you are working with material which will fray. Your stitches need not penetrate beneath the second layer of fabric, but it does not matter if they do.
5. Now that you have two colors exposed, the top layer and the second, you are ready to cut through to the third layer of material. To do this, cut around inside the shapes of the second layer, leaving a narrow border line around the inside of the design.
6. Stitch it down as before, and continue, cutting decreasing amounts from each layer of fabric so that borders of color are left inside each pattern, until finally the base layer is reached.

This is the very simplest form of reverse appliqué, described so that you can understand and practice the basic technique.

However, there are many sophisticated versions of the same thing. Instead of cutting all the way through to the base layer, one by one, you can leave some shapes with only the second color exposed, for instance. Or if you want the third color to be the only one to show in a certain area, slightly lift the top fabric so that you can snip the second layer far enough back underneath so that it will not show.

Alternatively, for variety in parts of the design, you can cut the top fabric into a network of openings, and underneath these you can push small pieces of fabric in different colors, lay them flat, and then stitch them down. And where the pattern is too narrow or the shapes too small to cut through easily, you can combine surface appliqué, stitching other colors on top.

The layers of colors need not be exposed in even bands, following the design, as in the simple form explained in detail, but different shapes and areas may be exposed to give limitless variations on this exciting theme.

SHISHA WORK

An unusual and fascinating type of needlework is done with mica or mirrors in the western part of India, in the provinces of Kutch, Kathiawan, and Sind. The nomadic herdsmen and farmers who live in these regions make richly encrusted skirts and bodices, trappings for sacred cattle, and hangings for doorways called "Toran." Since the Indian word for glass or crystal is "shisha," this seems a suitable name for the rich sparkling embroidery with its vivid yet subtle colors.

Because cutting mirror may be difficult (to say the least!), a good substitute for it is "Mylar," a mirror-like aluminum backed with linen or

Shisha work in wool and Mylar on blue jeans and pillow. *Designed and worked by author*

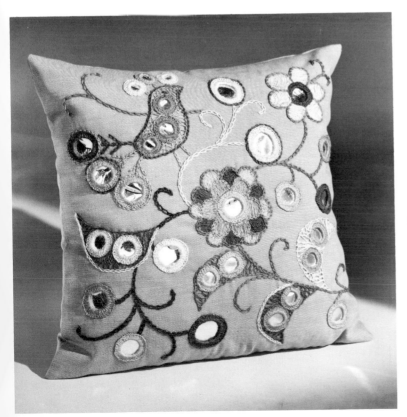

Headdress for a child. *Author's Collection*

A 17th century door hanging, Shisha work
from Kutch. *Author's Collection*

cotton. Soft and pliable, the Mylar can be easily cut into any size circle, making it easy to work with. Mylar is available at most art stores, but if it cannot be found, plastic disks called "glitters" would be a substitute. As a last resort you could cut cardboard circles from regular postcards and cover them with heavy-duty aluminum foil.

The mirrors are held down with a crisscross stitching worked right across the circle. This is then caught back by a combination buttonhole-chain stitch which borders the edges and holds the mirror firmly in place. Ovals or circles are therefore the simplest and most effective shape for this sort of embroidery, and these can be arranged in the design like jewels in elaborate settings.

The circles can either be worked closely together to make a geometric pattern or they can fill the silhouette shapes of any "free" design. Any crewel stitches could be combined with shisha work, but traditionally the stitches used were limited to herringbone, chain, cretan, and French knots. This seems to give the needlework an overall unity, allowing the mirrors to be the focal points of interest. The Indian embroidery is always done in strong cotton or silk thread, but working with matte wool makes an attractive contrast with the brilliant sheen of the Mylar.

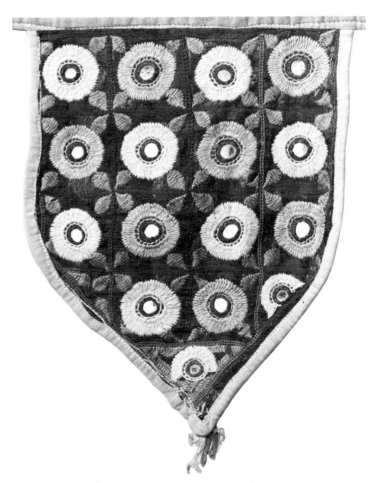

Detail from a door hanging, in orange and purple. *Author's collection*

SHISHA STITCH

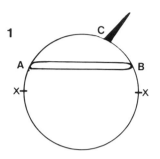

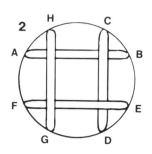

Place mylar circle in position and hold in place with two small stitches on either side (x). Then come up at A, close to edge of circle at left and go down at B close to edge, to make a horizontal stitch one third down from top of circle. Come up at C, one third in from right of circle.

Continue around circle, from C to D, E to F, G to H, making a square as shown.

Repeat around circle, making four more stitches from I to J, K to L, M to N, O to P, to make a diamond on top of the square as shown. These are the "holding" stitches, which keep the circle firm.

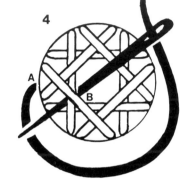

Using a blunt needle, come up at A (anywhere close to left hand edge of circle). Slide needle under the "holding" threads, and with the thread under the needle draw tight.

Then take a little stitch into the fabric, close to the edge of the circle, from C to D. With thread looped under needle as shown, draw tight.

Repeat 4, sliding needle under the "holding" threads, and draw tight with the thread under the needle.

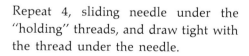

Repeat 5, but go down into the same hole, *inside* the loop at D. Come up at F with thread under needle. Continue, repeating steps 6 and 7 to make a close band of stitching around circle, catching in all the "holding" stitches so that they are completely concealed.

MIXED MEDIA

Gold, silk, and wool combined

Crewel stitches with needlepoint on canvas

White work in rug wool (needle weaving and drawn thread)

Black work stitches on needlepoint canvas

Stump work (raised wool) combined with flat crewel

Three-dimensional needlemade lace in linen thread pictures

Tent stitch in rug wool on coarse weave wool fabric, combined

    with crewel in various thicknesses of yarn

THIS chapter is included not only to show how mixed media can look entirely different but also to show how a traditional work can have new life breathed into it by taking it into another medium or scale. Since so much very fine work has been done in the past, the contemporary version is exciting when the stitches are exploded in size. Instead of fine linen thread for white work, for instance, try using knitted worsted, and instead of working lacy black work stitches in fine silk, stitch them with bold wool. Stay free, fluid, and flexible in embroidery techniques, letting your needle and the traditions of the past give you inspiration. Once you have mastered traditional stitches and are bent on adventure, there is no telling where experimentation will take you. It is amazing how quickly your imagination will lead you down new inventive paths. Stitches, textures, and fabrics have become a new dimension in art and the suggestions I have made for new combinations at the head of the chapter are only a start for your own creativity.

Once you have mastered and become familiar with crewel work and needlepoint, experimented with silk and gold threads; worked with contrasting textures and fabrics in appliqué, and tried out drawn thread and flat stitches on different materials in white on white embroidery, you can mix them all up with glorious freedom, combining many techniques in a single piece of needlework. Beware! the pitfalls are many! The result can become too intricate and cluttered if you try to do *too* much—without the strict guide lines of a traditional technique to keep you within bounds you may be tempted to fly off in too many directions and the design may lose its impact. When you combine and mix techniques your textures and stitches are going to be the predominant factor, so let them inspire the design; perhaps combining only two types of work with stylized simplicity. Try crewel and needlepoint stitches on canvas, or appliqué with stitchery, or silk and gold threads with wool, and so on.

/ 353

OPPOSITE
Detail from the Coq d'Or panel, showing gold couching combined with wool and silk stitching. Design adapted and worked by Mrs. Theodore Roosevelt. *Smithsonian Institution*

OVERLEAF
Needle lace in wool and linen threads. *Designed and worked by Bianca Artom*

Jacob's Coat. *Designed and worked by Alma Lesch*

Combinations are not new. The changing of styles in fashion always inspired cross pollination of techniques and very interesting hybrids often resulted. In Queen Anne's time in England, for instance, silk was combined with wool in the transition from Jacobean to all silk embroideries. "Crewelpoint"—the combination of crewel stitches with needlepoint on canvas—was done in the 18th century, and stump work combined numerous techniques and materials.

Sunflowers in linen lace stitches
Designed and worked by Merry Bean

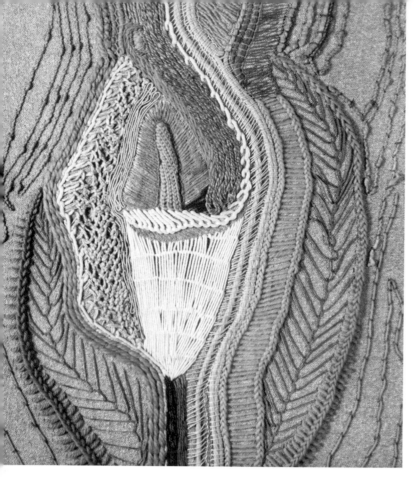

Panel by Mariska Karasz, showing a variety of textures and threads. *Cooper Hewitt Museum of Design, Smithsonian Institution*

Detail of a hanging showing tent stitch worked with rug wool on an even-weave wool fabric. *Designed and worked by the author*

DESIGN AND COLOR

Crewel work inspired by a French Book of Hours. *Designed by the author, worked by Mrs. E. Farrar Bateson*

WHEN Tolstoy said, "Art is not a handcraft, it is the transmission of feeling the artist has experienced," he was perhaps unaware that the craftsman by the same definition can find expression for his creativity and transform his craft into an art.

There are two ways of designing for embroidery. The first and probably the easiest is done by working out repeat or measured patterns geometrically. This simple approach is by no means limited to squares and triangles but can be used to create the most elaborate traditional or modern designs.

For example, there is the art of the American Indian, depicting animals, flowers, and birds, all having a geometric counted pattern as their base. Then there are the intricate and intriguing subtleties of oriental rug patterns, the unlimited beauty and variety of bargello and counted needle-point designs, and the charming storytelling and decorative patterns of peasant embroideries, used to embellish exquisite articles of clothing and household use.

In Roumania the peasant embroideries are classified in two groups: the "counted" or regular repeat geometric patterns and the "written," or free designs. This second type of pattern opens up the entire spectrum of the painter's artistic freedom, where expression can be as varied as classic pictorial representation, the impressionists' flow of color and form, and surrealistic and abstract expressionism. In fact, whatever can be done with pen, pencil, or paint can be interpreted equally with needle and thread. Interestingly, today's artists, searching for newer media, and frequently turning away from their paints, are exploring the medium of yarns, ropes, and fabrics to give dimension and texture to their creativity. There are no longer hard lines between the art of the painter and that of the sculptor, and frequently embroidery and weaving become the bridges between the two art forms.

But it is not necessary to think of yourself as an artist in order to   / *359*

OPPOSITE
The simplicity of many Oriental designs can provide inspiration for embroidery in any medium. *Designed by the author, worked by Mrs. William Lamb*

create your own embroidery designs. The entire spectrum of geometric and counted patterns lends itself superbly to the telephone doodler or person seeking expression with color, but who is perhaps lacking in freehand drawing ability. The easiest way to launch into geometric patterns is to work with a set of colors on graph paper. The illustration (see page 329) shows you how you can build by this means, from the simplest to the most sophisticated patterns.

For the "written" or freehand designs, the variety is endless, and this may seem at first more difficult because of the apparently complete freedom it gives the designer. But because you are working with fabrics, yarns, and textures, you do have limitations and must channel your creative efforts to use the almost infinite variety of stitches to their best advantage. In other words, your design should be more beautiful in needlework than in any other medium. Your stitches can become an alphabet with which you can make poetry or prose by arranging them in limitless combinations.

Here are ten down-to-earth suggestions that may help you with your embroidery design.

1. *Begin with small sketches* in the correct proportion, no matter what size your final piece is to be. You can always have the drawing photostatically enlarged, and it is so helpful to be able to see the overall final effect, rather than grappling with huge pieces of paper and with drawings that have to be seen from a distance.

Sisters aged 4 and 5, painted in 1590 by Isaac Oliver, a pupil of Nicholas Hillyarde, the famous Elizabethan "limner" or miniature painter. The girl holding a red carnation inspired the author's embroidery showing different techniques at the head of each chapter. *Victoria and Albert Museum*

2. *Photostating* may be useful not only for an original design but also when you are duplicating a painting or drawing from a book or magazine, or any other printed matter such as a photograph. Remember, photostats can be used to reduce as well as to enlarge a pattern, but keep in mind that the proportions will always remain the same. Therefore, don't try to give all-round measurements of the finished size you need; just determine the measurement of the most important side, and the rest will follow.

   While photostating may be somewhat expensive compared to enlarging by the graph method (below), it saves so much time and is so much more accurate it may well be worth the price.

3. *Enlarging* by squaring the design is certainly one of the most ancient methods, but it is still simple and useful today. It was quaintly but clearly described by Richard Schorleyker in "A Schole House for the Needle" quoted earlier. He says, "I would have you knowe, that the use of these squares doth showe how you may contrive to worke any Bird, Beast or Flower into biger or lesser proportions, according as you shall see cause: As thus, if you will enlarge your patterne, devide it into squares, then rule a paper as large as ye list, into what squares you will: Then looke how many holes your patterne doth containe, upon so many holes of your ruled paper drawe your patterne." In case the seventeenth-century English is too much for you, the illustration below will make things clear!

4. *Drawing your design freehand.* Suppose you wanted to do a wing armchair with a comparatively simple pattern. First, have a muslin pattern or "template" made by the upholsterer, then it will be sure to

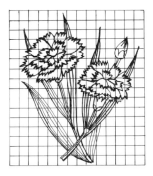
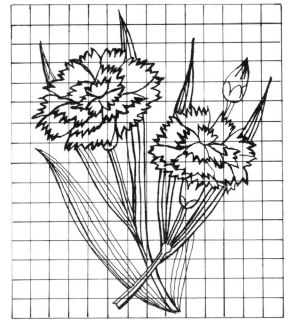

fit. Lay it in position on the chair and draw your design onto the muslin with colored chalk or pastel crayon. In this way you can see how the finished design will look on the chair and just how it will fit with an overall balance. You can go over the lines afterward with a felt marking pen to make them more definite. Then you can trace the pattern accurately on tracing paper and apply it to the fabric with carbon or the perforating method (page 19).

5. *Making designs with cutouts of colored paper* can help you restrain your drawing to the silhouette shapes ideal for stylized needlework, which gives full emphasis to the stitches.

6. *Drawing on layout paper* (a semi-transparent heavy form of tracing paper) makes your designing freer, and means that it's easier to trace one sketch from another instead of laboring on one drawing and constantly erasing it.

7. *Making a color sketch,* however rough, using crayons or felt markers, or cutout colored paper shapes, gives you a good idea of how the final design will look. It is so much quicker to change a color when it is

Sketch for a pillow, adapted from tapestry. Detail from the Hunt of the Unicorn Tapestry
The Metropolitan Museum of Art, the Cloisters Collection, Gift of John D. Rockefeller, Jr., 1937

only paint or crayon, rather than cutting out large areas of stitching. Overlay a sheet of paper which is the same color as your background fabric with a piece of transparent acetate and, using permanent felt markers or colored paper, work out your design on this clear surface. The background color showing through will influence your color selection and you will be able to see exactly how your design will look when it is completely finished.

8. *One idea leads to another.* Once you learn to translate designs into stitches you can develop a language of your own, finding inspiration from such things as china, wallpaper, pictures in magazines, greeting cards, children's books, the view from your window . . . a walk in the country . . . or in the city.

9. *Experiment with stitches,* taking another tack altogether, and allow them to guide your design. The forms the stitches can take may give you inspiration for all kinds of combinations of textures and may start you on a whole new set of ideas.

10. *Your background fabric will always influence you.* Whether your stitches become part of the background or whether they stand out as clear silhouettes upon it, the color and texture of your background material is generally one of the most important factors in the end result.

How do you decide what kind of embroidery to use for a certain design? Often the medium you choose will be decided by what you are making, and where it is to go. But sometimes you may choose the design first, and then be confronted with the decision as to whether it will look best in crewel, needlepoint, or perhaps silk or cotton. First ask yourself what is the essence of the design? Its lightness—its delicacy? Crewel or silk might therefore be best. Is the emphasis on brilliant, solid over-all masses of color? Then needlepoint should be excellent. Could it be effective in one color with textural pattern its main interest? Black work, white work, or silk and gold thread may be the ideal choice in that case.

However, often a design may work out well in several mediums. Geometric designs, which lend themselves well to the canvas of needlepoint or the even weave linen of black or white work, can also be excellent in crewel. When worked in crewel, geometric designs have the attractive "hand drawn" look of repeat patterns worked without counting the background threads, often found in peasant embroideries.

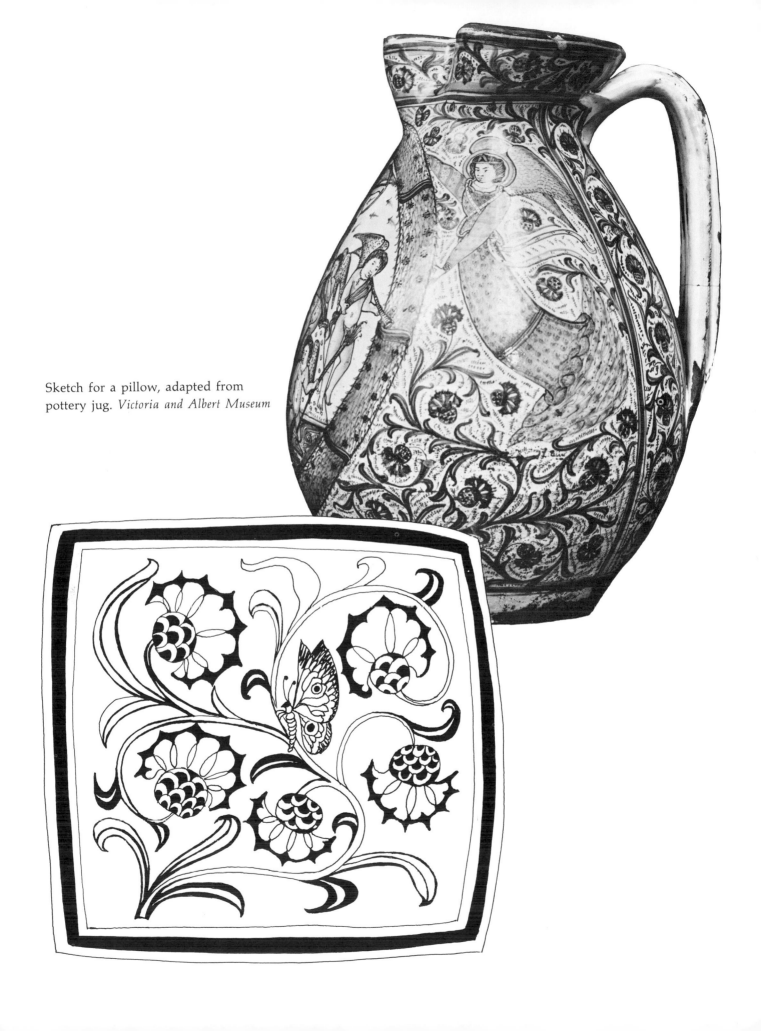

Sketch for a pillow, adapted from
pottery jug. *Victoria and Albert Museum*

COLOR

Most people have an innate natural color sense which they use every day without really knowing it. In deciding which piece of clothing to wear with which, in combining colors in a room, in making a flower arrangement or a table setting, everyone has to make color selections quite naturally and without a great deal of forethought and difficulty. But when it comes to choosing colors for a piece of needlepoint or crewel it's a different matter. Without being sure of the end result, the beginner is often fraught with indecisions and is apt to become too timid or too over-confident.

Sometimes it seems much simpler to gather a bunch of delicious colored skeins of wool in your hand, just like picking flowers, rather than arranging them in a design. So perhaps you could do just that, because if the colors look lovely all together in your hand, so they will when they are worked into the embroidery. You can add and eliminate by holding extra colors beside the main ones, and if they add excitement, keep them, but if they seem to contribute nothing, throw them out. This is one of the advantages wools, cottons, and fabrics have over paints: the colors are there for you; you don't have to mix them. Your color scheme can be bold and brilliant, or subtle and understated, but whichever it is, keep it simple. A design with a predominating color is often dynamic; too many colors, or too many close shadings could make a design look muddy, just like paints that have been mixed too much.

To give you an elementary course in color theory, here are a few basic laws which may be helpful when you are planning color schemes for your embroidery.

Red, blue, and yellow are the primary colors. The colors between are obtained by mixing the two adjacent colors: red and yellow make orange; yellow and blue make green; blue and red make purple. Therefore the colors next to each other around the spectrum will blend softly together. The colors opposite to one another have the strongest contrasts; red and green, blue and orange, yellow and purple. In other words, if you put them together each will shine out with its own intensity and neither will overpower the other. Therefore they are called complementary colors.

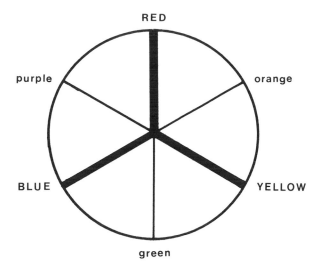

Color can be everything, but the absence of color can be the essence of the whole design, as for instance in black work where your embroidery becomes an etching or delicate line drawing. Or white work and monochromatic designs where nothing is allowed to interfere with the textured interest. But a design done in crewel, needlepoint, or appliqué may be more vibrant if it is worked in many shadings of the same color instead of just one. Using your color spectrum, you could work in reds, for instance, going as far toward the yellows on one side and the blues on the other as you can. Hence your color scheme will range all the way from persimmon and orange reds to scarlet, crimson, and magenta.

To extend the idea even further, your colors could range all round the spectrum, juxtaposing melodic hues in a rainbow which blends from blue to purple to red to orange to yellow and green. Or you could try working with complementary colors of the same depth and intensity: electric pink with khaki green; emerald with tangerine; aqua with burnt orange; so that they vibrate. As a complete contrast you could experiment with colors such as stone, sand, champagne, white, and tawny brown, varying the textures of the materials to give full dimension to this restrained palette.

Always consider your background fabric as an integral part of your color scheme, and your colors in relationship to one another. It may be easier for a beginner to start on a natural background to allow more freedom of choice for the coloring of the design. But whatever color your background is, lay out your threads on the fabric as you choose them. If your design is in needlepoint, do not put them on the white canvas (unless your ground will be white), but on a skein of the actual background color. Then you will really know the effect of your colors in the finished design. Remember that when you are working with a dark background everything will be in reverse, like the negative of a photograph, and the lightest colors will be the ones that stand out most. A dark ground tends to "swallow up" the design, making it look smaller.

The simpler the stitch, the more intense the color will be. A close-textured stitch breaks up the light and generally makes the color darker. An open lacy textured stitch will naturally blend more into the background and so the color will become more muted. The stitch which gives the effect of color closest to that in the skein is satin stitch; the threads are laid down with flat straight stitches with nothing to interfere with them, and so they remain clear and radiant. In needlepoint, Gobelin, or the brick stitch used for bargello, is the closest to satin stitch, so the color also remains very vivid.

Tent stitch, the stitch most often used in needlepoint, gives a rich velvety effect, a little darker than the original color. Turkey work, the tufted stitch with cut pile like velvet, works out at least two shades darker than that of the original skein. In order to match the color of a finished piece of Turkey work, you have to turn to the reverse side or hold the tufts back with your finger.

Color, like taste and smell, is a very personal thing. There are no hard and fast rules. Color combinations are constantly being discarded by greater freedoms, and the excitement of experimenting with color is all yours. The same is true of textures and stitches and the varied classical techniques described in this book are just a starting point for your own creativity.

BIBLIOGRAPHY

ASHTON, LEIGH. *Samplers*. The Medici Society, London and Boston, 1926

BEER, ALICE BALDWIN. *Trade Goods*. Smithsonian Institution Press, Washington, 1970

BRETT, GERARD. *European Printed Textiles*. Victoria and Albert Museum, London, 1949

CAULFEILD, S. F. A. and SAWARD, BLANCHE C. *The Dictionary of Needlework*. L. Upcott Gill, London, 1882

CUMMINGS, ABBOTT LOWELL. *Bedhangings*. Society for the Preservation of New England Antiquities, Boston, 1961

DIGBY, GEORGE WINGFIELD. *Elizabethan Embroidery*. Thomas Yoseloff, New York, 1963

DONGERKERY, KAMALA. *The Romance of Indian Embroidery*. Thacker and Company, Ltd., Bombay, 1951

GARDNER, HELEN. *Art Through the Ages*. Harcourt Brace and Company, New York, 1936

GEDDES, ELIZABETH and MCNEILL, MOIRA. *Blackwork Embroidery*. Mills and Boon, London

HARBESON, GEORGIANA BROWN. *American Needlework*. Coward-McCann, New York, 1938

HUGHES, THERLE. *English Domestic Needlework 1660–1860*. The Macmillan Company, New York, 1961

HUISH, MARCUS B. *Samplers and Tapestry Embroideries*. Longmans, Green and Company, London, 1913

JONES, MARY EIRWEN. *History of Western Embroidery*, Studio-Vista, London, 1969

KENDRICK, A. F. *English Needlework*, 2nd edition. A. and C. Black, London, 1967

STENTON, SIR FRANK, et. al. *The Bayeux Tapestry*. Phaidon Publishers, London, 1957

SWAIN, MARGARET. *Historical Needlework*. Charles Scribner's Sons, New York, 1970

SYMONDS, MARY and PREECE, LOUISA. *Needlework Through the Ages*. Hodder and Stoughton, London, 1928

TODD, CHARLES BURR. *Story of the City of New York*. Putnam, New York, 1888

WILLIAMS, JAY. *Life in the Middle Ages*. Random House, New York, 1966

The Old Testament, King James Version

The New York Gazette

SUPPLIERS

*Indicates mail order catalogues are available.

*C. M. Almy and Sons, Inc.
37 Purchase Street
Rye, New York 10580

Metal threads
(Japanese gold)
Real silk threads

La Lamé
1170 Broadway
New York, New York 10001

Lurex threads
Gold Bullion
Braids and Tinsels

*Merribbe Co.
4000 Saw Mill Run Boulevard
Pittsburgh, Pennsylvania 15227

"Binca" and "Panama" cloth suitable for counted stitches
Hardanger Linen

Singer Sewing Center 30 Rockefeller Plaza New York, New York 10020 (and at all local Singer centers)	"Stitchwitchery" bonding fabric
*Erica Wilson Needleworks 717 Madison Avenue New York, New York 10021	Metal threads (all varieties) Embroidery frames Linen Canvas Wool (French, English, Persian, Irish)
Haandarbejdets Fremme (Danish Handcraft Guild) Vimmelskaftet 38 1161 Copenhagen, Denmark	Yarns Linen thread Cotton thread Contemporary designs
The Royal School of Needlework 25 Prince's Gate Kensington, London S.W. 7 England	Appleton wool Knox's linen threads Canvas Linens
*The Needlewoman Regent Street London S.W. 1 England	Linens (all varieties) Cotton floss Wool Embroidery frames
*Clara Waever Ostergaade Copenhagen, Denmark	Cross stitch linens Threads Patterns
J. Whippel and Co., Ltd. Cathedral Yard Exeter, Devon, England	Metal threads, silk floss Damask Brocades
Jack Lenor Larsen 232 East 59th Street New York, New York 10021 or Space 6-40 Merchandise Mart Chicago, Illinois	Unusual fabrics in wool, linen, cottons and synthetics
Karl Mann 232 East 59th Street New York, New York 10022	Wall paper, (linen with paper backing)
Scalamandré 977 3rd Avenue New York, New York 10022	Antique satins Damasks Brocades Silk fabrics of all kinds

INDEX

Numbers in bold face refer to illustrations

371